Social Work and the Law in Scotland

2nd Edition

Edited by

Roger Davis

Jean Gordon

palgrave
macmillan

The Open
University

© The Open University 2003, 2011

The Open University, Walton Hall, Milton Keynes MK7 6AA, United Kingdom

All rights reserved. No reproduction, copy or transmission of this publication may be made without written permission.

No portion of this publication may be reproduced, copied or transmitted save with written permission or in accordance with the provisions of the Copyright, Designs and Patents Act 1988, or under the terms of any licence permitting limited copying issued by the Copyright Licensing Agency, Saffron House, 6–10 Kirby Street, London EC1N 8TS.

Any person who does any unauthorized act in relation to this publication may be liable to criminal prosecution and civil claims for damages.

First edition published 2003
Reprinted six times
Second edition published 2011 by
PALGRAVE MACMILLAN

Palgrave Macmillan in the UK is an imprint of Macmillan Publishers Limited, registered in England, company number 785998, of Houndmills, Basingstoke, Hampshire RG21 6XS.

Palgrave Macmillan in the US is a division of St Martin's Press LLC, 175 Fifth Avenue, New York, NY 10010.

Palgrave Macmillan is the global academic imprint of the above companies and has companies and representatives throughout the world.

Palgrave® and Macmillan® are registered trademarks in the United States, the United Kingdom, Europe and other countries.

ISBN: 978–0–230–27631–4

This book is printed on paper suitable for recycling and made from fully managed and sustained forest sources. Logging, pulping and manufacturing processes are expected to conform to the environmental regulations of the country of origin.

A catalogue record for this book is available from the British Library.

10 9 8 7 6 5 4 3 2 1
20 19 18 17 16 15 14 13 12 11

Printed and bound in Great Britain by
CPI Antony Rowe, Chippenham and Eastbourne

Contents

Notes on Contributors		vi
Acknowledgements		x
	Introduction *Jean Gordon and Roger Davis*	1
1	Legal Values and Social Work Values *Jeremy Roche*	6
2	Accountability, Professionalism and Practice *Kathryn Cameron*	20
3	Risk, Professional Judgement and the Law: Antinomy and Antagonism in an Age of Uncertainty *Mike Titterton and Susan Hunter*	35
4	The Role of Assessment in Social Work for Children and Families in Scotland *Jane Aldgate*	52
5	Law, Social Difference and Discrimination *Lena Robinson*	70
6	Children's Hearings in Scotland: Balancing Rights and Welfare *Janice McGhee*	85
7	The Voice of the Child *Kathleen Marshall*	101
8	Community Care and the Promotion of Independence *Alison Petch*	118
9	Vulnerability, Autonomy, Capacity and Consent *Kathryn Mackay*	136
10	Working with Adults who Use Services and Carers *Kirsten Stalker and Lisa Curtice*	152
11	Youth Justice *Bill Whyte*	167
12	Adult Criminal Justice *Trish McCulloch and Fergus McNeill*	184
13	Partnership with Service Users *Andrew Kendrick*	201
Index		217

Notes on Contributors

Jane Aldgate is a graduate of Edinburgh University and a trained social worker. She is Professor of Social Care at the Open University and Honorary Professorial Fellow at the University of Edinburgh. Jane has researched and written about a wide range of child welfare issues, including child development, direct work with children, family support, services for looked after children, and child protection. Jane is currently seconded to the Scottish Government's *Getting it right for every child* team as a professional adviser. She was awarded the OBE in 2007 for services to children and families.

Kathryn Cameron was formerly Senior Lecturer in the Glasgow School of Social Work, a joint school of the Universities of Glasgow and Strathclyde. She is qualified in both social work and law and has a particular interest in law and practice in relation to children and families.

Lisa Curtice has been Director of the Scottish Consortium for Learning Disability since its inception in 2001. She was Lecturer in Community Care at the University of Glasgow (1994–2001) and has recently completed her PhD thesis on the subject of citizenship, inclusion and people with learning disabilities who have high support needs.

Roger Davis has practised as a social worker and mental health officer. He has been involved in social work education since 1994, has taught a range of Open University courses since 1999 and is currently an academic staff tutor in the OU Faculty of Health and Social Care. He is also a member of the Mental Health Tribunal for Scotland.

Jean Gordon has worked in Scotland as a social worker and mental health officer in schools, hospitals and community mental health settings. She combines teaching on the Open University's social work programme in Scotland with research, writing and publishing in the fields of mental health, social work education, and practice learning.

Susan Hunter is a Senior Lecturer in Social Work at the University of Edinburgh where she has primary responsibility for teaching in community care, particularly in the fields of learning difficulties and ageing. She is also Programme Director of the MSc in Advanced Professional Studies (Adult Protection) aimed at qualified practitioners in health and social welfare. Her current research interests include an evaluation of self-directed support in three test sites in Scotland, supported employment and people with learning difficulties, and experiences of detention under the Mental Health (Care & Treatment) (Scotland) Act 2003.

Andrew Kendrick is Professor of Residential Child Care and Head of School of the Glasgow School of Social Work, a joint department of the Universities of Strathclyde and Glasgow. He is closely involved in the work of the Scottish Institute for Residential Child Care. He has published widely in the field of child welfare and child protection, and has particular research interests in residential childcare, decision making in childcare, and interdisciplinary work, particularly the relationship between education and social services.

Trish McCulloch is a Senior Lecturer in Social Work at the University of Dundee. Prior to joining the university in 2003, she worked as a social worker within youth and adult justice settings. Her publications have focused on various areas of criminal justice social work/probation practice and include a focus on the social and community contexts of change. Trish is currently completing her doctorate and has recently finished an evaluative study in the area of community service.

Kathryn Mackay is a Lecturer in Social Work with the Department of Applied Social Science at the University of Stirling. She has over 10 years of practice within community and mental health social work. Her teaching and research focus on law, policy and practice in these fields. Kathryn's current research projects include practitioners' and services users' experiences of adult support and protection work, mental health law and citizenship across the UK and the teaching of values within social work education.

Janice McGhee is Senior Lecturer in Social Work in the School of Social and Political Science at the University of Edinburgh. She has responsibility for law teaching on the undergraduate and postgraduate social work programmes. Her research interests lie in child welfare policy and law and child protection. She has extensive publications on the Scottish children's hearings system. Her most recent book (edited with Chris Clark) is *Private and Confidential? Handling Personal Information in the Social and Health Services* (2008).

Fergus McNeill is Professor of Criminology and Social Work at the University of Glasgow. His work addresses the interfaces between these two fields, including community sanctions, prisoner resettlement, sentencing and youth justice.

Kathleen Marshall is a solicitor and child law consultant. In April 2009, she demitted office as Scotland's first Commissioner for Children and Young People, an appointment created by the Scottish Parliament to promote and safeguard children's rights. She was formerly Director of the Scottish Child Law Centre. She chaired the Edinburgh Inquiry into Abuse and Protection of Children in Care, which reported in February 1999. She is the author of *Children's Rights in the Balance: The Participation–Protection Debate* (1997), and co-author of *Honouring Children: The Human Rights of the Child in Christian Perspective* (2004). She has undertaken research on many matters associated with children.

Alison Petch has spent most of her career involved with research and policy across a broad range of social work, health and housing issues. From 1985 to 1993, she worked at the Social Work Research Centre at Stirling University. She then moved to Glasgow University as Director of the Nuffield Centre for Community Care Studies. The opportunity to ensure that research was used in practice tempted her south in October 2005 to work with research in practice for adults. In October 2009, she returned to Scotland as Director of the Institute for Research and Innovation in Social Services.

Lena Robinson is Professor of Social Work, Faculty of Sciences, Engineering and Health, Central Queensland University, Australia, having recently left her previous post as Professor of Social Work at the University of the West of Scotland. Previously she was a Senior Lecturer in Psychology and Social Work at the University of Birmingham. She is an international scholar who has published and researched widely in the field of race, culture, ethnicity and psychology and social work.

Jeremy Roche is Dean and Director of Studies in the Faculty of Health and Social Care at the Open University. He has written extensively on how law and policy affects children and families and on children's rights. He has edited a number of books including *Youth in Society* (2004), *Children in Society: Contemporary Theory, Policy and Practice* (2001) and *Law and Social Work: Contemporary Issues for Practice* (2001) and was co-editor of *Social Work and the Law in Scotland* (2003).

Kirsten Stalker is a Professor in the Department of Applied Educational and Professional Studies at the University of Strathclyde. From 1991 to 2006, she worked in the Social Work Research Centre, University of Stirling and, prior to that, in the Norah Fry Research Centre at Bristol University. Much of Kirsten's research has focused on disabled children and people with learning disabilities. She is a member of the editorial boards of *Disability & Society* and the *British Journal of Learning Disabilities*. In a former life, she was a social worker, again working with people with learning disabilities.

Mike Titterton is Director of the charity HALE (Health & Life for Everyone), which assists children and adults at risk of harm in the UK and overseas. He has latterly worked on health, social care and educational projects in Eastern Europe and Central Asia, and previously worked for government, social work, NHS and third sector agencies in Scotland. He has also taught and undertaken research at three universities in the UK. He has been a consultant for the Open University, as well as a tutor for three of its courses. His PhD was on risk and resilience in socially excluded groups. He has two grown-up children and plays in a blues band in Edinburgh.

Bill Whyte is Professor of Social Work Studies in Criminal and Youth Justice at the University of Edinburgh and Director of the Criminal Justice Social Work Development Centre for Scotland. The centre is an independent national resource funded by the Scottish Government providing a range of research and practice development services to those working in, or concerned about, criminal and youth justice social work. The centre works in partnership with statutory and voluntary sector service providers and with central government to identify, promote, develop and disseminate good practice and management, based on the best available evidence. Bill has worked as a social work manager and field social worker in the Lothians area, as a residential care worker in a (former List D) residential school, and as an independent local authority chair of child protection.

Acknowledgements

The authors and publishers wish to thank the following for permission to use copyright material: Réné Schegg and the International Federation of Social Workers (IFSW) for permission to use the epigraph at the start of Chapter 2, originally from *Ethics in Social Work, Statement of Principles* (IFSW, 2004); and the Scottish Government for Figure 4.1, National Practice Model, originally from *A Guide to Implementing Getting it right for every child*, Scottish Government (2010), p. 49.

Every effort has been made to trace the copyright-holders, but if any have been inadvertently overlooked the publishers will be pleased to make the necessary arrangements at the first opportunity.

Introduction

JEAN GORDON AND ROGER DAVIS

Knowledge of the law and the skills to use this knowledge well are both central to social work practice. Social workers' legal powers and duties provide a mandate for practice that enables, and sometimes requires, them to take action to promote people's rights and, where necessary, to protect people from danger or harm. Law regulates social work practice, and holds social workers, and the organisations they work for, to account when services do not meet legal requirements. Legislation also provides service users, carers and social workers themselves with opportunities for redress, for example when people have been misinformed or discriminated against. Without an understanding of the law, social workers are unable to empower people by providing accurate information and advice about their entitlements, or to understand the legal options available to them and the consequences of taking legal action in different circumstances. Ultimately, a limited or flawed understanding of the law and its application to practice can have serious and even life-threatening consequences for service users and carers. At the same time, as many of the authors of the chapters in this book emphasise, law does not simply consist of a series of rules that have to be applied to particular situations to achieve particular outcomes. Service users and carers have wide-ranging and complex needs and live in diverse circumstances. Social workers, like other legal actors, have to exercise judgement and discretion in their work. One of the key dilemmas for social workers is how to negotiate tensions between legal principles and processes and the values and approaches that underpin social work practice in order to meet the needs of the people they work with.

The context for this book is social work practice as it relates to Scotland, its legal system and its statutes. While there are many parallels with the practice of the law in the rest of the UK, Scotland has a distinctive legal system, informed by its particular social, historical and cultural landscape, which impacts on its policy and law and therefore on the way in which, and the context within which, social work is practised. Of particular importance to modern social work practice has been the establishment of the Scottish Parliament in 1999. The Parliament is responsible for making laws that impact on many aspects of

1

Scottish social service provision, including community care and social work with children and families, as well as the structures and procedures of the legal system itself, including the courts, prosecution systems, legal aid, and the responsibilities of legal actors such as procurators fiscal and sheriffs. Some of these systems are significantly different from those in the rest of the UK, such as the children's hearing system, established by the Social Work (Scotland) Act 1968, explored by Janice McGhee in Chapter 6 and referred to in Chapters 7 and 11. Another important difference from other jurisdictions in the UK is that work with adult offenders in Scotland is undertaken by social workers employed by local authorities, a reflection of Scotland's particular focus on the promotion of welfare in its legislation (see Chapter 12). In some other respects Scotland has followed a similar path to the rest of the UK. One shared priority has been the regulation and registration of the social care workforce. This has included the establishment of the Scottish Social Services Council (SSSC) by the Regulation of Care (Scotland) Act 2001. The SSSC regulates the social service workforce through registration, quality assurance of education, and publication of codes of practice (SSSC, 2009). An important development since the first edition of this reader has been the introduction of honours degree-level training for social workers in Scotland (Scottish Executive, 2003). The degree is intended to increase social workers' competence and professionalism (Scottish Executive, 2006) and to equip them to respond effectively to future challenges through, for example, its emphasis on critical and evidence-based practice.

Since 1999 the Scottish Parliament has been extremely active in making and passing legislation, all of which must be compatible with the rights enshrined in the European Convention on Human Rights. The Parliament's busy programme has included further examples of distinctive policy and statute, including the introduction of free personal and nursing care for people over the age of 65 in 2001 (see Chapter 8) and, more recently, the passing of the Adult Support and Protection (Scotland) Act 2007 (see Chapters 3 and 9). At the same time, the UK Parliament at Westminster retains some important 'reserved powers', which include legislation in relation to immigration, defence, foreign policy and social security.

As law, like social work, is a dynamic and human process, it is constantly evolving and changing. Public debates around, for example, crime and society's response to it and the balance to be struck between private responsibility and public welfare as people live longer, as well as the voices of service users and carers themselves, who increasingly demand improved services framed by rights and not just needs, have all contributed to the pressure for reform.

This new edition recognises that much has moved on since the first was published in 2003. In 2006, the Scottish Executive published *Changing Lives: Report of the 21st Century Social Work Review*. This independent review concluded that increasing complexity and rising expectations of social work services was making the practice of social work in its current form unsustainable. It recommended new ways to design and deliver services, and make best use of social workers' skills (Scottish Executive, 2006, p. 8). Meeting the recommendations of *Changing Lives* through its ongoing change programme is a key challenge for social work practice at the start of the twenty-first century and forms a backdrop to the content of many of this book's chapters. For example, in Chapter 2, Kathryn Cameron discusses the increasing focus on social workers' accountability, and the tensions and dilemmas inherent in balancing this accountability with the Review's concern to promote social workers' professional autonomy. In Chapter 10, Kirsten Stalker and Lisa Curtice explore another central tenet of *Changing Lives*, the transformation of culture and systems required to make a reality of the Review's recommendations to build the capacity of social work to deliver personalised services. These themes, as well as other current drivers, such as an increasing emphasis on joint working and interagency practice, and the importance of the effective assessment and management of risk, appear in different guises in this book in relation to social work with a wide range of different service users and carers in a variety of contexts. These changing practices are set against a background of increasing globalisation, concern about climate change, debates about the extent of the role of the state in people's everyday lives, demographic change, and, at the time of writing, a global recession and threats to public services. An understanding of the 'big picture' of social change is key to understanding the social and economic contexts within which people live their lives, and therefore to the practice of social work and the law in Scotland.

This reader is structured around 13 contemporary thematic accounts of key areas of law and practice in social care and social work. In editing this collection of chapters about different aspects of the law, we have attempted to incorporate a sense of the complexity and breadth of the social work task in relation to the law in Scotland. In Chapter 1, Jeremy Roche introduces the book with a thought-provoking examination of values and ethics in relation to social work and the law and the ways in which social workers can maintain a commitment to values such as social justice in their practice. A number of the book's chapters build on these themes to reflect on a range of dilemmas that underpin ethical social work and social care practice. Key issues highlighted, and explored in relation to a range of different practice areas, include rights, accountability, partnership working, anti-oppressive practice, and the recognition of diversity and difference. In Chapter 2, Kathryn Cameron focuses on the question of accountability, what it means to be accountable as a social worker, and the issues that can arise when there are clashes between personal, professional and organisational accountabilities. In Chapter 3, Mike Titterton and Susan Hunter look at the question of risk 'in an age of uncertainty', posing searching questions about a series of key tensions for social workers such as the drive for regulation versus people's individual rights, and the standardisation of services versus the exercise of local discretion and initiative. The theme of assessment is taken up in Chapter 4 by Jane Aldgate, with an exploration of this key social work process, and a detailed examination of the ways in which assessment practice has changed and developed in Scotland in relation to children and families. Another central issue in understanding social work and the law is that of discrimination, taken up by Lena Robinson in Chapter 5. She uses the example of racial discrimination to illustrate how the law has developed over time, reflecting societal beliefs about the value of diversity and difference, and to suggest ways in which social workers can challenge discriminatory practices. Chapter 13, by Andrew Kendrick, considers the meaning of working in partnership with service users and carers and the extent to which partnership, as opposed to compliance, is possible within existing legal and practice frameworks.

The breadth of the social work role is represented through chapters that specifically address social work practice with particular groups of service users and carers. A number of chapters focus on children and young people. The philosophy, principles and procedures of the children's hearing system and the role of the social worker within that system are considered by Janice McGhee in Chapter 6. In Chapter 7, Kathleen Marshall develops the theme of participation, embedded in the United Nations Convention on the Rights of the Child and explains why, when and how social workers and other professionals should listen to children's voices. Three chapters specifically focus on social work with adults. In Chapter 8, Alison Petch traces the development of community care in Scotland and highlights legislation and practice issues in relation to the assessment of need and service provision. In Chapter 9, Kathryn Mackay addresses key questions about adult autonomy and the role of social workers in using the law to attempt to resolve tensions between people's rights to make their own choices about how to live their lives and the rights of vulnerable adults to be protected from harm. In Chapter 10, Kirsten Stalker and Lisa Curtice reflect on key practice issues for social workers working with adult service users and carers in the voluntary and statutory sectors, with a focus on ethical principles of practice such as the promotion of rights and anti-discriminatory practice. Social work practice in the justice system is discussed in relation to youth justice and adult criminal justice. In Chapter 11, Bill Whyte introduces the reader to competing and conflicting agendas in youth justice, including tensions between welfare and justice approaches, and different understandings of the nature and purpose of the justice system. In Chapter 12, Trish McCulloch and Fergus McNeil take up these central themes in relation to adult criminal justice, providing an overview of justice processes and a critical account of social workers' multiple accountability to stakeholders with valid and competing interests, including victims of crime, court, offenders, and members of the public.

This book aims to stimulate the debates that surround the contested areas of law and social work practice. It will have particular resonance for social work students and qualified workers as well as service users, carers and practitioners from other professions who are interested in updating and developing their understanding of the impact of the law and social work on the lives of children, young people, families and vulnerable adults in Scotland.

References

Scottish Executive (2003) *The Framework for Social Work Education in Scotland*, Edinburgh, Scottish Executive.

Scottish Executive (2006) *Changing Lives: Report of the 21st Century Social Work Review*, Edinburgh, Scottish Executive.

SSSC (Scottish Social Services Council) (2009) *Code of Practice for Social Service Workers, and Code of Practice for Employers of Social Service Workers*, Dundee, available online at www.sssc.uk.com/sssc/homepage/codes-of-practice.html [accessed 11 August 2010].

Chapter 1

Legal Values and Social Work Values

JEREMY ROCHE

This chapter explores the relationship between social work values and the law. *Changing Lives: Report of the 21st Century Social Work Review* (Scottish Executive, 2006, p. 9) referred to social work's 'passion for social justice' and social workers having 'a distinct set of knowledge, skills and values that need to be better used in supporting our most vulnerable people'. I argue that there is significant common ground between social work values and legal values. This includes a respect for the individual, a commitment to formal equality, the ending of prejudice and discrimination, and a concern with procedural fairness. There is much in the law in terms of its rules and procedures, including the law's insistence on certain forms of accountability, that can be supportive of social work, and issues of social justice and human rights are increasingly significant in contemporary social work discourse and the law. In this chapter, I consider the recent history of the relationship between the law and social work before moving on to explore social work values and images of law. I then consider the importance of the language of rights and conclude with a consideration of why law and the language of rights are important to social workers and service users alike.

Social work and the law

There are three aspects of the social work and law relationship that require some comment. First, while the law provided the mandate for social work practice in the sense that it accorded the local authority wide-ranging discretionary powers to intervene and regulate family life, for example to protect children, the law was not seen as being particularly important in social work education (Vernon et al., 1990): 'good practice' did not see the law as a key reference point. In other words, the law provided the authority upon which professional social work activity took place, and within which professional discretion could be exercised, but the law itself and a knowledge of the law were not seen as being integral to social work practice on a day-to-day basis. This situation has changed radically over the past two decades. Since the early 1990s, in part as a result of a series of scandals about the ways in which local authorities discharged their social service functions, the relationship between social work and the law has been redrawn (Kearney, 1992; Clyde, 1992; Marshall et al., 1999; O'Brien et al., 2003; SWSI/MWC, 2004). The law has an ever-increasing importance in social work education as well as day-to-day professional practice.

Today, not only is an understanding of the law seen as essential to professional social work practice but service users and carers are better informed about their rights, and social workers are specifically charged with promoting 'the independence of service users and assisting them to understand and exercise their rights' (SSSC, 2009, para. 3.1). The effective discharge of this professional responsibility requires social workers to know the extent of their powers and duties in a given situation and the range of entitlements that service users and carers can claim.

Second, despite the fact that today the law is an integral part of social work education and frames practice decision making, as Braye and Preston-Shoot (1997, p. 343) observed, 'deciding when to invoke the law is not a simple matter'. Knowledge of the law by itself is not enough. They go on to argue that competence in practice requires both knowledge of the law and assessment skills 'inspired by social work values, theoretical knowledge and practice wisdom'.

Third, the way in which professional social workers see and understand the law is important to their practice. Many social workers and academic commentators see the law as complicated, lawyers as unsympathetic if not hostile, and the courts as an unwelcoming and inappropriate environment for dealing with the complex human problems that lie at the centre of social work practice (King and Trowell, 1992). Furthermore, the courts are in the position of standing in judgement on social work decision making. It is important to acknowledge that the calling of social work practice to account, which is integral to many cases, can be unsettling and uncomfortable for the social work professionals involved. From the service user perspective however, legal accountability might bring some benefits, for example as a result of making a complaint, having a decision reversed and receiving services that the service user believed they were entitled to in the first place. So the law has come to assume a significance to social work practice that would have been hard to predict in the 1980s. Today, social work students are required to demonstrate their competence in applying the law. The argument of this chapter is that this is not merely a technical activity but an ethical one, an ethical activity framed by disagreements over values both within social work and the law.

Social work values

There are a number of different ways in which social work values are discussed in the social work literature. In the Central Council for Education and Training of Social Workers (CCETSW) *Revised Rules and Requirements* (1995), the section 'Values of social work' made it clear that meeting the core competences could only be achieved through the satisfaction of the value requirements. The position is that 'values are integral to rather than separate from competent practice' and that 'practice must be founded on, informed by and capable of being judged against a clear value base' (CCETSW, 1995, p. 18). The 'values requirements' included the need for students to 'identify and question their own values and prejudices and their implications for practice' and 'promote people's rights to choice, privacy, confidentiality and protection, while recognising and addressing the complexities of competing rights and demands' (p. 18). These are self-evidently complex and contradictory tasks; the promotion of the client's right to privacy may, for example, conflict with another client's right to protection, and both may be shaped by the social worker's own values. Social work practice is thus not simply a technical or administrative enterprise.

The Scottish Social Services Council (SSSC) *Code of Practice for Social Service Workers* (2009) resembles the CCETSW rules and requirements. While the language is at times different, it is clear that a positive respect for the rights and interests of service users is common to both documents, as is the promotion of the independence of service users while ensuring they are protected. The code of practice also emphasises the issue of public trust and confidence in social services – a theme echoed by the Scottish Executive report *Changing Lives* (2006; Chapter 2). What is distinctive about the code is the possibility that a social services worker might be deregistered as a result of failing to comply with the code. The issue of social work values thus links with the question of professional competence and accountability.

In 2002, the British Association of Social Workers (BASW) published *The Code of Ethics for Social Work*, which it described as binding on all BASW members. It has strong persuasive power, even though a minority of social workers are BASW members. It makes links between global and social interests and professionalism. It is essentially an aspirational document of guidance for practitioners that sets out what the members of the profession themselves expect of their peers. BASW has adopted the 2001 International Federation of Social Workers and the International Association of Schools of Social Work definition of social work, which should be used as a reference point for considering the code of ethics: it is included in the preamble to *The Code of Ethics for Social Work* (BASW, 2002), which states that:

The social work profession promotes social change, problem solving in human relationships and the empowerment and liberation of people to enhance well-being. Utilising theories of human behaviour and social systems, social work intervenes at the points where people interact with their environments. Principles of human rights and social justice are fundamental to social work.

Thus the BASW (2002, p. 1) code of ethics is centrally concerned with the values and principles underlying ethical practice, asserting that:

Social work is a professional activity. Social workers have obligations to service users, to their employers, to one another, to colleagues in other disciplines and to society. In order to discharge these obligations they should be afforded certain complementary rights.

The BASW code focuses on the protection of individuals, including protection from state and institutional abuses. It asserts a reciprocal duty on the state and employers to support social workers in the exercise of their professional functions.

Braye and Preston-Shoot (1997) saw the value base as being central to social work but also saw its definition as open. It might refer to 'a commitment to respect for persons, equal opportunity and meeting needs' or, more radically, to a 'concern with social rights, equality and citizenship'. They are not the only commentators who have identified an uncertainty in the meaning of social work's value base. Banks (1995, p. 6) observed that 'values' is 'one of those words that tends to be used rather vaguely and has a variety of different meanings'. Shardlow (2002, p. 30), however, took the argument further. It is not just a question of the openness or vagueness of the word 'values', he argued, but that 'no consensus exists about value questions in social work'. He referred to debates within social work over whether the contract culture empowers clients, the extent to which social work is predicated on a respect for the individual person, the significance of ideology in social work, for example the impact of feminism on social work knowledge and practice in the 1980s and 90s, and the extent to which social workers should be held responsible when something goes wrong. Shardlow (2002, p. 31) wrote:

These debates are inevitably open-ended where social work itself is intrinsically political, controversial and contested, and where the nature of practice is subject to constant change.

The argument about the controversial and changing nature of social work's value base was taken up by Smith (1997), who observed that the application of values is not without difficulty and noted the change in 'values talk' that had taken place, for example the reference to service users rather than clients. Nonetheless, whatever the significance of such shifts in language, Smith argued that it is still the case that a respect for persons and self-determination remain central to social work practice. The complexity of the social work task relates in part to how the professional social worker negotiates the tension between these values and the decision-making dilemmas that are integral to social work. Smith's concern is that 'rights are in danger of becoming dislocated from values' (p. 6), such that values become invisible; what is required is a confirmation of the relationship in particular terms. While Smith sees values and rights as conceptually distinct, she also sees in the idea of fundamental human need, itself predicated upon a respect for the person, a positive link in the values–rights relationship. She argues that a renewed commitment to values does not entail ignoring rights and that values and rights are proper partners in the social work project.

So it is possible to identify agreement on three issues. First, there is no dispute that values are central to social work practice. Second, these values are at times contradictory, and in themselves do not resolve the dilemmas inherent in the social work task. Third, there have been significant changes over the past few years, one of which is the increasing importance accorded to law within the education and practice of social workers. This said, there is almost a note of regret in the writing, as if social work has taken a wrong turning. As the law has come to assume a greater importance in both social work education and practice, with increasing accountability to the courts, some would argue that it is this trend that threatens to undermine good practice. How can social workers get on with their job if they are always having to look over their shoulders? The complaint is that 'defensive practice' is the result of law's new prominence, of the new relationship between the social work profession and the courts. This is, however, only one dimension of the law–social work relationship, one that is constantly subject to change. Before exploring this further, I want to consider some key images of law and the significance of the language of rights.

Images of law

Just as I have argued that there are competing images of social work practice, the same can be argued about the law. There is a debate about the values underpinning social work and how these find expression (or otherwise) in everyday practice; similarly, the law is properly characterised by contest and change. In other words, law is, like social work, a dynamic and contested set of discourses. There are a number of ways of seeing the law. The law can be viewed as a means by which the socio-economic status quo is maintained and guaranteed. The machinery of justice can be viewed as a charade or a genuine attempt to grapple with complex issues and arrive, however imperfectly, at a reasoned decision. Judges can be seen as disinterested adjudicators of disputes whose only allegiance is to the law or as biased individuals whose decisions reflect their class interests and preferences. The law can also be seen as a champion of the unprivileged and dispossessed. Within this tradition, contests around the law are part of the struggle for social justice, for example for equal treatment. Williams (1991, p. 153) saw the law and the language of rights as playing a part in the fight against discrimination:

> For the historically disempowered, the conferring of rights is symbolic of all the denied aspects of their humanity: rights imply a respect that places one in the referential range of self and others, that elevates one's status from human body to social being.

This progressive imagery of the law is strangely absent from social work. So the law is not just about, for example, the right to property, it also concerns human rights such as the right to liberty and the right to a fair trial. In this sense, the law concerns us all, irrespective of our social identity and location. When it comes to discussing the meaning of rights, there is no less debate. Positivists argue that the law is simply those rules laid down by the proper law-making procedures. There is thus no necessary moral content to the law – in the past, some legal regimes have sanctioned slavery, others the 'rights of man'. For utilitarian thinkers like Bentham, the question of 'what the law is' is distinct from the question of 'what the law ought to be'. A critique of the law was not to be confused with an accurate account of what the law was. Events in the twentieth century, however, rendered this neat distinction problematic. The state in Nazi Germany had all the trappings of the rule of law (referred to as the 'tinsel of legality'), yet unimaginable horrors were committed. Natural law thinkers such as Fuller and Dworkin argued that unless the law satisfied certain criteria in terms of its content and procedures, it could not properly be called law. While Fuller (1969) was mainly concerned with procedural questions, for example whether the rules of law were known to those who were required to obey them, whether they were comprehensible and whether obedience to them was possible, Dworkin addressed the issue of law's content. Dworkin (1980) argued that, in a democracy, individuals require rights and that the interests of the minority cannot be sacrificed to those of the majority. He then argued that such a belief in the importance of rights requires a respect for persons and a commitment to political equality; it is this that makes rights so important. While Dworkin conceded that there are circumstances in which rights can be overridden, for example because it is necessary in order to uphold another's rights or because the cost of not doing so is excessive, it is only if rights are seen as special that there can be said to be any real constraint on the power of government.

This argument is important because it opens up a number of issues, two of which concern us here. First, it alerts us to debates surrounding state power. When the state proposes new legislation in the field of social care, it often raises controversial issues concerning, for example, a redistribution of resources or new powers to intervene in the private sphere. Second, it serves as a reminder that when we are talking about social work and the law, we are also talking about human relationships in which a commitment to an equality of concern and respect is important.

However, what also needs to be made explicit is the idea that the public power of the state may be needed in order to correct a past injustice, to prevent discriminatory and oppressive behaviour in the 'here and now', and, practically and symbolically, to signal that certain forms of behaviour are not acceptable. All legal systems have a value base. The important question about the law is: what are the values upon which the laws are built? Some legal regimes have been built on values that have been explicitly discriminatory, for example the law in apartheid South Africa or the legal regime in Nazi Germany. In the UK, with the passing of the Human Rights Act 1998, the law has embraced more directly the fundamental freedoms in the European Convention on Human Rights (ECHR). The freedoms contained in the ECHR are those commonly associated with parliamentary democracies, for example the right to a fair trial and the right to family life, both of which are issues central to social work practice.

The question of rights

According to some, however, talk of rights does not progress the interests of the disadvantaged in our society. The critical legal studies movement argued that rights talk is unable to address structural oppression and often serves to depoliticise social issues, while some feminist critiques of rights include the charge that they are abstract, impersonal, atomistic and induce conflict. Others suggest that rights talk 'obscures male dominance', while its strategic implementation 'reinforces a patriarchal status quo and, in effect, abandons women to their rights' (Kiss, 1997, p. 2).

Perhaps the most sustained arguments against the language of rights come from those who embrace an ethic of care, influenced by the work of Gilligan (1982), with which they seek to supplement or even supplant the ethic of rights. The ethic of care is based on the idea of connectedness and thus focuses on caring as moral action (see Tronto, 1993; Heckman, 1995). As such, an ethic of care is as concerned with welfare as it is with justice – what is important is the ambiguity and context of the action in question rather than simply the application of abstract legal principles. Thus the proper response to dependency and vulnerability is a rethinking of caring relationships. Sevenhuijsen (1998) argued for the recognition of vulnerability to be 'incorporated into the concept of a "normal" subject in politics'. She observed, however, that (p. 146):

> Clearer ideas about what constitutes necessary care can be gained by granting those who are the 'object' of care cognitive authority over their needs and giving them the opportunity to express these in a heterogeneous public sphere which allows open and honest debate.

Minow and Shanley (1997, p. 99) agreed with feminist critics of rights theory 'that a political theory inattentive to relationships of care and connection between and among people cannot adequately address many themes and issues facing families'. However, they went on to observe that rights-based views require 'public articulation of the kinds of freedoms that deserve protection and the qualities of human dignity that warrant societal support' and that 'rights articulate relationships among people'. There are a number of important distinctions to be made about the different ways in which rights are considered. First, at a theoretical level, rights can be a source of protection, allowing one to make claims on others, for example for services, and allowing people to change relationships, via, for example, divorce law. Kiss (1997, p. 4) argued that rights can also be seen as being concerned with mutual obligations:

> There is nothing isolating about a right to vote, to form associations, or to receive free childhood immunisations. And while many rights, like political rights and rights to free expression, do enable people to express conflicts, they also create a framework for social co-operation ... Rights define a moral community; having rights means that my interests, aspirations and vulnerabilities matter enough to impose duties on others.

Kiss (1997, p. 4) argued that the problem is not so much with rights but with 'the tendency to cast the State in the role of exclusive rights violator': employers, service users and colleagues can all threaten one's rights. What we need to consider is the effect of rights – whether or not they make a practical and valuable difference to people's lives and the quality of their relationships. It is in the political aspects of rights that the link with social work values becomes most clear-cut. How, for example, are we to understand the failure of social work to engage with service users in the sense of showing respect for them and their choices? The example of social work and confidentiality is revealing here.

The traditional argument for respecting confidentiality is that without such an assurance, people would not seek help, they would be reluctant to make any significant disclosures and hence there would not be a relationship of trust: this would undermine the professional–service user relationship. There is a critical professional interest in working in part-nership and building a positive relationship with the service user. Where the service user is a child, there is also the issue of ensuring that working in partnership with parents and carers does not deflect attention from the needs and rights of the child, and there is evidence that some social welfare professionals find it hard to work with children in a way that takes their rights seriously (Roche and Tucker, 2003; Tucker, 2010).

In his analysis of confidentiality in contemporary social work prac-tice, Swain (2006) reminded us that the right to confidentiality is an integral part of one's privacy rights. He argued that, while a commit-ment to respecting client confidentiality is as central to effective social work practice as allowing a trusting and helping relationship to develop between professional and service user, in reality the commitment to confidentiality is misleading. Swain questioned whether practitioners are sure that clients expect confidentiality to be respected, and cited Ormrod and Ambrose's research (1999), which found that the profes-sion with 'the greatest discrepancy between what should happen in respect of confidentiality and what actually happened was social work' (Swain, 2006, p. 91). He asked what the promise of confidentiality actu-ally means in the context of working with children and families, and concluded that social work needs to come clean and recognise that the 'commitment' is so qualified that the social work professional should instead simply commit to respectful and open dealings with the client. It is clear that absolute confidentiality is not sustainable and that 'the protection afforded by an ethical commitment to confidentiality is argu-ably diminished by the increasing community demands for professional accountability, by legislative obligations across various practice areas, by the mandated duties to protect and warn' (Swain, 2006, p. 99).

This echoes in some ways the work of McLaren (2007) in her analysis of 'forewarning' in the context of Australian social work practice. McLaren (2007, p. 23) observed that 'many human service associations require their members to inform clients of the parameters of confidenti-ality, including their child abuse reporting obligations, at the onset of worker–client relationships'. However, her research found that workers avoided forewarning because they believed that clients would feel threatened and that to do so would put obstacles in the way of relationship building. McLaren (2007, p. 30) observed that most social workers in her study thought that 'forewarning clients may be received by clients as an authoritarian act, thus creating suspicion and mistrust'. This research captures the complexity of the social work task, the different ways in which social workers negotiate the professional–service user relationship and charts how difficult it can be to work according to the ethical ideals of the profession. It is, however, not just a matter of individual social work professionals experiencing difficulty in working with service users and carers in particular circumstances. At times, the accepted practices of their agency can give rise to problems.

Braye et al. (2005) have noted that managers can provide misleading advice and that agencies can refuse to listen to another agency's concern about risks to children and adults. Recognising that there are few absolute duties in social work law, that social work professionals do have discretion, they argue that the key task is to ensure that students and social workers know how that discretion should be exercised, drawing on values, knowledge and statutory guidance, and are skilled in its use to support sensitive, innovative and informed practice.

It is clear from Braye et al.'s discussion that they see part of the social work task as having the skill to challenge unfair or illegal policies and procedures. When faced with unlawful action on the part, for example, of their employer, the social work professional might feel they have no choice but to blow the whistle. 'Whistle-blowing' can be seen as a way of enabling an organisation to take responsibility for poor practice and to be more accountable for the actions of its employees. To be a whistle-blower involves individuals taking responsibility for highlighting problems within an organisation that they are not in a position to rectify by themselves. In 2009, in the wake of the death of Baby P (who died in Haringey, north London, in 2006), a confidential 'whistle-blowing hotline' was set up in England so that employees and former employees of local authorities could contact Ofsted to raise concerns about practice in relation to safeguarding children. The SSSC's *Code of Practice for Social Service Workers* (2009) specified that the requirements of a professional social services worker include:

- Bringing to the attention of your employer or the appropriate authority resource or operational difficulties that might get in the way of the delivery of safe care (para. 3.4)
- Informing your employer or an appropriate authority where the practice of colleagues may be unsafe or adversely affecting standards of care (para. 3.5).

This is reflected in a requirement that employers must be prepared to address any such issues brought to their attention, and that they must have:

> systems in place to enable social service workers to report inadequate resources or operational difficulties which might impede the delivery of safe care and [work] with them and relevant authorities to address those issues. (para. 2.3)

On whistle-blowing, the British Association of Social Workers' code (BASW, 2002, p. 11) says that social workers should 'uphold the ethical principles and responsibilities of the Code, even though employers' policies or instructions may not be compatible with its provisions' and that they should 'familiarise themselves with the complaints and whistle-blowing procedures of their workplace, and with the relevant provisions of the Public Interest Disclosure Act'.

Conclusion

Social work and law are properly characterised as contested and multiple discourses. The value of law and rights resides not in the idea that the law has the answer or that the language of rights makes social conflict disappear – on the contrary, the latter is a key part of making it visible. Rights talk is the language in which differently positioned people can articulate their own definitions of their needs and interests. I would thus argue that law and the language of rights is a necessary but not sufficient condition for good practice. As Banks argued (1995, p. 4):

> The law does not tell us what we ought to do, just what we can do ... most decisions in social work involve a complex interaction of ethical, political, technical and legal issues which are all interconnected.

The law by itself cannot and does not provide a clear guide to action in a whole host of complex circumstances. To argue that it did would be to misrepresent the importance of law. The law is open textured and contested, and when this is considered, alongside the detail of social work decision making, it is clear that the law cannot and does not provide the answer. Instead, it provides the framework within which social work knowledge is applied. Nor, it must be conceded, does the law always provide an immediate practical remedy – often, some would say too often, the law lags behind, failing to support anti-oppressive practice. Thus the law might at times deny the legitimacy of a claim, for example proscribing discrimination on the basis of age. At other times, however, it is not the law that fails to provide a remedy, but the actions of officials working within the authority of the law that deny the remedy, as in, for example, police inaction over instances of domestic violence. However, because the law can be seen as, among other things, an expression of the power of the state to meet certain outcomes, and one which can be mobilised to secure a wide range of objectives, it is important not to underestimate its power. Individual decisions of the courts, some existing practices of the legal system and indeed some statutory provisions might all be vulnerable to criticism when considered in the context of social work's commitment to respect for persons and self-determination. Yet, like social work itself, the law is the site of contest and debate, and one must not lose sight of the fact that one of the distinctive aspects of modern developments is the deployment of the language of rights by service users and service user organisations. Braye et al. (2005, p. 183) pointed out that social workers have to engage with the law, recognising its potential to oppress and often seek to minimise 'the negative constraints it might place upon people'. They argued that the concept of proportionality is important in this context, that law might be used to challenge oppression and that it is important to develop a perspective on law 'that is not confined to coercive intervention'. For social work today, the relation between social work values and rights need not be seen in exclusively negative terms. This is not to deny that there are court decisions that disadvantage socially marginalised people or to claim that recourse should always be had to the courts and lawyers. It is instead to recognise that, for some service users and professionals, the language of rights is the only means by which their perspective can be heard. The language of care might not allow the object of care to break free of their dependent, being-cared-for status. The language of rights is also about values – not necessarily in the form of a preferred list of 'correct' values but through the recognition of different viewpoints and through the hearing of different and perhaps unfamiliar voices on questions of need and respect.

References

Banks, S. (1995) *Ethics and Values in Social Work*, Basingstoke, Macmillan – now Palgrave Macmillan.

BASW (British Association of Social Workers) (2002) *The Code of Ethics for Social Work*, London, Venture Press.

Braye, S. and Preston-Shoot, M. (1997) *Practising Social Work Law*, Basingstoke, Macmillan – now Palgrave Macmillan.

Braye, S., Preston-Shoot, M. with Cull, L. et al. (2005) 'Teaching learning and assessment of law in social work education', *Social Work Education Knowledge Review*, Bristol, SCIE.

CCETSW (Central Council for Education and Training of Social Workers) (1995) *Revised Rules and Requirements: Assuring Quality in the Diploma in Social Work I – Rules and Requirements for the Dip. SW*, London, CCETSW.

Clyde, J.J. (1992) *Report of the Inquiry into the Removal of Children from Orkney in February 1991*, HC Papers 1992–3, No.195, London, HMSO.

Dworkin, R. (1980) *Taking Rights Seriously*, London, Duckworth.

Fuller, L. (1969) *The Morality of Law*, New Haven, CT, Yale University Press.

Gilligan, C. (1982) *In a Different Voice*, Cambridge, MA, Harvard University Press.

Heckman, S. (1995) *Moral Voices, Moral Selves*, Cambridge, Polity Press.

Kearney, B. (1992) *Report of the Inquiry into Child Care Policies in Fife*, Edinburgh, HMSO.

King, M. and Trowell, J. (1992) *Children's Welfare and the Law: The Limits of Legal Intervention*, London, Sage.

Kiss, E. (1997) 'Alchemy of fool's gold? Assessing feminist doubts about rights', in M. Shanley and U. Narayan (eds) *Reconstructing Political Theory: Feminist Perspectives*, Cambridge, Polity Press.

McLaren, H. (2007) 'Exploring the ethics of forewarning: social workers, confidentiality and potential child abuse disclosures', *Ethics and Social Welfare*, 1(1): 22–40.

Marshall, K., Jamieson, C. and Finlayson, A. (1999) *Edinburgh's Children: The Report of the Edinburgh Inquiry into Abuse and Protection of Children in Care*, Edinburgh, Edinburgh City Council.

Minow, M. and Shanley, M. (1997) 'Revisioning the family: relational rights and responsibilities', in M. Shanley and U. Narayan (eds) *Reconstructing Political Theory: Feminist Perspectives*, Cambridge, Polity Press.

O'Brien, S., Hammond, H. and McKinnon, M. (2003) *Report of the Caleb Ness Enquiry*, Edinburgh, Edinburgh and Lothians Child Protection Committee.

Ormrod, J. and Ambrose, L. (1999) 'Public perceptions about confidentiality in mental health services', *Journal of Mental Health*, 8(4): 413–21.

Roche, J. and Tucker, S. (2003) 'Extending the social inclusion debate: an exploration of the family lives of young carers and young people with ME', *Childhood: A Global Journal of Child Research*, 10(4): 439–56.

Scottish Executive (2006) *Changing Lives: Report of the 21st Century Social Work Review*, Edinburgh, Scottish Executive.

Sevenhuijsen, S. (1998) *Citizenship and the Ethics of Care: Feminist Considerations on Justice, Morality and Politics*, London, Routledge.

Shardlow, S. (2002) 'Values, ethics and social work', in R. Adams, L. Dominelli and M. Payne (eds) *Social Work: Themes, Issues and Critical Debates* (2nd edn), Basingstoke, Palgrave Macmillan.

Smith, C. (1997) 'Children's rights: have carers abandoned values?', *Children and Society*, 11: 3–15.

SSSC (Scottish Social Services Council) (2009) *Code of Practice for Social Service Workers, and Code of Practice for Employers of Social Service Workers*, Dundee, Scottish Social Services Council, available online at www.sssc.uk.com/sssc/homepage/codes-of-practice.html [Accessed 11 August 2010].

Swain, P.A. (2006) 'A camel's nose under the tent? Some Australian perspectives on confidentiality and social work practice', *British Journal of Social Work*, **36**(1): 91–107.

SWSI/MWC (Social Work Services Inspectorate/Mental Welfare Commission) (2004) *Investigations into Scottish Borders Council and NHS Borders Services for People with Learning Disabilities: Joint Statement from the Mental Welfare Commission and the Social Work Services Inspectorate*, Edinburgh, Scottish Executive.

Tronto, J. (1993) *Moral Boundaries*, London, Routledge.

Tucker, S. (2010) 'Listening and believing: an examination of young people's perceptions of why they are not believed by professionals when they report abuse and neglect', *Children & Society*, DOI:10.1111/j.1099-0860.2010.00291.x.

Vernon, S., Harris, R. and Ball, C. (1990) *Towards Social Work Law: Legally Competent Professional Practice*, London, CCETSW.

Williams, P. (1991) *The Alchemy of Race and Rights*, Cambridge, MA, Harvard University Press.

Chapter 2

Accountability, Professionalism and Practice

KATHRYN CAMERON

Introduction

> Social workers need to acknowledge that they are accountable for their actions to the users of their services, the people they work with, their colleagues, their employers, the professional association and to the law, and that these accountabilities may conflict. (IFSW, 2004)

Good practice has always dictated that social workers and the agencies that employ them should be answerable to those to whom they offer services. However, possibly as a consequence of high-profile inquiries into a number of tragic deaths of children, the call for social workers and other professionals to be accountable for their deeds (and their omissions) has become both a preoccupation of society and a demand. The inquiry into the tragic death of Victoria Climbié (Laming, 2003a) brought the concept of accountability into sharp focus. Although in his report Lord Laming aimed his most trenchant criticisms at those in senior positions, the inquiry itself and the surrounding media interest ensured that issues of accountability were examined and discussed. He recently revisited this in his report following the death of Baby P, when he was commissioned to provide an urgent report on the progress being made across the country to implement effective arrangements for safeguarding children (Laming, 2009). The kernel of the task was to evaluate the good practice that had been developed since the publication of the report following the death of Victoria Climbié, to identify the barriers that were preventing good practice becoming standard practice, and to recommend actions to be taken to make systematic improvements in safeguarding children across the country. One of the key areas in his remit was to look at effective systems of accountability. In Scotland, the need for an accountable social work profession has been highlighted in *Changing Lives: Report of the 21st Century Social Work Review* (Scottish Executive, 2006). This report sees accountability as an essential plank in the building of 'high quality, accessible, responsive and personalised services' (p. 2). It made recommendations not only about the accountability of social workers but also of their managers and employers.

What do we mean by the term 'accountability'? Broadly speaking, being accountable means being obliged to give an explanation or being held to account for one's actions or inaction. Shardlow (1995, p. 67) defined accountability as arising 'where social workers give an explanation and justification for their actions to somebody else who might reasonably expect to be given such an explanation'. This encapsulates what Braye and Preston-Shoot (2001, p. 43) have described as 'the twin concepts of "accountability to" – to those on whose authority professionals act – and "accountability for" – the range of activity that is open to scrutiny'. It could be argued that in relation to social workers there are two forms of accountability present, namely professional and public accountability. Social workers are accountable to service users for the quality of the work they do, for promoting and protecting their rights, treating each service user as an individual and adhering to the core values of social work. However, their accountability also requires them to be accountable to the wider community and to public bodies such as the courts. There can be tensions inherent in meeting these differing demands and, according to Banks (2009, p. 33), 'notions of professional and public accountability are at the heart of social work and, in both areas, demands are increasing'. Pollack (2009, p. 838) argued that as social work has become more professionalised, 'the public has scrutinised our performance and raised its expectations'.

Is accountability the same as responsibility? It has been said (Clark, 1985, p. 41) that the two are synonymous in conventional usage, but Banks (2009, p. 34) argued that the two are not synonymous and that it is unhelpful to use them interchangeably. Rather, she claimed, responsibility is only one sense of accountability. The term can encapsulate notions of duty, blame and liability. Each of these needs to be distinguished from the other. Accountability is just one dimension of the meaning of responsibility. For example, we say that someone is responsible for something in the sense that he or she caused it to happen. A car accident might be such an example. The person causing the accident may have a duty of care towards others and so should act responsibly. Their failure to do so may be blameworthy and they may then be liable for the outcome. They may ultimately be accountable to a court for their actions. These are all different and distinct forms of responsibility, none of which is identical to the others. It may be important to further distinguish responsibility from blame. We increasingly live in a blame culture in which society looks for scapegoats for things that go wrong. Workers may be held to account by their employers, by society and by courts and inquiries for failing to follow procedures. This is discussed later in the chapter. However, it has to be remembered that human error or misjudgement may not be the only reasons why things go wrong. It could be that the procedures themselves will be found to be inadequate. Eby and Morgan (2008, pp. 197–8) further suggest that professional accountability 'relies on 2 interrelated concepts; ability and competence. Is the practitioner able and competent?' Ability encompasses the knowledge, skills and values that are required to make decisions and act upon them, while competence 'is the capacity to perform a responsibility with appropriate knowledge and skill'.

Why is an awareness of accountability important in social work practice? Social workers interact most frequently with the most vulnerable in society. These service users are often those who, for a number of reasons, do not have a voice or who cannot make their voice heard. They are disadvantaged and frequently experience discrimination. They are oppressed and at risk of being overlooked and denied services. Many of those who make use of social services are the members of society who are least likely to hold the providers of those services to account. Social work values of openness, partnership and empowerment are crucial factors in ensuring accountability to service users, as is an awareness of the inequality of power within the relationship between service users and service providers. The rights discourse, which emerged strongly in the 1990s and culminated in the passing of the Human Rights Act in 1998, has contributed to the increasing significance of accountability in all public services. If individuals have rights, then there needs to be a clear understanding of how these rights will be guaranteed, and a discernible system that can deal with infringements and breaches of these rights. Such a system requires that there be transparency at all levels. Only when there is such transparency can there be an identification of possible areas where things have gone wrong and, consequently, the opportunity for challenge to take place.

Accountability within social work is complex. It involves the social worker being accountable to a number of individuals, groups, agencies and institutions. It encompasses public accountability to the state and to society. It embraces legal accountability in terms of the mandate to practise and the duties imposed by statute. It also requires accountability to professional bodies. There can often be tensions between the different demands made by all of these and it behoves social workers to be clear about where and to whom the accountability for their practice lies. Social workers are, on the whole, creatures of statute and are consequently closely bound up with the state and carry out their functions on behalf of the state and society. Clark (2000, p. 78) stated that since social work receives its mandate and funds from the state, 'it is quite properly expected to demonstrate that it is responsive to the wider political community'. The complexity of the task faced by workers is evident in the fact that workers can find themselves faced with a range of different responsibilities, which may, at times, conflict with one another.

Workers often find themselves working within families or other groups where there are conflicts of interest and opinions. Being clear to whom one owes allegiance can be problematic and the role of the worker can appear to be somewhat ambiguous. Social workers could, therefore, find themselves having to manage the tension between their duties to their agency and to their personal and professional values. Susan Banks (2004, p. 8) argued that in the social professions, there has been the development of a 'new accountability', which encapsulates the growth of accountability requirements in terms of procedures, targets, outcomes and monitoring systems to measure performance. These can sometimes be at odds with the principles of the professional codes of ethics or practice. Add to this the blame culture in which we live, and the web of accountability (rather than the supposedly clear lines) becomes potentially strangling for the social services worker caught in its threads.

Forms of accountability are present in all areas of service delivery but one area of practice, namely community care, will be used to illustrate some of the aspects of accountability of which workers should be aware in relation to their practice with service users. While there is a seductive simplicity in drawing lines of accountability that give a clear picture of the ways in which it is possible to hold someone to account, this belies the complexity of the tensions that exist. The different forms (or threads) of accountability will be explored in some detail using the device of a fictional case study to highlight the different lines of accountability. Although a community care case is used, the issues raised are applicable to other areas of practice as well:

> Mrs J is an 85-year-old woman who was widowed 10 years ago. She has one son aged 60 who lives thirty miles away. He has his own health problems but he tries to visit as often as he can to help his mother. Mrs J has lived on her own since her husband's death and has made it clear to everyone that she wishes to remain independent. She has recently had a fall and had to be admitted to hospital. While there, she began to show signs of forgetfulness and disorientation. A social worker was asked to do a community care assessment to determine what resources and support Mrs J might need if she were to return home.

The accountability owed by the worker in this case would encompass accountability to her employer, to other agencies and to the service user as well as legal, public and professional accountability.

Lines of accountability

Accountability to the employer

The policies and procedures of the local authority that is their employer bind the social worker undertaking the assessment. Failure to work within these policy guidelines could leave the social worker open to disciplinary action and even personal liability for their actions. In undertaking their work, social workers act as agents for their employer, be that a statutory or voluntary agency. They are accountable to their employers for the work undertaken in their name and so must abide by the conditions of their employment and the policies of the agency. This, therefore, represents an unequal balance of power between the employer and the worker and could place the worker who speaks up against policies or practices in a vulnerable situation. In such situations, the issue might arise of conflict between the professional duties of the worker and what they see to be ethically sound practice and the requirements of their employer. The worker may decide that they have no alternative but to speak out and bring the matter into the public arena. Whistle-blowers have often been represented, at worst, as villains or, at the very least, as deluded. The passing of the Public Interest Disclosure Act in 1999 has set out a clear framework for raising genuine concerns about malpractice and provides protection against victimisation for those workers who do make disclosures. It provides legal protection against dismissal or victimisation.

Social workers are anxious about the extent to which, if any, they might be held to be personally liable if things go wrong. In the past, local authorities were protected by the courts from being held to account for the mistakes of their employees, at least in so far as being sued was concerned. This did not prevent local authorities from being investigated through the process of inquiry. However, a number of decisions in recent years have altered the trend and local authorities can now be sued in the courts for negligence if they have failed in their duty of care towards service users (*A and another* v *Essex County Council* [2003] EWCA Civ 1848). An individual social worker who fails to carry through the policies and procedures of the agency or who has not acted in a professionally competent manner might be disciplined or dismissed. They might also become the subject of an inquiry. However, if the worker has followed procedures, has recorded diligently and has acted professionally, then they will be in a strong position to explain their decisions. The frontline workers in the Victoria Climbié and Baby P cases were vilified by sections of the media. However, in the former, a Care Standards Tribunal (2005), which heard the appeal brought by Lisa Arthurworrey, Victoria Climbié's social worker, against the decision of the Secretary of

State to place her on the list of those deemed unsuitable to work with children, found at the end of the day that although mistakes had been made because of a lack of adequate training, experience and supervision, there was no professional misconduct. It is important to realise that accountability and responsibility do not equate with culpability.

Accountability also belongs to those who are in managerial and supervisory capacities, even though they may not have had direct face-to-face contact with a service user. Lord Laming (2003b) made this clear in his speech given to the inquiry on 25 January 2003, when he stated that:

> Those in senior positions carried, on behalf of us all, the responsibility for the quality, efficiency and effectiveness of the services delivered. They must be accountable for what happened. That is why their posts exist.

He took this argument further in his most recent report (2009, p. 4), when he stated that: 'The personal accountability of the most senior managers in all of the public services now needs to be fully understood.' This viewpoint has been echoed in the report *Changing Lives* (Scottish Executive, 2006, p. 49), which states that to develop personalised services that revitalise and refocus services on the core values of social work will mean 'making full and effective use of the whole social service workforce, building capacity, developing confidence and trust at all levels and allowing a significant shift in the balance of power and control'. This will mean that managers will have to develop 'trust in their staff, making sure that they are enabled and empowered to practise professional autonomy in their day-to-day work, within a framework that promotes personal accountability and enables safe yet creative practice'.

Accountability to other agencies

In line with joint working in the area of work with older people as envisaged in the Joint Future Group agenda (Scottish Executive, 2000), the social worker in the above case would be involved in a single shared assessment and may be making recommendations that will involve health and other professionals. Collaborative working of this kind requires that there need to be adequate arrangements for accountability and this is often achieved through the application of interagency agreements and protocols. Lines of accountability need to be transparent because in situations of collaborative practice there can sometimes be a lack of a clear hierarchical structure with no easy way of establishing who is responsible for particular aspects of the case and what they are accountable for. It can then be difficult for service users to hold anyone to account for a failure to provide services. The mixed welfare economy has contributed to a blurring of lines of accountability. In many cases, there is no one person of whom it could be said 'the buck stops here'. Pollack (2009, p. 839) talked about 'the prevalence of a multiplicity of accountability relationships which may lead to accountability overload and an overall fragmented and fuzzy accountability'. This can lead to confusion not only for service users but also for all agencies involved because the responsibility for decision making is not clearly understood. Many service users find themselves in touch with a bewildering array of professionals whose roles and responsibilities are dimly understood, if at all.

In such situations, there is little transparency and so the ability to hold individual professionals accountable is diminished. One way to address this would be the use of case reviews at which service users and their carers are present. These can be a useful mechanism for demonstrating accountability to service users by ensuring their presence and providing them with copies of relevant reports and action plans detailing the work of various agencies and clarifying the roles and responsibilities of all involved.

Legal accountability

Local authorities derive their mandate to deliver services from statutory duties and responsibilities and these in turn are delegated to their employees. The social worker undertaking this community care assessment will, therefore, require to work within the appropriate legislative framework and may be held accountable for a failure to carry out duties. In this case, there will be duties under s. 12A of the Social Work (Scotland) Act 1968 to undertake an assessment of needs. Failure to carry out duties could lead to legal challenge. This could be by way of a judicial review, a process that can be pursued through the Court of Session and can be raised where there are allegations that a decision taken was illegal, procedurally unfair or irrational. Alternatively, an action could be raised based on s. 6 of the Human Rights Act 1998 that might allege that the local authority has acted in a way that breaches an individual's human rights as laid down in the European Convention on Human Rights.

Public accountability

Public scrutiny of social work practice is now much more rigorous and more subject to regulation than it was in the past. The provision of social work services in the area of community care as in other areas is monitored through a national system of monitoring and inspection. National Care Standards have been established which ensure that the provision of services will meet identified standards and will enable the public to know what those standards are. The public can, therefore, hold authorities to account if the care they provide falls below the required standards in any way. The Scottish Council for the Regulation of Care, known as the Care Commission, which was set up by the Regulation of Care (Scotland) Act 2001, was given responsibility for the registration and inspection of care provision. In addition, the Social Work Inspection Agency (SWIA) was set up in 2005 to inspect local authority social work functions and suggest and encourage improvements in the provision of services. The Public Services Reform (Scotland) Act 2010 received royal assent on 28 April 2010. Among other provisions, s. 44 of this Act establishes Social Care and Social Work Improvement Scotland (SCSWIS), a new body that brings together the Care Commission and the SWIA. It will have the general duty of furthering improvement in the quality of social services in Scotland, and will encompass registration of the social services work-force, inspections of local authority social work functions and the regula-tion and inspection of care services.

If Mrs J was admitted to residential care or offered a package of care to sustain her in her own home, then not only will the standards for her care be established but there will be regular inspection to ensure that these standards are met. If they are not, then the agency will be held to account for its failure. In addition, there is now a public services ombudsman in Scotland. The Scottish Public Services Ombudsman Act 2002 established a one-stop shop to deal with complaints, which relate to the public sector. While a full list of such authorities is set out in Schedule 2 to the Act, those which would have relevance to social work in particular include all Scottish public authorities, health boards, SCSWIS and the Scottish Social Services Council. Mrs J, or her son as her authorised representative, could make a complaint about any maladmin-istration in respect of her case to the ombudsman. She could also complain to the newly established body, SCSWIS. Section 77 of the Public Services Reform (Scotland) Act 2010 requires SCSWIS to establish a procedure by which a person, or someone acting on a person's behalf, may make complaints (or other representations) in relation to the provision to the person of a care service or about the provision of a care service generally. The description of what constitutes a care service is widely defined and covers almost all local authority services including services to children, support and day care, residential care, fostering and adoption.[1]

Accountability to service users

The ethos of empowerment that underpins social work practice has resulted in a significant move towards accountability to service users.

The idea of the service user as consumer rather than as the passive recipient of services has been crucial in this development. However, there is a tension here for social workers who formerly had a role in advocating for their clients where these same social workers are now gatekeepers to scarce resources and are also constrained by statutory powers. For some service users, negotiating their way through the labyrinth of services and agencies is a major problem. They have to understand different systems and structures as well as the jargon used by professionals, which is often baffling. Service users can also feel that they are isolated and fear that, if they complain, services might be withdrawn. For these reasons, pressure groups and user-led services now have an important role to play in holding service providers to account.

Service users, such as Mrs J, could use the complaints procedures that have been set up by social services departments. Each local authority is bound to set up and publish details of a complaints procedure (s. 5B(1) of the Social Work (Scotland) Act 1968). This allows an individual to make representations concerning the discharge of local authority functions under the 1968 Act and other designated statutes. However, this limits the range of individuals who can raise a complaint in law, namely those to whom the local authority owes a duty under the Act. Local authorities are required to designate officers who will receive and investigate representations made. Authorities are expected to assist people to make complaints and direct them to sources of independent advice. Each formal complaint must be investigated by an independent officer of the local authority and responded to within a specified period of time. A complaint may be made by anyone for whom the local authority provided or should provide a service or anyone who has had that service withdrawn. Local authorities are required to designate a complaints manager who will receive and investigate representations made. Authorities are expected to assist people to make complaints and direct them to sources of independent advice. Each formal complaint must be investigated in the first instance informally, responded to within a specified period of time and a report issued giving findings, conclusions and recommendations. If the complainant is still dissatisfied, they can ask for an investigation. Again, if the outcome of the investigation is not satisfactory to the service user, an independent review panel will be set up. The decision of the review will be communicated to the local authority which will set out in writing what it intends to do. Ultimately, if the local authority still does not act, the decision could be reported to the local authority ombudsman or challenged by way of a judicial review or in the courts under the Human Rights Act 1998.

Service users can always hold local authorities to account by using the procedures available to them within legislation such as the Social Work

(Scotland) Act 1968 to challenge decisions that have been made. In addition, it should be remembered that service users can take action against any public authority on the grounds that their rights under the ECHR have been breached.

Professional accountability

There are aspects of professional accountability that link with public accountability. Social service professionals in Scotland now have to adhere to the *Code of Practice for Social Service Workers* drawn up by the Scottish Social Services Council (SSSC, 2009), which sets out the standards of professional conduct and practice required of them. The SSSC was set up by the Regulation of Care (Scotland) Act 2001. It has three objectives:

- To strengthen and support the workforce
- To raise standards of practice
- To protect those who use services.

To fulfil these objectives to protect service users and their carers, the SSSC has responsibility for key areas:

- To establish registers of key groups of social services staff
- To publish codes of practice for social service employees and employers
- To regulate the training and education of the workforce.

Among the other standards, social service workers must be 'accountable for the quality of their work and take responsibility for maintaining and improving their knowledge and skills'. It is a condition of employment that workers are registered with the SSSC and they may be disciplined or deregistered for misconduct. This ensures that social service workers will be held personally accountable for their failure to carry out their professional role.

In addition, the British Association of Social Workers has a code of ethics, which outlines the values and principles that are integral to social work (BASW, 2002). *The Framework for Social Work Education in Scotland* (Scottish Executive, 2003, p. 19) asserts that 'social work is a moral activity' and goes on to say that social workers 'should be able to understand moral reasoning and make decisions in difficult ethical situations, especially where there are conflicting moral obligations'. This position was further explored by Braye and Preston-Shoot (2001, p. 53), who stated: 'Employing agencies clearly have a claim on social work's accountability', but as Wilmot (1997) argued, in situations where allegiance conflicts with ethical practice in relation to an individual, the moral accountability is to the person rather than the agency. Together, these codes of practice and ethics convey a message that workers are accountable at a personal and professional level for the services that are offered. In addition, the ethical code of the International Federation of Social Work (IFSW, 2004) highlights the ethical conflict and dilemmas that may arise between the accountability to service users, colleagues, agency and society.

These tensions between accountability to one's employer, to service users and to professional values could be illustrated by returning to our fictional case study. Let us imagine that the worker has undertaken the assessment. She has been influenced by the ethos of community care and her assessment has been needs rather than resource led. In her meetings with Mrs J, the latter has been distressed at the idea that she might be placed in residential care. She is also worried about her son's health and does not want to make unreasonable demands on him. The social worker has identified a package of care for Mrs J. However, her line manager has stated that it is not possible to meet all the expenses that would be incurred because the budget is already overstretched. He suggests that Mrs J's son will have to do more for his mother and that the worker should put in place a much reduced care package. The worker feels that Mrs J and her son will be so pleased to get any kind of package that allows her home that they will accept what is offered, but she fears they will both suffer in the long term. The worker is torn between the professional value of protecting the rights and promoting the interests of Mrs J and her son. She is also accountable to them for the assessment that has been made and the plan for the kind of care that will be offered. Should she explain to them what has happened and inform them of their right to challenge the decision that has been made? There is also her accountability to her employer to abide by agency policies. The social worker has a difficult task in finding an accommodation between these conflicting accountabilities.

Social work in the past two decades seems to be increasingly affected by outcome-driven imperatives. Public accountability in terms of performance indicators, targets and procedures is demanded. Alongside these demands we have to factor in the requirements for regulation and inspection of workers and the services they provide. Many of the changes that have come about in relation to social work practice have been introduced as a consequence of recommendations made following inquiries into cases where there have been tragic outcomes. Public confidence has been affected by the publicity surrounding these inquiries and the emphasis on procedures is one way of holding workers to account for what they have done, or for what they have failed to do.

The question for social workers in the twenty-first century is how they will juggle these conflicting demands and constraints and follow them through, while still taking account of the principles set out in professional codes of ethics. The code of practice demands that social workers should be accountable for their work. The ethical code of the IFSW reflects on the challenges and dilemmas that face social workers as they make ethically informed decisions about how to act in each particular case. The IFSW (2004) noted that some of the problem areas include:

- The fact that the loyalty of social workers is often in the middle of conflicting interests
- The fact that social workers function as both helpers and controllers
- The conflicts between the duty of social workers to protect the interests of the people with whom they work and societal demands for efficiency and utility
- The fact that resources in society are limited.

Accountability and professional autonomy

Changing Lives (Scottish Executive, 2006) stated that social work services must develop a new organisational approach to managing risk, which ensures among other things that there be 'clear accountability frameworks which make explicit the accountabilities of the social worker and that social workers ... exercise professional autonomy within a clear framework of accountability' (p. 50). It refers to social workers as autonomous professionals but the question needs to be asked if accountability and autonomy are conflicting imperatives. Clark (2000, p. 155) argued that professional autonomy refers to 'freedom of choice of the individual professional practitioner to make decisions about how to act', although this freedom has to be understood to lie within the framework as defined by the professional group. Therefore, this freedom is not about acting according to one's own values or judgements, but rather it means working within the professional code of conduct as well as within guidance, rules and procedures. Social workers use discretion in their decision making and they balance conflicting needs, decide on the allocation of frequently scarce resources and manage risk. It was argued in *Changing Lives* that the opportunity for social workers to exercise professional judgement has been constrained by tighter management accountability, itself a response to increasing requirements placed on organisations in response to high-profile cases. It is possible to identify two different elements of accountability, namely personal accountability for decision making and professional judgement. Social workers need to be able to justify their decisions, calling on their knowledge base and their understanding of risk. To do this, they will need to be offered adequate supervision, which is not just about factual information about their caseloads, but is an opportunity to reflect on their practice.

Changing Lives (Scottish Executive, 2006, p. 59) noted that one of the strengths of social work had traditionally been that professional supervision had been used 'to challenge practice and discuss complex problems and their solution'. The writers of the report were concerned by the evidence that suggested that supervision was, in effect, often being used as a means for the manager to take accountability for the social worker's actions rather than promoting and enabling personal professional accountability. They concluded that if the social services workforce was to develop professional autonomy within a framework of accountability, a new approach to supervision will have to be found and they consider that a new term will have to be used to convey this new approach. The new term they have chosen is 'consultation', which should include three core elements, namely performance management, staff development and staff support.

Conclusion

There is a danger that the present focus on the concern about public accountability is overshadowing the regard for professionalism. There will continue to be a dilemma for social workers to act as professionals, their interventions informed by their professional values, and at the same time to remain accountable to the bureaucracies of which they are a part.

Trust is hugely important. It becomes eroded when inquiries into tragedies question the competence of social workers and the blame culture contributes to this. However, there could be a danger that the lines, or threads, of accountability might become chains, which will stifle the professionalism of workers and their ability to make informed and holistic decisions. In addition, these structures that have been put in place will only work if there is openness towards all the stakeholders who have an interest in the delivery of social services, and, in particular, there is real commitment towards ensuring that accountability to service users is not, in the final analysis, empty rhetoric.

References

Banks, S. (2004) *Ethics, Accountability and the Social Professions*, Basingstoke, Palgrave Macmillan.

Banks, S. (2009) 'Professional values and accountabilities', in R. Adams, L. Dominelli and M. Payne (eds) *Critical Practice in Social Work* (2nd edn), Basingstoke, Palgrave Macmillan.

BASW (British Association of Social Workers) (2002) *The Code of Ethics for Social Work*, London, Venture Press.

Braye, S. and Preston-Shoot, M. (2001) 'Social work practice and accountability', in L.A. Cull and J. Roche (eds) *The Law and Social Work*, Basingstoke, Palgrave Macmillan.

Care Standards Tribunal (2005) *Lisa Arthurworrey-v-Secretary of State for Education and Skills* [2004] 268.PC, available online at www.carestandardstribunal.gov.uk/Judgments/j196/Lisa%20Arthurworrey%20v%20Secretary%20of%20State%20for%20Education%20and%20Skills.doc [accessed 6 July 2010].

Clark, C.L. (2000) *Social Work Ethics: Policies, Principles and Practice*, Basingstoke, Macmillan – now Palgrave Macmillan.

Clark, C.L. with Asquith, S. (1985) *Social Work and Social Philosophy*, London, Tavistock.

Eby, M. and Morgan, A. (2008) 'Accountability', in S. Fraser and S. Matthews (eds) *The Critical Practitioner in Social Work and Health*, London, Sage.

IFSW (International Federation of Social Workers) (2004) *Ethics in Social Work, Statement of Principles*, available online at www.ifsw.org/f38000032.html [accessed 15 June 2010].

Laming, H. (2003a) *The Victoria Climbié Inquiry: Report of an Inquiry by Lord Laming*, Cm 5730, London, TSO.

Laming, H. (2003b) Speech to the inquiry, 25 January 2003, available online at www.nationalarchives.gov.uk/ERORecords/VC/2/2/keydocuments/lordstate.htm [accessed 1 September 2010].

Laming, H. (2009) *The Protection of Children in England and Wales: A Progress Report*, HC 330, London, TSO.

Pollack, D. (2009) 'Legal risk, accountability and transparency in social work', *International Social Work*, 52: 837–42.

Scottish Executive (2000) *Community Care: A Joint Future:* Report of the Joint Future Group, Edinburgh, Scottish Executive.

Scottish Executive (2003) *The Framework for Social Work Education in Scotland*, Edinburgh, Scottish Executive.

Scottish Executive (2006) *Changing Lives: Report of the 21st Century Social Work Review*, Edinburgh, Scottish Executive.

Shardlow, S. (1995) 'Confidentiality accountability and the boundaries of client–worker relationships', in R. Hugman and D. Smith (eds) *Ethical Issues in Social Work*, London, Routledge.

SSSC (Scottish Social Services Council) (2009) *Code of Practice for Social Service Workers, and Code of Practice for Employers of Social Service Workers*, available online at www.sssc.uk.com/sssc/homepage/codes-of-practice.html [accessed 11 August 2010].

Wilmot, S. (1997) *The Ethics of Community Care*, London, Cassell.

Note

1. The situation following devolution has meant that each jurisdiction within the UK has a different set of regulatory institutions. The Care Quality Commission is the independent regulator of health and social care in England and regulates care provided by the NHS, local authorities, private companies and voluntary organisations. The General Social Care Council is the body responsible in England for the registration of the social care workforce, although it was announced in July 2010 that the functions of the GSCC will be taken over by the Health Professions Council; Wales has the Care and Social Services Inspectorate, Northern Ireland has the Regulation and Quality Improvement Authority and the Northern Ireland General Social Care Council. All these bodies have similar though not identical responsibilities but in general they are responsible for the registration and inspection of care provision and ensuring that National Care Standards are met.

Chapter 3

Risk, Professional Judgement and the Law: Antinomy and Antagonism in an Age of Uncertainty

MIKE TITTERTON AND SUSAN HUNTER

In history, in social life, nothing is fixed, rigid or definitive. And nothing ever will be. (Gramsci, 1985, p. 31)

Introduction

The most pressing task that any welfare professional faces, when working with vulnerable individuals, is that of making decisions about risk. Professionals are increasingly called upon to account for, and to justify, the judgements they make concerning the welfare of their clients in health and social care settings (Titterton, 2005a; Carson and Bain, 2008). It is difficult to conceive of a more interesting, if deeply challenging, time for social work students and practitioners to be studying risk and the law in respect of the health and social services within the UK, and specifically in Scotland, which has introduced new safeguarding legislation, the Adult Support and Protection (Scotland) Act 2007 (ASPA), which is unique in the UK.

Risk has come to dominate professional and social life in the twenty-first century, in ways that are only now coming to be appreciated and understood by social scientists and practitioners alike. The recent surge in official documents is testimony to the growth in importance of this topic (see for example Mental Welfare Commission for Scotland, 2006). The Multi-Agency Public Protection Arrangements in relation to serious offenders also reflect this, as do the new proposals for the protection of vulnerable adults in England and the Protection of Vulnerable Groups (Scotland) Act 2007. Moreover, the remarkable flourishing of the academic literature on risk underlines this trend (see for example Barry, 2007; Mitchell and Glendinning, 2007; Heyman et al., 2009).

Risk-related incidents throw into sharp relief issues to do with public trust and professional expertise, while deftly delineating demarcation disputes about the scope and competency of the law. From a legal point of view, questions are posed about the respective domains of individual and common rights, of the citizen and the state, of the private sphere and public sphere, of civil society and what Habermas (1962) conceived as the *Offentlichkeit* – the arena where meanings are articulated and, as is often the case, disputed by social actors or, in our context, the various stakeholders.

In one sense, social work is similar to law; social work can be seen as mediation (Philp, 1979; Warner and Gabe, 2004). The law is both a product and an expression of changing social values as is social work but, in many situations, social work practice is constrained by the law as well as underpinned by it in the process of individualising its application. While the law may be perceived as the societal realm par excellence for mediating this discord, there are limitations with respect to the topic of 'risk'; the contention here is that it is the public sphere that supplies the proper forum for this. Moreover, the authors will examine a choice selection of tensions, which form intriguing aspects of the contested nature of these domains. These sets of tensions will be deployed here as organising motifs for the discussion:

1. Regulation agenda versus rights agenda
2. Personalisation of service versus personalisation of risk
3. Greater flexibility and freedom for the user versus requirement for protection from forms of abuse
4. Limits of public law versus scope of the private sphere
5. Standardisation of service versus local discretion and initiative
6. Professional judgements about risk versus private interpretation and choice.

These tensions, antagonisms and doctrinal clashes over risk represent manifestations of the construction of 'uncertainty' and mirror aspects of the efforts to anticipate, manage and regulate risk in complex, 'postmodern' societies. They also involve competing narratives of risk. Health and social care practitioners and their managers are faced with such risks on a daily basis. In this chapter, it is argued that in order to make sense of them, individuals need to develop a critical understanding of these tensions and the issues at stake. It will be contended that lawyers and welfare professionals need to embrace this uncertainty, in what is termed a 'positive risk-taking approach', in order to improve health and welfare outcomes for vulnerable children and adults (Titterton, 1999, 2005a, 2010).

The authors will first consider the regulatory landscape now to be found in Scotland. They will then attempt to clarify the main terms of debate, before moving on to discuss the central issues, tensions and dilemmas arising from professional judgements concerning risk in an age of uncertainty.

The changing landscape of regulation

Core tensions:

1. Regulation agenda versus rights agenda
5. Standardisation of service versus local discretion and initiative

In his comparative look at trends within the public sector of the four countries of the UK, particularly with respect to community care and social care policy, Titterton (2001, 2005a) noted that as well as intriguing divergences, there are commonalities (see also Hunter and Wistow, 1987). With its distinctive legal and social policy traditions, Scotland and its Parliament, which was given a new lease of life in 1999, has the ability to innovate. In terms of legislative measures in the social work and social care field, Scotland has pressed ahead with legislation, such as the Adults with Incapacity (Scotland) Act 2000 (AwIA), the Mental Health (Care and Treatment) (Scotland) Act 2003 (MHCTA), and the Adult Support and Protection (Scotland) Act 2007; it has the ability to introduce variations in proposals, such as those relating to the protection of vulnerable adults within the UK.

Common features include the shared emergence of the regulation agenda. The landscape of regulation of health and social care systems for adults, and for children, is in constant flux in the UK (Adil, 2008). As Adil (2008, p. 199) noted, there is a 'lack of agreement as to how risks should be defined and identified', as well as duplication and confusion as agencies attempt to respond to these differing interpretations. Alongside equivalent changes in England, this approach can also be witnessed in recent developments in Scotland. Yet further reform has taken place in the shape of a new regulatory commission, Social Care and Social Work Improvement Scotland. These changes have their genesis in the Crerar Review of public service scrutiny (Scottish Government, 2007) and will come into effect now the Public Services Reform (Scotland) Act 2010 has become law.

Stirred by the results of the independent inquiries such as that commissioned by Dundee's Children and Young Person's Child Protection Committee, tragic cases such as Brandon Muir, Caleb Ness and Dylan

Lockerbie have raised difficult questions in Scotland about the failures of regulatory systems, the blame culture, the training of social worker and healthcare staff, and indeed the parental roles and responsibilities of parents who misuse drugs. Issues to do with recording and communication systems within and between agencies have also been highlighted, as well as the heavy caseloads and administrative burdens placed on social workers. The shortage and uneven spread of experienced staff has also been identified.

The question of *quis custodiet custodiens*, who regulates the regulators when they fail to identify weaknesses in systems for protecting the public is a moot one, although from a legal point of view, final accountability must rest with the government (Heyman et al., 2009). Criticisms of 'overregulation' and 'overprotection' of vulnerable people have been made, especially in terms of the negative perceptions of risk that some recent legislative and policy measures have embodied. Titterton (2005a) was critical of the top-down approach used across the four countries, where scarce public funds have been deployed to fuel the growth of regulatory mechanisms, rather than investing in the capacity of staff, users and informal carers.

The construction of risk and rise of positive risk taking

Core tension:

6. Professional judgements about risk versus private interpretation and choice

There is no space here to comment on the burgeoning literature on risk (for commentaries, see Stalker, 2003; Titterton, 2005a; Barry, 2007; Mitchell and Glendinning, 2007; Heyman et al., 2009). A major issue within the literature concerns the definition and understanding of 'risk' (Heyman et al., 2009). Described by Titterton (2010) as having five faces or aspects, risk is:

- *politically contested* – including over issues of trust, authority and expertise
- *socially constructed* – in that there are social factors that shape and influence perceptions of risk
- *culturally aspected* – that is, variable across countries and regions
- *experiential* – a quintessential element of the subjective experience of being human
- *dual natured* – featuring both positive and negative features.

In their work, professionals need to acknowledge the diversities of personal experience, as well as strategies for managing uncertainty in everyday life, respecting competing narratives and framing interpretations across the life course.

'Risk-taking' in healthcare and social work has been defined as 'a course of purposeful action based on informed decisions concerning the possibility of positive and negative outcomes of types and levels of risk appropriate in certain situations' (Titterton, 2005a, p. 25). This definition highlights the elements of purpose, the setting of objectives and informed decision making by service users, alongside the appraisal of options, particularly in relation to potential harms and benefits. It sets boundaries for decision making about risk-taking, although these are subject to negotiation and, where relevant, some legal constraints such as substitute decision making under the provisions of the AwIA 2000.

This definition presents risk-taking within the context of welfare services, not as a spontaneous activity but as something undertaken following careful consideration of the context within which the activity is to occur. There should be a purpose or reason for any action related to the taking of risks. It should be an informed choice as far as possible. Indeed, recently modernised legislation, in the form of the AwIA 2000, established capacity as a situation-specific concept rather than an all-or-nothing state that adds to the complexity of professional task and judgement.

Making judgements in uncertain times and unloved places

Core tension:

3. Greater flexibility and freedom for the user versus requirement for protection from forms of abuse

If any doubts lingered about the arrival of an era shorn of comforting certainties, the inconclusive outcome of the UK general election in 2010 and resultant coalition government should have dispelled them. 'Welcome to the age of uncertainty', proclaimed one national newspaper (Beckett, 2010); the article also cited the financial meltdown, expenses scandal, devolution, Europe, energy and spending cuts. As it is becoming abundantly clear that lightly regulated capitalism (with its financial sector lightly regulated in contrast to the social welfare workforce) is failing, what will it be like to practise social work in such circumstances?

Risk work conducted by social workers and allied professions in relation to the care of children and adults at risk of harm is increasingly taking place in what are referred to here as 'uncertain times and unloved places'. Intriguingly, Warner and Gabe (2004) pick up on Lupton's seminal work on risk and 'otherness' and develop notions of space, place and the 'street', and how mental health service users are being increasingly identified with those 'marginal spaces and unloved places' (Wolch and Philo, 2000, p. 144, cited in Warner and Gabe). Ellis and Davis (2001, p. 138) referred to this as a 'means of governing the dangerous welfare "other"'. Social work is perceived as a 'liminal' profession since it deals with the 'in-between' areas of the public and private spheres (Christie, 2001; Warner and Gabe, 2004). In this sense, it becomes a form of 'edgework', precariously balanced within the nexus of tensions described in this chapter. It is within this indeterminancy that social workers must make judgements concerning the welfare of individuals who may be deemed to be 'vulnerable' or at risk of harm in some way.

Risk-taking should be acknowledged as presenting opportunities for learning and development and as an essential feature in contributing to the quality of life of individuals, as well as involving potential harms for children and families.

New laws, new issues

Core tensions:

2. Personalisation of service versus personalisation of risk
4. Limits of public law versus scope of the private sphere

In her discussion of vulnerability, Fawcett (2009) provided a critique of the dominant construction as providing a narrow definition that relies on certainty and rigid interpretations. As she argued, vulnerability is a concept with 'many meanings and applications' (p. 482). Building upon the work of Grenier (2004), she contended that recognising this allows social workers and health professionals to open up 'critical space', and especially to open the spaces for 'lived experiences and stories' (p. 479). She criticised the construction of 'frailty' and added that professionals dwell on the weaknesses of older people at the expense of their strengths and abilities. Professionals are encouraged to recognise 'uncertain experiences', to learn to live with these and, in our view, to work with them. Perhaps one of the most contentious provisions in the ASPA 2007 is the one that allows the sheriff to dispense with consent in a capable adult who meets the three-point test of an 'adult at risk' where circumstances of 'undue pressure' can be established from a third party, without which the adult would make different decisions.

Waterson (1999) and Kemshall (2002) have argued that risk is displacing need as the dominant concern of social policy. Brown (2006) also highlighted the clash between risk and need in his review of the revising of England's 1983 Mental Health Act, which eventually led to the Mental Health Act 2007, and accused the government of producing a muddle. Spencer-Lane (2010, p. 43), among others, points to the 'confusing patchwork of conflicting statutes and soft law enacted over 60 years' that characterise adult social care law in England. In February 2010, the Law Commission published its consultation paper on adult social care, which put forward proposals for reform of the law. While England and Wales use the terms 'vulnerable adults' and 'safeguarding', Scotland has opted for the terms 'adults at risk of harm' and 'adult protection', and Scotland's MHCTA 2003 also avoided indefinite detention of patients, providing for compulsory community-based treatment orders. The decision of the Scottish Parliament to mandate in relation to adult protection with the ASPA 2007, however, meant that Scotland 'reentered the controversial borderland of state intervention into the private lives and private homes of adults with its associated ethical dilemmas' (Mackay, 2008, p. 27).

In Scotland, there is now legislation on which professionals can draw to intervene to protect individuals at risk of harm and to protect their human rights to autonomy and privacy. If a social work, welfare or health professional considers an adult is at risk and in need of protection, what provisions are at their disposal? If the adult in question lacks capacity and remembering that decisions must be situation specific under the legislation, professionals can use the Adults with Incapacity (Scotland) Act 2000 (AwIA). If the individual has a 'mental disorder', professionals may intervene under the terms of the Mental Health (Care and Treatment) (Scotland) Act 2003 (MHCTA). Nonetheless, there has long been recognition of a gap in provision covering adults who are able to make decisions for themselves but who might be vulnerable to exploitation or harm.

The Adult Support and Protection (Scotland) Act 2007 (ASPA) was introduced as an attempt to respond to this concern. This Act is the third plank in this raft of legislation and provides the duty for 'council officers' to investigate the circumstances of adults who can be shown to be 'at risk of harm', the duty on public bodies to collaborate, including the creation of adult protection committees, and intervention orders as a last resort. Once across the threshold, professionals can only proceed with the adult's consent, a proviso that supports autonomy.

These three legislative measures interact with one another offering a repertoire of intervention powers that complement each other; a detailed comparison of their commonalities and differences can be found in a government document (Scottish Government, 2009; see also Chapter 9). They are underpinned by a set of principles that clarify the ethical basis and with which professionals are expected to comply in its implementation. These include respect for individual wishes, benefit (not 'best interests') to the individual, least restrictive option, respect for the views of significant others, participation and non-discrimination. The principles are intended to provide a counterbalance to the power of state and professional intervention to overrule the wishes of individuals. Further, they are in line with the provisions and intent of the Human Rights Act 1998 (HRA), which, in addition to specific articles such as Article 5 'liberty and security of person' and Article 8 'right to privacy and a family life', set out some principles of its own, namely that any interference must be 'lawful, necessary and proportionate'. All legislation must not only be what is called 'HRA compliant' but also applied in a consonant manner; professionals must understand this in making their decisions to intervene.

While there is no concept of risk in law, this 'suite of legislation' (Mackay, 2008), taken together with the HRA, provides a framework of options for intervention on behalf of vulnerable adults at risk from others or themselves, and of protections against overzealousness on the part of professionals and public agencies who have a 'duty of care'. Although the rest of the UK has not opted to mandate on behalf of individuals with capacity but who are 'vulnerable', the legislation in Scotland provides a window of opportunity to begin, if not resolve, a dialogue about the nature of the risks in an individual's life. This legislation and its underpinning principles are an addition to the professionals' decision-making armoury.

Since the introduction of direct payments in 1997 in the Community Care (Direct Payments) (Scotland) Act, offering service users cash in lieu of services has been at the heart of the government's personalisation agenda. This policy was favourably reviewed in *A Review of Self Directed Support in Scotland* (Scottish Government, 2008) and in consultative proposals for legislation. Local authorities are expected to offer this option to service users as a first step; in other words, individuals will have to opt out rather than opt in to managing an individual budget (Scottish Government, 2008, 2010). Expressions of concern about the risks of financial exploitation and the burden of responsibility have been raised, along with practicalities of operating direct payments (Scourfield, 2005; Manthorpe et al., 2009). These arrangements pose new challenges and risks for professionals and service users alike. The possibility of abuse in the low pay rates, unsocial hours and demanding work among the unregulated market of personal assistants, with the dilemma of encroachment on the powers and choices of service users, has been raised (Scourfield, 2005).

The Scottish legislation, like the legal proposals in England, skirts around the concept of 'risk' and where it is touched on, it tends to be dealt with in a negative and restrictive manner; this remains a key problem. Given that 'risk' is not a legal concept, it is not typically clarified within the law; however, legal conceptualisation of the issues can be used by practitioners to assist in justifying risk strategies (Titterton, 2005a; Carson, 2008). What the law does do is offer a range of lenses through which to test these judgements but it should not be expected to clarify the boundaries of risk. Since, as was suggested above, risk is a multi-aspected concept of a political and social nature, it can be expected to be subject to negotiation within a societal and civil discourse, rather than a legal one per se.

Centrality of uncertainty

Core tensions:

3. Greater flexibility and freedom for the user versus requirement for protection from forms of abuse
4. Limits of public law versus scope of the private sphere

Taylor and White (2006) suggested that professionals should avoid creating certainty where none exists and instead go for 'respectful uncertainty'. It is often the case that the 'certain thing is not the right thing' (p. 944). Since making a decision is influenced by moral judgements, it is necessarily to be contested and is provisional in nature. Taylor and White, Grenier, and Fawcett all contest the assumption that knowledge is linear in form, in other words something that practitioners can simply apply in a straightforward way to the problems of their clients. Thus there needs to be a reframing and reorienting by practitioners towards:

> respecting and acknowledging the stories, narratives and accounts of service users, focusing on what is important to them and working in partnership to build on the resources they utilize to counteract adversity. (Fawcett, 2009, p. 480)

The concept of the social construction of risk suggests that factors such as values and beliefs, age and background, professional training, the media, social/cultural norms and so on are significant in framing 'risk'. This can sometimes lead to the adoption of a safety first approach, which can, in turn, result in additional problems for individuals and practitioners. Risk work with children and adults can be constrained by limited understandings of risk, an absence of risk policies and guidance, a lack of managerial support, and a shortage of appropriate training. The failure to treat risk holistically leads to defensive practice and the blame culture (Titterton, 1999, 2005a; Parton, 2001; Carson and Bain, 2008). Parton (2001, p. 69) stated that it is 'perhaps not surprising ... that risk is ... often defensive and concerned with safety'. Parton (1998) had earlier pressed for the recognition of the role of uncertainty and ambiguity in the case of child welfare.

Defensible practice, not defensive practice, is what professionals should strive for, where it can be demonstrated that the evidence regarding risk has been carefully considered and where professionals can justify their decision making.

Dealing with dilemmas

Core tension:

6. Professional judgements about risk versus private interpretation and choice

The interrelationships among ethics, moral judgements and professional decision making are important to consider. Stanford (2008) has argued that social workers can get stuck in a morass of 'moral conservatism of risk' and warned that they can become 'unreflective co-conspirators' of the conservative 'politics of risk' and the status quo. However, citing Ericson and Doyle (2003), Stanford contended that risk is an 'intensely moral construct': discourses and practices of risk are deeply imbued with a moral language and ethical basis. For writers such as Webb (2006, p. 233), social work ethics help to counter the 'hegemony of neo-liberalism'. Social workers are enabled to engage with their clients as morally significant actors, and as such, Stanford argued, can help to combat and resist moral conservatism.

A recent genre in the literature has identified user expertise in assessment as another challenge for professional perspective (Hunter and Kendrick, 2009). Hunter and Kendrick write of the ambiguities that arise when practitioners are confronted with the 'messy' realities of users' own experiences and knowledge. The expertise that users have needs to be taken on board by professionals, for example in the field of learning disabilities, as a significant part of the problem-solving dialogue and intervention.

Osmo and Landau (2001) called for explicit argumentation in making ethical decisions in social work. Ethical dilemmas are 'frequently encountered ... as part of their regular practice' (p. 483). Given this, it is surprising that more effort is not made to guide and assist practitioners, supporting them in developing the skills and knowledge required for this. Despite the existence of codes of ethics, these authors claim that 'there is no evidence that social workers know and use them in any organised or systematic fashion' (p. 484). Guidance is available from codes of ethics for social workers (for example from the British Association of Social Workers and the International Federation of Social Workers; see Chapter 2) and regulatory standards now exist in the four countries of the UK, including Scotland (SSSC, 2009).

There is consensus in the literature that ethical decisions are not simple, right or wrong, black or white choices: social workers will often face difficult choices with no specific direction where there is a clash of professional values (Reamer, 2005; Sexton et al., 2006). In this case, developing skills for decision making and ethical review is important for the social worker and for trainers and educators. Sexton et al. (2006) pointed to the value of analysing personal values and life experiences. Reamer (2005) discussed conflicts between ethical duties and legal standards that social workers can come across. These provide ethical dilemmas in that 'they entail conflicts among professional values, duties and obligations' (p. 168). There are no simple solutions then: social workers need to engage in a series of steps, he argues, based on the best available knowledge and an understanding of ethical issues. These need to be morally defensible and consistent with ethical standards. This is the approach that HALE (Health and Life for Everyone, www.haletrust. com) adopts in its training with practitioners, with steps outlined to guide good practice (Titterton, 2005b). As Reamer and others note, social work practitioners will always face 'difficult and controversial' decisions. Banks and Williams (2005, p. 1020) argued that social workers could arm themselves by 'practising ethical reflexivity' when thinking through their dilemmas, subjecting values and claims to knowledge to critical analysis.

The question of how social workers make judgements in complex circumstances has been raised in the literature (O'Sullivan, 1999; Titterton, 2005a; Taylor, 2006). The dilemmas and choices often faced by social workers and those in risk work have been described by Titterton (2005a) as 'welfare dilemmas'. Practitioners should take cognisance of the fundamental dilemmas behind the presenting risk; identifying these and weighing the options is a necessary skill for practitioners to foster. They need to develop the techniques and expertise necessary for this. Such ethical dilemmas are at the root of these welfare dilemmas and there is a range of factors that influence decision making about risk in health and welfare settings (Figure 3.1).

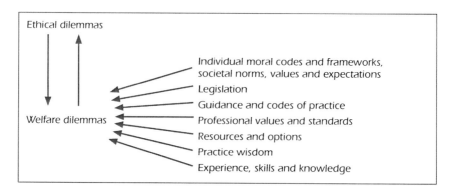

Figure 3.1 What guides us when we try to resolve dilemmas?

The notion of 'risk literacy' or the capacity for critical understanding of and reflective judgements about risk and risk-taking, based on evidence and experiential learning, helps to promote a critical understanding of risk (Titterton, 2010). What this implies, inter alia, is that in risk work with children and adults, efforts should focus on capacity building among users, informal carers and practitioners, through the building of skills, including understanding, evaluating and managing risks through negotiation in partnership. In addition, social workers can use devices such as metaphors and models to help reframe and conceptualise the issues, and to be much more aware of how they think through the decisions they make (Taylor, 2006; Baker and Wilkinson, 2010).

Social work, risk and the law: the role of the public sphere

Core tension:

4. Limits of public law versus scope of the private sphere

Earlier, reference was made to the role of the public sphere, to Habermas's concept of the *Offentlichkeit*. It is this public arena that forms the proper arena for the articulation and consideration of risk and expectations placed by society on social workers and health professionals. These will be subject to negotiation and debate among the social actors involved, including those with a stake in risk decisions. Primarily this is the welfare professional and their client in the first instance. In addition, there needs to be a broader discussion of risk involving members of the public, including informal carers, other professionals, advocates and legal advisers, media representatives and politicians. The weight of legal statutes and quasi-legal advice is on the side of the risk takers, not the risk dodgers (Titterton, 2005a; Carson, 2008; Carson and Bain, 2008). Risk can be used to reinvigorate the debate about the boundaries between social work and the law.

Risk can be expected to rise in prominence on the agenda, while the limits of the legislative domain will become increasingly blurred. There will be even greater pressures on social workers, accompanied by even more efforts for the reform and regulation of social welfare, which may only exacerbate the problems. One of the ways of avoiding this is through the public conducting of an honest and open rethinking of risk, along with an acknowledgement of the six tensions discussed here.

Certain ethical dilemmas likewise require public airing. Consider the emotive issue of the possibility of 'tagging' older people with dementia, which former Scottish minister Malcolm Wicks had floated as a means of keeping them safe (*The Scotsman*, 2007). This, along with the rise of new technology such as 'telecare' for monitoring the welfare of older people, raises issues of risks versus rights. Such thorny issues need further deliberation publicly and it is here that the realm of the public sphere can perform a vital and critical role.

Referring to the 'exhilarating and liberating' times of the 1970s, Beckett (2010, p. 9) evokes a time when 'the country seemed to be bursting out of stifling old structures, history seemed to be being made daily, and people formed improbable dreams and alliances'. In the age of uncertainty, social welfare workers, legal workers and service users can form such a liberating alliance to break out of the confines of overregulation and overprotection to take ownership of risk and forge new critical understandings within this *Offentlichkeit*.

Conclusion

The need for more nuanced understandings of risk and the roles that social work and health professionals can play has been emphasised in this chapter. The celebration of uncertainty, and ambiguity, taking into account the life experiences, fragmented accounts and multiplicities of lived realities of people at risk of harm has been proposed here. Such indeterminacy may appear to sit uneasily in respect of the law; however, the role of the law in terms of justifying decisions can be helpful. There is also a lack of fit with the prescriptive, top-down, overly rationalist world of regulation and risk management, understood in a restrictive sense. Moreover, knowledge is not linear but is contested. Uncertainty sits at the heart of the enterprise. Positive risk-taking has been put forward here as a valuable approach for practitioners to follow, forming risk partnerships with their clients, and with their colleagues in other agencies.

In this chapter, the authors have identified and deliberated upon some of the main tensions that run like live wires through debates surrounding risk and professional judgements. The role of the law is still very much a developing one but one which is unfolding within the limits outlined here with respect to risk. The lines between state intervention and the private sphere are not drawn and fixed, rather, they are shifting, realigning and changing constantly. One factor is public fear, which is so often misplaced and which is fuelled by the media and by governments. This in turn places professionals under the microscope and adds to an already stressful and difficult job. By celebrating uncertainty and advocating the positive taking of risks in partnership with service users, social workers and their legal advisers can combat this fear and promote more innovative, creative and empowering ways of working.

Social work in the twenty-first century will increasingly feature risk, as the government-sponsored report *Changing Lives: Report of the 21st Century Social Work Review* (Scottish Executive, 2006) made clear. Therein lies an opportunity for the social work profession to demonstrate leadership in respect of this highly charged topic. This can be done in close association with other professions, with service users and with local communities to form partnerships for risk, in order to creatively and imaginatively bring choice and change into the lives of vulnerable children and adults.

References

Adil, M. (2008) 'Risk-based regulatory system and its effective use in health and social care', *Journal of the Royal Society for the Promotion of Health*, **128**(4): 196–201.

Baker, K. and Wilkinson, B. (2010) 'Professional risk taking and defensible decisions', in H. Kemshall and B. Wilkinson (eds) *Good Practice in Risk Assessment and Risk Management*, vol. 3, London, Jessica Kingsley.

Banks, S. and Williams, R. (2005) 'Accounting for ethical difficulties in social welfare: issues, problems and dilemmas', *British Journal of Social Work*, 35: 1005–22.

Barry, M. (2007) *Effective Approaches to Risk Assessment in Social Work: An International Literature Review*, Edinburgh, Scottish Executive.

Beckett, A. (2010) 'Into the great unknown', *The Guardian*, 11 May, G2, pp. 6–9.

Brown, P. (2006) 'Risk versus need in revising the 1983 Mental Health Act: conflicting claims, muddled policy', *Health, Risk & Society*, 8(4): 343–58.

Carson, D. (2008) 'Editorial: justifying risk decisions', *Criminal Behaviour and Mental Health*, 18: 139–44.

Carson, D. and Bain, A. (2008) *Professional Risk and Working with People: Decision-making in Health, Social Care and Criminal Justice*, London, Jessica Kingsley.

Christie, A. (2001) 'Gendered discourses of welfare, men and social work', in A. Christie (ed.) *Men and Social Work: Theories and Practices*, Basingstoke, Palgrave – now Palgrave Macmillan.

Ellis, K. and Davis, A. (2001) 'Managing the body: competing approaches to risk assessment in community care', in R. Edwards and J. Glover (eds) *Risk and Citizenship*, London, Routledge.

Ericson, R.V. and Doyle, A. (2003) 'Risk and morality', in R.V. Ericson and A. Doyle (eds) *Risk and Morality*, Toronto, University of Toronto.

Fawcett, B. (2009) 'Vulnerability: questioning the certainties in social work and health', *International Social Work*, **52**(4): 473–84.

Gramsci, A. (1985) *Selections from Cultural Writings*, London, Lawrence & Wishart.

Grenier, A. (2004) 'Older women negotiating uncertainty in everyday life: contesting risk management systems', in L. Davies and P. Leonard (eds) *Social Work in a Corporate Era: Practices of Power and Resistance*, Ashgate, Burlington.

Habermas, J. (1962) *The Structural Transformation of the Public Sphere: An Inquiry into a Category of Bourgeois Society*, Frankfurt am Main, Suhrkamp.

Heyman, B., Alaszewski, A., Shaw, M. and Titterton, M. (2009) *Health Care Through the Lens of Risk: A Critical Guide to the Risk Epidemic*, Oxford, Oxford University Press.

Hunter, D. and Wistow, G. (1987) *Community Care in Britain: Variations on a Theme*, London, King Edward's Hospital Fund.

Hunter, S. and Kendrick, M. (2009) 'The ambiguities of both professional and societal wisdom', *Ethics & Social Welfare*, **3**(2): 158–69.

Kemshall, H. (2002) *Risk, Social Policy and Welfare*, Buckingham, Open University Press.

Law Commission (2010) *Adult Social Care*, Consultation Paper No. 192, Law Commission, London.

Mackay, K. (2008) 'The Scottish adult support and protection legal framework', *Journal of Adult Protection*, **10**(4): 25–36.

Manthorpe, J., Stevens, M., Rapaport, J. et al. (2009) 'Safeguarding and system change: early perceptions of the implications for adult protection services of the English Individual Budgets Pilots – a qualitative study', *British Journal of Social Work*, 39: 1465–80.

Mental Welfare Commission for Scotland (2006) *Rights, Risks and Limits to Freedom: Principles and Good Practice Guidance for Practitioners Considering Restraint in Residential Care Settings*, Edinburgh, Mental Welfare Commission for Scotland.

Mitchell, W. and Glendinning, C. (2007) *A Review of the Research Evidence Surrounding Risk Perceptions, Risk Management Strategies and their Consequences in Adult Social Care for Different Groups of Service Users*, York, Social Policy Research Unit, University of York.

Osmo, R. and Landau, R. (2001) 'The need for explicit argumentation in ethical decision-making in social work', *Social Work Education*, **20**(4): 483–92.

O'Sullivan, T. (1999) *Decision Making in Social Work*, Basingstoke, Macmillan – now Palgrave Macmillan.

Parton, N. (1998) 'Risk, advanced liberalism and child welfare: the need to rediscover uncertainty and ambiguity', *British Journal of Social Work*, 28: 5–27.

Parton, N. (2001) 'Risk and professional judgement', in L.-A. Cull and J. Roche (eds) *The Law and Social Work: Contemporary Issues for Practice*, Basingstoke, Palgrave – now Palgrave Macmillan.

Philp, M. (1979) 'Notes on the form of knowledge in social work', *The Sociological Review*, **27**(1): 83–111.

Reamer, F.G. (2005) 'Ethical and legal standards in social work: consistency and conflict', *Families in Society*, **86**(2): 163–9.

Scotsman, The (2007) 'Elderly patients could be tagged', *The Scotsman*, 20 April.

Scottish Executive (2006) *Changing Lives: Report of the 21st Century Social Work Review*, Edinburgh, Scottish Executive.

Scottish Government (2007) *The Crerar Review: The Report of the Independent Review of Regulation, Audit, Inspection and Complaints Handling of Public Services in Scotland*, Edinburgh, Scottish Government.

Scottish Government (2008) *A Review of Self Directed Support in Scotland: Research Findings*, Edinburgh, Scottish Government.

Scottish Government (2009) *Comparison of the Adult Support and Protection (Scotland) Act 2007 (ASP) with the Adults with Incapacity (Scotland) Act 2000 (AWI) and the Mental Health (Care and Treatment) (Scotland) Act 2003 (MHCT)*, Edinburgh, Scottish Government.

Scottish Government (2010) *Proposals for a Self-Directed Support (Scotland) Bill: Consultation*, Edinburgh, Scottish Government.

Scourfield, P. (2005) 'Implementing the Community Care (Direct Payments) Act: will the supply of personal assistants meet the demand and at what price?', *Journal of Social Policy*, 34: 469–88.

Sexton, C., Jacinto, G.A. and Dziegielewski, S.F. (2006) 'Self-determination and confidentiality: the ambiguous nature of decision-making in social work practice', *Journal of Human Behaviour in the Social Environment*, **13**(4): 55–72.

Spencer-Lane, T. (2010) 'A statutory framework for safeguarding adults? The Law Commission's consultation paper on adult social care', *Journal of Adult Protection*, **12**(1): 43–9.

SSSC (Scottish Social Services Council) (2009) *Code of Practice for Social Service Workers, and Code of Practice for Employers of Social Service Workers*, Dundee, Scottish Social Services Council, available online at www.sssc.uk.com/sssc/homepage/codes-of-practice.html [Accessed 11 August 2010].

Stalker, K. (2003) 'Managing risk and uncertainty in social work: a literature review', *Journal of Social Work*, **3**(2): 211–33.

Stanford, S. (2008) 'Taking a stand or playing it safe?: resisting the moral conservatism of risk in social work practice', *European Journal of Social Work*, **11**(3): 209–20.

Taylor, B.J. (2006) 'Risk management paradigms in health and social services for professional decision making on the long-term care of older people', *British Journal of Social Work*, 36: 1411–29.

Taylor, C. and White, S. (2006) 'Knowledge and reasoning in social work: educating for humane judgement', *British Journal of Social Work*, 36: 937–54.

Titterton, M. (1999) 'Training professionals in risk assessment and risk management: what does the research tell us?', in P. Parsloe (ed.) *Risk Assessment in Social Work and Social Care*, London, Jessica Kingsley.

Titterton, M. (2001) *Social Care Policy in Scotland*, York, Joseph Rowntree Foundation.

Titterton, M. (2005a) *Risk and Risk Taking in Health and Social Welfare*, London, Jessica Kingsley.

Titterton, M. (2005b) 'One step at a time: the steps to better risk taking', *Community Care*, 26 May–1 June, pp. 42–3.

Titterton, M. (2010) 'Positive risk taking with people at risk of harm', in H. Kemshall, and B. Wilkinson (eds) *Good Practice in Risk Assessment and Risk Management*, vol. 3, London, Jessica Kingsley.

Warner, J. and Gabe, J. (2004) 'Risk and liminality in mental health social work', *Health, Risk and Society*, 6(4): 387–99.

Waterson, J. (1999) 'Redefining community care: needs led or risk led?', *Health and Social Care in the Community*, 16(3): 299–309.

Webb, S.A. (2006) *Social Work in a Risk Society*, Basingstoke, Macmillan.

Wolch, J. and Philo, C. (2000) 'From distributions of deviance to definitions of difference: past and future mental health geographies', *Health and Place*, 6(3): 137–57.

Chapter 4

The Role of Assessment in Social Work for Children and Families in Scotland

JANE ALDGATE

Introduction

From very early days, social workers have drawn on knowledge and observations to make professional judgements about how best to help people who are using their services. In her ground-breaking book, *Social Diagnosis*, published in the USA, Mary Richmond (1917) wrote about social workers building up a body of knowledge from their cases, and being able to draw on this to inform their practice. She successfully created a model for social casework and the approach now known in social work as the 'ecological approach' to assessment.

This chapter considers briefly what constitutes assessment in social work, looking at a definition of what it is, the processes that it involves and some of the key theories that are used in assessments in social work. It will then use the *Getting it right for every child* (Scottish Government, 2008) programme of assessment and planning in Scotland to discuss the merits of a national assessment framework.

What is assessment?

From the early beginnings of social work arose the idea that, in order to provide the best possible social work services, workers needed to be able to gather information about a person and their environment, make sense of this information using knowledge and research and then use their professional judgement to decide upon a course of action. From early on, assessment has been seen as a process, not an event. Meyer (1993, p. 2) suggested that assessment is a complex skill. It is:

> The thinking process that seeks out the meaning of case situations, puts the particular case in some order and leads to appropriate inter-

ventions ... Assessment is the intellectual tool for understanding the client's psycho-social situation, and for determining 'what's the matter?'

Meyer (1993, quoted in Austrian, 2002, p. 204) outlined the process of assessment in five steps:

1. Exploration
2. Inferential thinking
3. Evaluation
4. Problem definition
5. Intervention planning.

Austrian (2002, p. 206) summarised the different components of assessment and how each assessment needs to be tailored to the individual person and their situation:

> Assessment, while grounded in professional knowledge and skill, is an individualized process that demands recognition of the uniqueness of person and situation. It is an ongoing process, with intervention possibly subject to some modification as new data emerges. Knowledge of cultural, class, and gender differences and perceptions of problems, emotional or situational, is essential to providing a thorough assessment and good intervention planning. Knowledge of developmental stages, personality theories, and a range of family structures can also be important.

Two key points emerge from this summary:

- The actual process of conducting the assessment, including the relationship between service user and worker, will be as important as the outcome.
- Assessment will always be underpinned by knowledge and research and informed by professional judgement.

Rose (2010) has suggested that assessment is a relational activity and that the development of trust and confidence between family members and the social worker will influence the process. It is necessary that everyone has a clear understanding of the purpose of the assessment, how it is to be done, the information being sought, who will see this and what will happen next.

In their research on kinship care of looked after children, Aldgate and McIntosh (2006) found that families appreciated being treated with respect and being given clear information by social workers and the children's hearings. Writing about empowerment and participation of families, Shemmings and Shemmings (2001, p. 116) pointed out that professionals and families may have different preoccupations:

> Professionals tend to stress procedural aspects of empowerment – for example, sharing records, attending meetings, knowing about complaints procedures – whereas family members usually stress both the procedural and the relational aspects – typically developing trust, being transparent, genuine and even-handed, and being direct, yet sensitive.

There are many contemporary theories that underpin assessment in social work. These have evolved over time and are subject to some degree of social construction. There has been a revolution in thinking about mental health and learning disability, with a move from a medical model of 'what's wrong with this person?' to a social model that recognises that the issues may lie in the circumstances surrounding the person and the reaction of others to them (French and Swain, 2002). Psychological theory has also embraced a more positive approach, moving from a negative diagnostic model to one which emphasises strengths rather than weaknesses (Aldgate, 2006). Related to a strengths approach is the emergence of resilience theory (Seden, 2002; Daniel and Wassell, 2002).

One enduring theory, which has basically not changed as a foundation for assessment, is ecological theory (Bronfenbrenner, 1979). The interplay between person and environment permeates much developmental theory relating to children and adults (see, for example, Aldgate et al., 2006) and has become integral in assessing the wellbeing of individuals.

The law and assessment

Legislation that relates to protecting the rights and promoting the wellbeing of individuals has increasingly influenced the way social work is practised. Children's legislation in the UK, including the Children (Scotland) Act 1995, has embraced the United Nations Convention on the Rights of the Child (United Nations, 1989), emphasising the rights of children to be consulted about decisions affecting their lives. The Children (Scotland) Act 1995, used by social workers and others to give a mandate for services to protect and support children, also makes connections between eligibility for services and the wellbeing of individuals. Children are defined as 'in need' if their health and development are impaired or likely to be impaired without the provision of services (s. 22). The law also allows for immediate intervention if risk of harm is significant (s. 57).

Assessment of risk

Assessing risk is an important part of the social work role across different areas of practice. The principle of identifying risk, responding immediately and looking towards protection of individuals in the long term is embedded in much of the legislation implemented by social workers. What needs to be assessed therefore is the risk of current and future harm to an individual and what services need to be put in place to address that risk. Furthermore, there needs to be consideration of the risk to the individual if services are not available as the risk from not providing services may be extremely serious.

Stalker (2003) suggested that risk has taken priority over welfare in social care services. The increasing emphasis on risk in social work is a reflection of 'the impact of globalisation', which has 'dislocated many areas of social and economic life, giving rise to uncertainties, fears and insecurities: more importance is now attached to calculating choices of individuals' (Stalker, 2003, p. 216). Additionally, professionals in health and social work working in this 'risk society' have become 'increasingly reliant on complex systems of audit, monitoring and quality control' (p. 217). Risk assessment models have tended to focus on this bureaucratic approach (see, for example, literature reviews on the subject by Hagell, 1998; Cleaver et al., 1998).

As Seden (2000, p. 10) pointed out, the development of risk assessment models has also been influenced by a quest for more certainty in predicting harm. Highly publicised 'failures' to protect children from danger, for example, have led professionals to develop checklists of indicators and predictors, which claim to measure the safety of a child within a family or the recurrence of offending behaviour. This approach also lends itself to a concentration on immediacy, neglecting areas of risk where effects may be more evident in the longer term.

The desire to seek a fail-safe method of risk assessment has led to a move towards defensible decision making. Parton (1998) and Stalker (2003) have suggested that 'defensible' has been interpreted as workers wanting to defend their backs. In a more measured context of risk assessment, defensible decision making has an important part to play in managing risk. Recently, some writers have suggested a move away from a negative approach to one that includes an emphasis on recognising 'signs of safety' as well as risk (Turnell and Edwards, 1999). Calder (2002, p. 8) suggests that, in realms other than social work, a risk equation also calculates possible benefits, and he therefore urges that any risk assessment should include weighing up the pros and cons of an individual's circumstances 'in order to inform decision making as to what should happen with regard to intervention and protection'.

While Calder is talking about children, his views apply equally well to adults who are at risk.

Since assessing risk is so important, it is helpful to look at the most commonly used risk assessment models, highlighting their strengths and weaknesses. As Calder (2002, p. 13) suggested, 'there is no ideal risk assessment method or framework'. Practitioners wanting a fail-safe checklist will fail to find one and practitioner judgement will always need to play a part in identifying and responding to risk. In spite of this, there are several identifiable approaches to risk assessment.

Unstructured clinical assessment

Unstructured clinical assessment relies on assessments being made without any structured aide-mémoires, relying on the clinical judgement of professionals. Decisions are justified on the basis of the qualifications and experience of the professional making them but this has led to criticisms of subjectivity and lack of reliability and validity. However, its strength is that it allows assessments to take into account the particular circumstances and context of the situation, and interventions to be tailored accordingly. This approach gives considerable professional discretion but as Douglas and Kropp (2002, p. 624) suggested, it 'is vulnerable to missing important factors that require intervention'.

Actuarial methods of risk assessment

Actuarial methods are designed to predict specific behaviours within specific timescales. Interest in this approach has grown in order to counteract what was seen as the idiosyncratic and intuitive approach of individual clinical assessments. It has also been influenced by the wish to find a way to predict and prevent the likelihood of serious harm to children and adults (Seden, 2000). In youth justice, actuarial scales have been used to predict rates of reoffending. Barry (2007) suggested that such scales may foster a culture of blame towards individuals, for example those with mental health difficulties or parents of children at risk, and fail to bring into the equation external factors in the individual's ecology, such as poverty or neighbourhood.

Munro (2002, p. 881) suggested that actuarial calculations 'have an air of authority and objectivity that can mislead people into crediting them with more accuracy than they deserve'. There are a number of disadvantages to the actuarial approach. First, although there is merit in using factors that have been shown to be predictors in research studies, use also needs to be made of theories of human growth and development, for example understanding the relationship between patterns of attachment in childhood and their application in adults who are parents.

Second, actuarial models tend to develop an inflexible list of factors that cannot take into account the unique set of circumstances for a particular individual: 'To properly apply the actuarial approach, the evaluator is forced to consider a fixed set of factors and cannot consider unique, unusual, or context specific variables that might require intervention' (Douglas and Kropp, 2002, p. 625). The 'dynamic' risk factors Douglas and Kropp are talking about need to be taken into account and cannot always be accurately predicted.

Third, one of the most significant omissions of the actuarial model is that the checklist can only be applied to the specific current or past situations and does not allow for patterns of interactions and transactions over time. Current thinking suggests that risk is more contextual, dynamic and continuous (Seden, 2000).

Fourth, writing about children who have been abused, Jones et al. (2006) suggested that there is no reliable way of weighting the scores for particular factors to develop an aggregated picture of risk. The evidence base can do no more than guide decision making and is not 'a short cut to be reduced to mere numbers' (Jones et al., 2006, p. 278). Furthermore, the scores do not provide a fail-safe way of predicting that an individual is unsafe (Seden, 2000). Calder (2002) concluded that risk assessment is not an exact science. There will be consequential dangers of false positives and false negatives that could have serious consequences for child and family because actions taken by professionals could be based on false premises.

A structured professional judgement approach

Because of the limitations of actuarial approaches to risk assessment, a combination of approaches to risk assessment may, in the end, be most helpful. Douglas and Kropp (2002, p. 651) have taken forward this idea in what they call a 'prevention-based approach' to risk assessment 'characterised by the use of structured professional judgement'. Their work has been developed in relation to risk assessment of violent behaviour but has application to other services users in social work. The model uses scales or tools judiciously, but does not rely on them entirely. An important part of the assessment will be to look at an individual's ecology. The professionals will need to work in partnership with the service user to identify all the strengths and risks. They will then need to weigh the information gathered and bring their professional judgement into the decision making. This model has been adopted by the Scottish Government in the *Getting it right for every child* (GIRFEC) approach to assessment and planning (Aldgate and Rose, 2008).

Policy context for Scotland's framework for assessing and planning for children and families

Since devolution in 1999, Scotland's policies for all children have increasingly been driven by rights, social justice and children's wellbeing, with a growing coherence between different policies for all aspects of children's lives (Stewart, 2004). There are four strategic pillars of the government's vision for children's well-becoming as adults. Children should grow up to be 'successful learners, confident individuals, responsible citizens and effective contributors'. To achieve these outcomes throughout childhood, services should make sure that all children meet eight Well-being Indicators: that they are 'safe, healthy, achieving, nurtured, active, respected, responsible and included' (Scottish Government, 2008, p. 4). Scotland's overarching strategic plan for all children was published in 2001 as *For Scotland's Children* (Scottish Executive, 2001). This document spelt out the circumstances for improving outcomes for all Scotland's children. It addressed honestly Scotland's failure to coordinate services for vulnerable children leaving them 'born to fail' (Vincent and Morgan-Klein, 2008, p. 50). *For Scotland's Children* was distinctive in promoting the role of universal services in early intervention through suggesting every child should have a 'named individual' (p. 90) in health or education, who would be a point of contact for children and families and who could assess and activate additional help for them. This role has been introduced into the GIRFEC framework, to be applied in health and education.

Getting it right for every child

Getting it right for every child has been described by the Minister for Children and Early Years Adam Ingram as 'the golden thread that knits together our policy objectives for children and young people' (Scottish Government, 2010, p. 3). It is the methodology by which all agencies work singly or together. It begins in the universal services of health and education but also applies to targeted help, including additional educational support and social work services. It is directly relevant for children in need of child protection measures and supports a wide range of compulsory measures through the children's hearings system. GIRFEC is, therefore, much more than an assessment framework for social workers and others for children 'in need', including those at risk of significant harm, as in England and Wales (DH, 2000). It gives all practitioners across Scotland a common set of values and principles that can be applied in any circumstance. The GIRFEC values and principles stress the inclusion of children and families in the helping process and underpin the 10 core components that can be applied in any circumstance and setting:

1. A focus on improving outcomes for children, young people and their families based on a shared understanding of well-being.
2. A common approach to gaining consent and to sharing information where appropriate.
3. An integral role for children, young people and families in assessment, planning and intervention.
4. A coordinated and unified approach to identifying concerns, assessing needs, agreeing actions and outcomes, based on the Well-being Indicators.
5. Streamlined planning, assessment and decision-making processes that lead to the right help at the right time.
6. Consistent high standards of cooperation, joint working and communication where more than one agency needs to be involved, locally and across Scotland.
7. A Lead Professional to co-ordinate and monitor multi-agency activity where necessary.
8. Maximising the skilled workforce within universal services to address needs and risks at the earliest possible time.
9. A competent and confident workforce across all services for children, young people and their families.
10. The capacity to share demographic, assessment, and planning information electronically and within and across agency boundaries through the national eCare programme where appropriate. (Scottish Government, 2008, p. 14)

The Scottish Government's aim is to change the culture, systems and practice in all agencies, to introduce child and family-friendly assessment that is consistent, and to ensure that any help is proportionate to the child's needs and risks. To this end, a *Guide to Implementing Getting it right for every child* has been published, drawing on evidence from pathfinders and learning partners (Scottish Government, 2010).

The National Practice Model for assessment and planning

Assessing, planning and reviewing children's progress are built into the GIRFEC methodology through the National Practice Model (Scottish Government, 2008, 2010). It is important to stress that this model is for *all* practitioners and is genuinely multidisciplinary. It can be used to assess any child about whom a practitioner may have concerns. It applies to children at risk of significant harm as well as to children who may have educational or health needs and risks. Risk and need are both built into the model to be used as circumstances dictate. There is no separate assessment framework for social workers or different frameworks for different circumstances as in England, Wales and Northern Ireland. The Scottish National Practice Model has built on and incorporated what was previously known as the Integrated Assessment Framework (see Scottish Government, 2008). The National Practice Model is evidence based, using an ecological, whole child approach, based on long-term evidence of what helps children flourish in their development (Aldgate et al., 2006), thus providing a common language and understanding of children's development that can be shared by all agencies. It also incorporates the concept of resilience in a matrix that helps practitioners make sense of any information they gather (Scottish Government, 2008).

Assessment is seen as the means of identifying help for children and families that is timely (early intervention), proportionate (using as much or as little information as needed) and child and family centred (actively seeks their views and responds to their circumstances).

The National Practice Model is based around eight Well-being Indicators in the strategic vision for all children described earlier, that children should be safe, healthy, achieving, nurtured, active, respected, responsible and included. Any practitioner, as well as children and their families, can use these wellbeing indicators as an aide-mémoire to identify concerns, to help formulate a plan for a child, either in a single agency or on a multi-agency basis, and to measure outcomes after a review of progress has taken place. The Scottish system expects every practitioner to take responsibility for providing help, reprising the title of the Child Protection Audit and Review, *It's Everyone's Job to Make Sure I'm Alright* (Scottish Executive, 2002). There are five questions every practitioner should ask if they have concerns about a child:

1. What is getting in the way of this child or young person's well-being?
2. Do I have all the information I need to help this child or young person?
3. What can I do now to help this child or young person?
4. What can my agency do to help this child or young person?
5. What additional help, if any, may be needed from others? (Scottish Government, 2010, p. 35)

Unlike the other UK countries, there are no fixed templates for professionals to use in more detailed assessments and it is left to individual agencies to decide if they want to use a standard form. The model allows for detailed specialist and risk assessments to be incorporated into the generic assessment (Aldgate and Rose, 2008). There are no timescales set for completion of assessment, indicative of the attitude of the Scottish Government towards valuing the skills and judgement of profes-

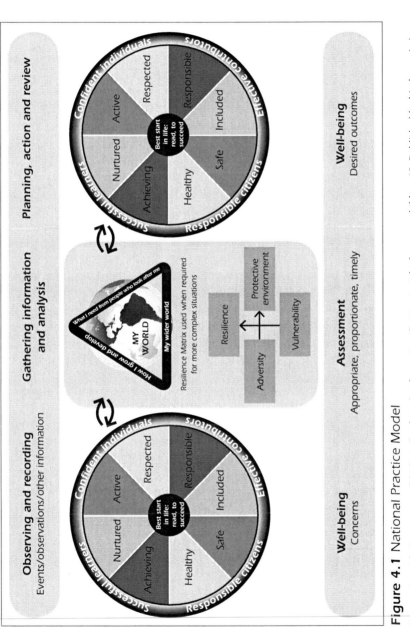

Figure 4.1 National Practice Model

Source: Scottish Government (2010) *A Guide to Implementing Getting it right for every child*, p. 49. Published by kind permission of the Scottish Government

sionals. This means that much will depend on the responsibility of everyone to understand and implement assessment in practice. Training has been found to be essential in implementing GIRFEC in practice (Scottish Government, 2010).

There is an emphasis on agencies streamlining meetings and bureaucracy. If one agency makes an assessment, any other agencies that become involved will trust the judgement of the first agency, thus avoiding elaborate and repetitious referral systems. There is a 'one child, one plan' system. A child who is looked after by the local authority needs a child protection plan, and a plan for additional educational support will have all these elements incorporated into one multi-agency 'child's plan', coordinated by a lead professional. This person will not necessarily be a social worker. It depends on the child's needs.

The normal sequence of using the National Practice Model is as follows:

1. *Identification of concerns using the Well-being Indicators:* In cases where needs are straightforward, and are mainly within the universal services, a plan can be put in place by a named person, using the Well-being Indicators. It is expected that agencies will cooperate on a basis of trust without elaborate referral systems.

2. *Gathering further detailed information:* If agencies need further information, practitioners can use the child-centred 'My World Triangle' to gather information, supplemented by any specialist reports. This is adapted from the Assessment Framework in England and Wales (DH, 2000) with one major difference. It looks at assessment from the perspective of the child, for example 'What do I need from the people who look after me?' This can be used by any agency. It has been incorporated into the hand-held maternal health record that midwives and other health professionals in Scotland use with parents. It is especially helpful for agencies working together on more complex cases of need and risk. It is expected that the My World Triangle will be used proportionately and it is not intended that social workers and others will need to gather information on every aspect of a child's life in every case. During this stage, specialist information such as that needed for assessing additional support for learning or health issues can be incorporated, as well as using risk assessment tools if the child is in need of child protection measures (Aldgate and Rose, 2008).

3. *Analysing information using the Resilience Matrix:* Learning from the problems social workers have had in England in analysing information gathered round the Assessment Triangle, Scotland has added a Resilience Matrix to help practitioners make sense of information they have gathered (Scottish Government, 2008).

4. *Using the Well-being Indicators to construct a child's plan:* The child's plan should include details of what is to be done, by when and by whom and the expected outcomes for the child against the wellbeing indicators. The plan will form the evidence social workers use to refer a child to the reporter for consideration of compulsory measures by a children's hearing.

5. *A review of the child's plan against the Well-being Indicators:* At an appropriate point, the child's progress will be reviewed against the child's plan, using the Well-being Indicators. The emphasis here is not on what has been done, but what outcomes have been achieved for the child. The review incorporates any statutory reviewing requirements such as those for looked after children.

Implementing *Getting it right for every child*

In January 2006, a two-year Pathfinder was established by Highland Council in Inverness to develop and test out an all systems and all agency programme of GIRFEC, with a plan for national implementation by 2011. Implementation nationally is being done gradually, with community planning partnerships opting in as they are able. The government has, to date, taken a low-key approach, believing that it is better to win hearts and minds by persuasion rather than legislation, so, at the time of writing, there is no equivalent of the Children Act 2004, as in England, to underpin the sharing of information and budgets. There are, however, annual targets for local authorities in the form of single outcome agreements between local authorities, the government and the Convention of Scottish Local Authority Services (Scottish Government/COSLA, 2007). Full implementation will depend in large part on this partnership and COSLA's role in supporting GIRFEC. This could be a strength or a hindrance. It is, as yet, too early to judge.

The Scottish Government has concentrated on recommending changes in practice and culture, as well as urging community planning partnerships to streamline their systems but it has left alone the organisational structures of each local authority, which provide the governance for implementing GIRFEC (Scottish Government, 2010). This could be helpful in targeting local issues but it could also lead to councils and health service trusts partially implementing GIRFEC rather than going for a whole systems change approach.

By 2010, Highland Council had rolled out GIRFEC throughout children's services across Highland. It has aligned the National Practice Model with its child protection procedures. Children in need of care and protection, looked after children, children who have offended and others who need compulsory measures are now assessed by the same National

Practice Model, as well as others who need single or multi-agency support (Stradling et al., 2009). Most importantly, each child who needs multi-agency support has one child's plan, based on evidence-led assessment. Where legislation demands certain actions, as where a child may need an educational support plan, this is incorporated into an overarching child's plan.

Where two or more agencies are working together, a lead professional is appointed. A significant feature of the Highland implementation has been to introduce the recommendation in *For Scotland's Children* (Scottish Executive, 2001) that every child should have a named individual (now called a 'named person') in health or education, who is a contact point for early intervention assessment and action. Other local authorities are beginning to incorporate these roles into their implementation of GIRFEC (Scottish Government, 2010).

Although it is the intention to have national computer systems to help in the sharing of information, this has been slow to develop. It will be on a need-to-know basis, and each agency will keep its own records of the child.

Does *Getting it right for every child* fulfil its promise?

A comprehensive external evaluation of the implementation of the Highland Pathfinder by the University of Edinburgh shows the green shoots of significant improvements in the delivery of children's services, beyond what might have been expected in such a short timescale (Stradling et al., 2009; MacNeil and Stradling, 2010a, 2010b). Many service users are getting a more appropriate, timely and proportionate service. The named person is effective in identifying unmet need at an earlier stage. More children and young people with concerns or unmet needs are receiving appropriate and proportionate support within universal services or are receiving targeted interventions for shorter periods of time. This includes using the early warning system identified through concerns to provide effective early intervention, reducing targeted support from social work. The quality of the information being shared across children's services has improved greatly. Significantly fewer children have been referred to the children's reporter on non-offence grounds, a change attributed to more effective screening and more evidence-based decision making. Police and children's services are working more closely together. Social work, the schools and the health service have had to produce fewer reports for the children's hearings. Observations have shown that planning meetings address the need of the whole child (Stradling et al., 2009; MacNeil and Stradling, 2010a).

Strengths and weaknesses of a national framework

So far, the experience of implementing GIRFEC is undoubtedly prom-ising. What is particularly striking is the way all agencies are using the same language for assessment, planning and action through the National Practice Model. This has standardised the use of an evidence-based approach to practice. As MacNeil and Stradling (2010b, p. 14) have suggested:

> A sizeable and growing group of practitioners (mainly those who have been trained and get regular opportunities to apply the practice model) are using these processes to make professional judgements that are based on evidence which can be reviewed by others in terms of its soundness, the way in which it is interpreted and the validity of the conclusions that were drawn.

The adoption of the My World Triangle by Scottish maternal health services and the use of the wellbeing indicators by many agencies, including the police, to identify concerns endorses the spread of this common evidence-based approach, although only a future, detailed evaluative case analysis of multi-agency usage by different professionals would really confirm that.

Introducing a single system has streamlined services and seems to have helped the delivery of services:

> With a single system, it is easier for children and families to access services without complex referral systems to different agencies. Path-finder evaluation is also showing that universal services having easier access to early intervention support has helped to prevent the likeli-hood of more complex targeted services being needed later on. It has also been found that the common system promotes trust and respect for the professional expertise and judgement of colleagues in other services. (Scottish Government, 2010, p. 36)

Implications of *Getting it right for every child* for social work

What, then, are the implications of this new system for social work in Scotland? A significant factor in national implementation has to be the political and economic context in which social work services in Scotland are practised. There has been universal cross-bench endorsement for GIRFEC from the Scottish Parliament (Scottish Government, 2010, p. 3).

In a time of recession, the major problem seems not to be with the vision or even the complexity of changes in culture, systems and practice that GIRFEC demands. Rather there are concerns that progress towards earlier and clearer involvement of the universal services will be thwarted by cutbacks and loss of posts. MacNeil and Stradling (2010b) have pointed out that this is an area that needs more embedding. Reducing the role of universal services in early intervention would put in jeopardy the role of the named person, with knock-on impacts on social work. Local authority cuts are inevitable and, although there is strong political will from the Scottish Parliament in 2010 to continue to safeguard frontline services, it is easy to see how social work services could be cut back to immediate child protection investigations. Even if these investigations are undertaken using GIRFEC values, principles and core components, the positive and longer term critical interventions of social workers might be eroded for all but those at immediate risk of significant harm, for whom compulsory measures are absolutely necessary. A wider range of children with long-term needs may be excluded from help even if the assessment evidence that indicates the imperative to responding to children's needs to avoid long-term consequences of not doing so are quite clear.

The beginnings of implementing GIRFEC are fragile. In a time of scarce resources in public services, the will to change culture, systems and practice to embrace GIRFEC may be severely challenged. It is to be hoped that the early progress in efficiency savings and streamlining systems to support social work are enough to win the day. One major step forward is that Highland Council Social Work Services, at least, are getting far fewer inappropriate referrals. Highland Council, in turn, is also able to present more appropriate evidence-based reports to the children's reporter if compulsory measures are being sought and there has been a significant reduction in the number of non-offence concerns referred to the children's reporter in the Highland Pathfinder as a result of more effective screening and more evidence-based decision making (MacNeil and Stradling, 2010b, p. 9). This means that social workers are able to target their help more effectively.

Child protection work with the police has been strengthened in the early investigation phases by making communication about the child's history easier and more efficient through the named person. The single child's plan can encompass risk and need and identify how each agency will contribute to risk management (see Aldgate and Rose, 2008).

Social workers are able to continue to exert their skills of coordination in complex cases by becoming lead professionals, especially where social work services have a statutory responsibility, such as for a looked after child, but are not expected to take on that role in every case where two or more agencies are working together. A child with complex health and social needs where there are no child protection issues may well have a more appropriate lead professional in health. Where social workers are lead professionals, the single child's plan means that it has become easier and more efficient to enlist the cooperation and actions of other agencies to the benefit of the child and the family by building a network of support around the child. It would be a tragedy if this progress is lost.

The last word has to be with the children and families who have experienced GIRFEC in action:

- They feel they have a clearer idea of what is going on, what is intended and when it will happen.
- Overall, they are more included in the processes of planning and getting help.
- They have a point of contact they can turn to when they have a concern (*Named Person*) and someone who has overall responsibility for their plan (*Lead Professional*) instead of going from one service to another to find out what is happening regarding different aspects of the support package. (Scottish Government, 2010, p. 9)

Acknowledgement

This chapter has been updated and developed within a Scottish context from Jane Aldgate (2010) 'The role of assessment in social work', in L.-A. Long, J. Roche and D. Stringer (eds) *The Law and Social Work: Contemporary Issues in Practice* (2nd edn), Basingstoke, Palgrave Macmillan.

References

Aldgate, J. (2006) 'Children, development and ecology', in J. Aldgate, D.P. Jones, W. Rose and C. Jeffery (eds) (2006) *The Developing World of the Child*, London, Jessica Kingsley.

Aldgate, J. and McIntosh, M. (2006) *Looking After the Family: A Study of Children Looked After in Kinship Care in Scotland*, Edinburgh, Social Work Inspection Agency.

Aldgate, J. and Rose, W. (2008) *Assessing and Managing Risk in Getting it right for every child*, Edinburgh, Getting it right for every child team, Scottish Government.

Aldgate, J., Jones, D.P., Rose, W. and Jeffery, C. (eds) (2006) *The Developing World of the Child*, London, Jessica Kingsley.

Austrian, S.G. (2002) 'Guidelines for conducting a biopsychosocial assessment', in A.R. Roberts and G.J. Greene (eds) *Social Workers' Desk Reference*, Oxford, Oxford University Press.

Barry, M. (2007) *Effective Approaches to Risk Assessment in Social Work: A Literature Review*, Edinburgh, Scottish Executive.

Bronfenbrenner, U. (1979) *The Ecology of Human Development: Experiments by Nature and Design*, Cambridge, MA, Harvard University Press.

Calder, M.C. (2002) 'A framework for conducting risk assessment', *Child Care in Practice*, 8(1): 7–18.

Cleaver, H., Wattam, C. and Cawson, P. (1998) *Assessing Risk in Child Protection*, London, NSPCC.

Cleaver, H. and Walker, S. with Meadows, P. (2004) *Assessing Children's Needs and Circumstances: The Impact of the Assessment Framework*, London, Jessica Kingsley.

Daniel, B. and Wassell, S. (2002) *Assessing and Promoting Resilience in Vulnerable Children: 1. The Early Years; 2. The School Years; 3. Adolescence*, London, Jessica Kingsley.

DH (Department of Health) (2000) *Assessing Children in Need and their Families: Practice Guidance*, London, TSO.

Douglas, K.S. and Kropp, P.R. (2002) 'A prevention-based paradigm for violence risk assessment: clinical and research applications', *Criminal Justice and Behaviour*, **29**: 617–58.

French, S. and Swain, J. (2002) 'The perspective of the disabled person's movement', in M. Davies (ed.) *The Blackwell Companion to Social Work* (2nd edn), Oxford, Basil Blackwell.

Hagell, A. (1998) *Dangerous Care, Reviewing the Risks to Children from their Carers*, London, Policy Studies Institute.

Jones, D.P., Hindley, N. and Ramchandani, P. (2006) 'Making plans: assessment, intervention and evaluating outcomes', in J. Aldgate, D.P. Jones, W. Rose and C. Jeffery (eds) *The Developing World of the Child*, London, Jessica Kingsley.

MacNeil, M. and Stradling, B. (2010a) *The Impact on Services and Agencies Part 1, Getting it Right for Every Child Evaluation Briefing 2*, Edinburgh, Scottish Government.

MacNeil, M. and Stradling, B. (2010b) *Green Shoots of Progress, Getting it Right for Every Child Evaluation Briefing 6*, Edinburgh, Scottish Government.

Meyer, C.H. (1993) *Assessment in Social Work Practice*, New York, Columbia University Press.

Munro, E. (2002) *Effective Child Protection*, London, Sage.

Ofsted (2008) *Safeguarding Children: The Third Joint Chief Inspectors' Report on Arrangements to Safeguard Children*, London, Ofsted.

Parton, N. (1998) 'Risk, advanced liberalism and child welfare: the need to rediscover uncertainty and ambiguity', *British Journal of Social Work*, 28: 5–27.

Richmond, M. (1917) *Social Diagnosis*, New York, Russell Sage Foundation.

Rose, W. (2010) 'The assessment framework', in J. Horwath (ed.) *The Child's World* (2nd edn), London, Jessica Kingsley.

Scottish Executive (2001) *For Scotland's Children*, Edinburgh, Scottish Executive.

Scottish Executive (2002) *It's Everyone's Job to Make Sure I'm Alright: Report of the Child Protection Audit and Review*, Edinburgh, Scottish Executive.

Scottish Government (2008) *A Guide to Getting it right for every child*, Edinburgh, Scottish Government.

Scottish Government (2010) *A Guide to Implementing Getting it right for every child: Messages from Pathfinders and Learning Partners*, Edinburgh, Scottish Government.

Scottish Government/Convention of Scottish Local Authorities (COSLA) (2007) *Concordat between the Scottish Government and Local Government*, available online at www.scotland.gov.uk/Resource/Doc/923/0054147.pdf [accessed 13 July 2010].

Seden, J. (2000) 'Assessment of children in need and their families: a literature review', in Department of Health, *Studies Informing the Framework for the Assessment of Children in Need and their Families*, London, TSO.

Seden, J. (2002) 'Underpinning theories for assessment of children's needs', in H. Ward and W. Rose (eds) *Approaches to Needs Assessment in Children's Services*, London, Jessica Kingsley.

Shemmings, Y. and Shemmings, D. (2001) 'Empowering children and family members to participate in the assessment process', in J. Horwath (ed.) *The Child's World* (2nd edn), London, Jessica Kingsley.

Stalker, K. (2003) 'Managing risk and uncertainty in social work: a literature review', *Journal of Social Work*, 3(2): 211–33.

Stewart, J. (2004) *Taking Stock: Scottish Social Welfare after Devolution*, Bristol, Policy Press.

Stradling, B., MacNeil, M. and Berry, H. (2009) *Changing Professional Practice: An Evaluation of the Development and Early Implementation Phases of Getting it right for every child in Highland, 2006–2009*, Edinburgh, Scottish Government.

Turnell, A. and Edwards, S. (1999) *Signs of Safety: A Solution and Safety Oriented Approach to Child Protection*, New York, WW Norton.

United Nations (1989) *United Nations Convention on the Rights of the Child*, Geneva, United Nations.

Vincent, S. and Morgan-Klein, N. (2008) 'From 2000: a period of significant reform', in A. Stafford and S. Vincent (eds) *Safeguarding and Protecting Children and Young People*, Edinburgh, Dunedin Press.

Chapter 5

Law, Social Difference and Discrimination

LENA ROBINSON

Introduction

Discrimination exists in many forms. In Britain, it is legislated against in the areas of race, sex and disability. The Race Relations Act 1976 and the Sex Discrimination Act 1975, both now repealed by and incorporated into the Equalities Act 2010, were phrased in similar terms, outlawing direct and indirect discrimination and making overtly discriminatory behaviour a criminal offence. This chapter will focus on discrimination in the area of race. It will outline the ways in which the law in relation to racial discrimination has developed over time in the UK. It will explore how diversity influences practice and examine issues that social workers may encounter, for example in relation to attitudes to smacking children.

Social work texts on child development make little reference to culture. The body of literature representing the deficit view of black children and families has most strongly influenced the professional and personal perceptions of social workers in Britain (see Robinson, 2008).

In this chapter, I have argued that discipline strategies are closely related to the values and goals of socialisation. Individualism and collectivism shape the processes of development through the ways in which parents socialise their children. Differences in discipline strategies are frequent sources of misunderstanding between minority/black and dominant/European cultures.

The chapter will assist social work students and practitioners in reflecting on issues of cultural diversity and avoiding discrimination. It will also examine the impact of institutional discrimination in relation to race and examine ways in which social workers can challenge discrimination and exclusion.

Setting the scene

The size of the black and minority ethnic (BME) population was 4.6 million in 2001 or 7.9% of the total population of the UK. Indians were the largest minority group, followed by Pakistanis, those of mixed ethnic backgrounds, black Caribbeans, black Africans and Bangladeshis. The remaining minority ethnic groups each accounted for less than 0.5% but together accounted for a further 1.4% of the UK population (ONS, 2001). Ethnic group data were not collected in the Northern Ireland Census in 1991. In Great Britain, the BME population grew by 53% between 1991 and 2001, half of the total BME population were Asians of Indian, Pakistani, Bangladeshi or other Asian origin. A quarter of BME people described themselves as black, that is, black Caribbean, black African or other black. Of the BME population, 15% described their ethnic group as mixed. About a third of this group were from white and black Caribbean backgrounds (ONS, 2001).

Scotland's BME population is small, but growing. At the 2001 census, 2% of the country's 5 million people were from BME backgrounds (ONS, 2001). Asian groups make up 1.4% of Scotland's population, with the largest single ethnic group being people of Pakistani background, followed by Chinese and Indians and those of mixed backgrounds. Those in BME groups in Scotland have a younger age profile, with more people under the age of 35 and fewer aged 55+ than in the white population of Scotland. More than 40% of non-white ethnic minorities (rising to one-half of Pakistanis and other South Asians) were under the age of 25 at the time of the 2001 census, compared with one-third (32%) of the white population. BME communities in Scotland encompass a diverse range of religious, cultural and economic groups, who make a valuable contribution to Scottish life. There are mixed views on the extent to which Scotland is accepting of migrants. Wren (2007) has argued that the Scottish Executive Fresh Talent initiative to attract new migrants (formally introduced by a statement in the Scottish Parliament by First Minister Jack McConnell on 25 February 2004, when he laid out the actions to be taken to address Scotland's population decline and support Scotland's continuing economic prosperity) indicates that public discourse in Scotland is less exclusionary than in England. However, others have taken a different view of Scottish multi-culturalism, claiming that it is characterised by complacency and a reluctance to recognise racism as a problem (Williams and de Lima, 2008). Supporting this view, a recently published report found that Scotland is 'still home to deeply rooted prejudice based on fear, perhaps even dislike, of difference' (Gordon et al., 2010, p. 1). A number of studies suggest that BME communities experience significant racism and greater isolation compared to the wider population (Netto et al., 2001; NHS Greater Glasgow, 2006). In the wider UK context, since the attacks on the New York World Trade Center in 2000, British Muslims have experienced a range of threatening responses – from increasing racist attacks and Islamophobic hostility to direct and indirect questions being raised about 'loyalty' to the state and the nature and direction of British Muslim 'citizenship' (Abbas, 2005). Recent urban disturbances in the northern England towns of Bradford and Oldham have given rise to concerns about deeply divided societies living parallel lives, stemming from mistrust and prejudice.

The law

In the 1960s, one of the first British national policy interventions to tackle racism was through legislation. A series of studies in the 1960s and 70s established the extent of discrimination faced by BME people, particularly in getting jobs. Evidence of racial discrimination experienced by black people in employment and in housing, as well as the overrepresentation of black people in the criminal justice system (Hall et al., 1978), led to the passing of the 1965, 1968 and 1976 Race Relations Acts.

The 1976 Race Relations Act, like the Sex Discrimination Act 1975, made it unlawful to discriminate either directly or indirectly on the grounds of race, colour, nationality or ethnic origin in the provision of housing, employment, education or the provision of goods, services or facilities to the public. A person discriminates against another if 'on racial grounds he/she treats that other less favourably than he/she treats or would treat other persons' (Race Relations Act 1976, s.1(1)(a)).

Following the Macpherson Report (1999) into the killing of Stephen Lawrence, the Race Relations (Amendment) Act 2000 (RR(A)A), now repealed by and incorporated into the Equalities Act 2010, extended the application of legislation on race relations to the police, and places an enforceable duty on public bodies to promote racial equality and outlaw racial discrimination in all public services. However, a substantial body of research has examined BME communities' experiences of accessing and using public services and found inequalities in service provision in the areas of housing, education, health, social care and social work in Scotland, and concerns about recruitment and progression in the labour market (Netto et al., 2001). In Scotland as well as other parts of the UK, research has repeatedly shown that a major factor influencing housing decisions among BME communities is fear of racial harassment (Netto, 2006). Changes in policy following from these findings have included the recommendation of ethnic monitoring of service provision and recruitment procedures, increasing the availability of racial equality training, enhancing the cultural sensitivity of public services and more sensitive letting policies in public housing (REAF, 2001).

The RR(A)A 2000, which requires public sector bodies to actively promote race equality, has been hailed as a key change in British social policy on race equality. Instead of a framework based on negativity, there is an emphasis on the 'positive'. The Act laid down the conditions not only for possible indirect or direct discrimination, but also for actively examining potential discrimination and advocates steps to tackle potential exclusion. For social work agencies, the RR(A)A 2000 required 'attention to race relations issues to be embedded in the organisation and its policies and procedures' (Ball and MacDonald, 2002, p. 25).

Although the 1976 and 2000 Race Relations Acts were breakthroughs in creating 'positive action' as a strategy to tackle racism, immigration policy together with the 1981 Nationality Act continued to entrench the idea of excluding 'coloured' immigrants. More particularly, the Nationality Act 1981 included a definition of 'British' as having a father or grandfather born in Britain. In British social policy responses to racism, one common pattern has been the link between the limiting of 'black' immigration resulting in good 'race' relations. Since 1990, at least five laws have been passed on restricting immigration and controlling citizenship and nationality. The connections in policy have been based on two issues of concern to governments. First, there has been a negative response by the white majority in Britain to the arrival of ex-colonial black migrants. These negative responses have been reinforced by government discourses on immigration. Second, ex-colonised groups, because of racial discrimination, have felt excluded from full participation in British society (Schuster and Solomos, 2003).

The Immigration Act 1988 made residents in Britain prove that they could maintain their relatives without recourse to public funds, implying that black people were a burden on the welfare state. The Asylum and Immigration Appeals Act 1993 made it more difficult for visitors to enter Britain. The Immigration and Asylum Act 1999 encompassed carriers' liability for illegal passengers, and introduced visa sanctions before entry. Refugees who did arrive were subject to poverty, exclusion and separation from a supportive community (Dominelli, 2008). Vouchers were introduced for food. The dispersal policy forced asylum seekers to be spread out over the country, where they were isolated and more vulnerable to hostility. A series of restrictions on immigration have continued to be passed. Dominelli (2008, p. 97) noted that immigration controls have made it difficult for 'black family units to be reconstructed in their traditional totality'.

The attacks on refugees and asylum seekers continued to be reported in Liverpool and Glasgow, and we saw the first murder of an asylum seeker (Schuster and Solomos, 2003). The Race Relations (Amendment) Act 2000 seemed ineffective in this context, particularly since it was not extended to cover the racist role of public authorities in relation to immigration, asylum and refuge. November 2002 saw the passing of the Nationality, Immigration and Asylum Act, preceded by a government White Paper entitled *Secure Borders, Safe Havens: Integration with Diversity in Modern Britain* (Home Office, 2002). The White Paper proposed a migrant-only oath of allegiance and suggested the introduction of English tests that migrants would have to pass. The White Paper reproduces the idea of racialised minorities as problematic.

Discrimination

Institutional racism is defined as:

> the collective failure of an organisation to provide an appropriate and professional service to people because of their colour, culture or ethnic origin. It can be seen or detected in processes, attitudes and behaviour which amount to discrimination through unwitting prejudice, ignorance, thoughtlessness and racist stereotyping which disadvantage minority ethnic people. (Macpherson, 1999, p. 28)

The Macpherson Report emphasises the need for institutions to inspect their practices, policies and strategies and actively consider how they may disadvantage BME communities. Its conclusion also confronts the view that equality can be achieved by 'treating everybody the same', a premise that fails to acknowledge the diverse forms of need and disadvantage experienced by BME people.

In a study of local authority provision for BME families, Richards and Ince (2000, p. 7) found that the 'overall picture remains extremely bleak'. Services had few of the most basic structures, for example comprehensive equal opportunities policies and ethnic record keeping and monitoring services. Also, very few had placement policies for black children and effective programmes for black foster carers (Richards and Ince, 2000). However, there were a few examples of good practice. For example, in one local authority, anti-racist practice and culturally sensitive service provision were kept consistently on the agenda, with rolling programmes of training and responsibility on team managers to ensure that culturally sensitive services were not seen as an 'add on' (Richards and Ince, 2000).

In another study, *Inspection of Services for Ethnic Minority Children and Families*, O'Neale (2000, p. 33) found that 'many of the case files examined failed to indicate that issues of race and culture had been taken into account by [social] workers when they undertook assessments'. O'Neale (2000, p. 33) pointed out that social workers also need to take into account the fact that 'the experience of racism is likely to affect the responses of the child and family to the assessment process'.

The main themes emerging from studies of BME communities in Scotland were that there were high levels of unmet needs, knowledge of existing services was weak, a lack of culturally appropriate services, communication difficulties and ineffective referral systems, which were all barriers to accessing services (Netto et al., 2001). Bowes and Dar (2000) found that despite community care plans demonstrating a principled commitment to meeting the needs of BME communities, in practice, local authority services were not. Under the Children (Scotland) Act 1995, social workers need to 'have regard to children's religious persuasion, racial origin and cultural and linguistic background' when working with BME families in Scotland.

In general, social work has operated within a 'problem-oriented' framework, which is characterised by deficit and dysfunctional theories of black families. Dominelli (2008, p. 166) argued that:

> Black children and families are over represented in the controlling aspects of social work ... We need a shift from a deficit model of social work control to a strength model of social work empowerment.

Many social work texts in the UK have painted crude cultural stereotypes of black families. The 'norm' against which black families are, implicitly or explicitly, judged is white. The norm presents a myth of the normal family as nuclear, middle class and heterosexual. Black families are seen as strange, different and inferior. The pathological approach to black family life is evident in the British research on black people. It is also evident in social workers' perceptions of black families. Social workers tend to rely on Eurocentric theory and practice that devalues the strength of black families (Robinson, 2008). The traditional method of studying black families in the social science literature has often focused on the pathological rather than on the strengths of the black family (Robinson, 2008). Barn (2002, p. 9) stated: 'Negative thinking feeds into policy and practice, leading to discriminatory behaviour and poor outcomes for black families.' Social work models have tended to pathologise black families and encourage practitioners to perceive the families as being the 'problem'. Consequently, social work interventions focus almost exclusively on clients' weaknesses, inabilities and inadequacies.

Socialisation practices

In this section, I will outline the differences in socialisation practices within BME communities. BME groups in multicultural societies may use different child-rearing practices to those of the dominant group and their appropriateness may be questioned by social workers not familiar with that particular culture.

Socialisation has been defined as 'the process by which children acquire the beliefs, values and behaviours deemed significant and appropriate by older members of their society' (Shaffer, 1999, p. 558. There are cultural differences in child-rearing values, beliefs and goals. Thus, parents and other carers foster behavioural capacities in their children that maximise their cultural values (LeVine, 1974). Different cultures provide various ways in which child-rearing practices socialise children for adult life (Whiting and Edwards, 1992). Socialisation practices in various cultures have been studied from a number of different perspectives. These studies have focused on cultural differences in such areas as infant care, autonomy, discipline and attachment behaviour. Other research, especially within subcultures of a given society, has focused on specific parenting styles.

Two fundamental values that have been shown to differentiate European and American culture from most non-Western cultures are 'individualism' and 'collectivism'. Individualism refers to 'the subordination of the goals of the collectivities to individual goals, and a sense of independence and lack of concern for others', and collectivism refers to 'the subordination of individual goals to the goals of a collective and a sense of harmony, interdependence, and concern for others' (Hui and Triandis, 1986, pp. 244–5). These constructs reflect individual societal values regarding self, others, family and community, and thus are related to attitudes and social behaviour. Individualistic societies value autonomy, independence, achievement, identity, self-reliance, solitude and creativity. Collectivistic societies value loyalty to the group, dependence, tradition, harmony, respect for authority and cooperation (Triandis, 1990, 2001). In individualistic cultures, 'people are supposed to look after themselves and their immediate family only', and in collectivistic cultures, 'people belong to ingroups or collectivities which are supposed to look after them in exchange for loyalty' (Hofstede, 1984, p. 419). In individualistic cultures, the development of the individual is foremost, even when this is at the expense of the group, whereas in collectivistic cultures, the needs of the group are more important, with individuals expected to conform to the group (Gudykunst, 2003). Conformity is valued in collectivistic cultures, but diversity and dissent are more esteemed in individualistic cultures. The 'I' identity has precedence in individualistic cultures over the 'we' identity that takes precedence in collectivistic cultures. The emphasis in individualistic societies is on individuals' initiative and achievement, while emphasis is placed on belonging to groups in collectivistic societies. Collectivistic cultures stress the needs of a group; individuals are identified more through their group affiliation than by individual position or attributes. Hierarchical differences and vertical relationships are emphasised, and role, status and appropriate behaviours are more clearly defined by position. Collectivistic cultures require a greater degree of harmony, cohesion and cooperation within their ingroups and place greater burdens on individuals to identify with the group and conform to group norms. Sanctions usually exist for nonconformity. Individualistic cultures, however, depend less on groups and more on the uniqueness of their individuals. The pursuit of personal goals rather than collective ones is of primary importance. As a result, individualistic cultures require less harmony and cohesion within groups and place less importance on conformity of individuals to group norms.

These underlying values shape the processes of development through the ways in which parents socialise their children. Extended families and respect for elders are important in collectivistic cultures. Parents emphasise interdependence and sharing as socialisation goals for children. Greenfield and Cocking (1994, p. 7) hypothesised that:

> a value orientation stressing interdependence would characterize the cultural and cross-cultural roots of socialization practices and developmental goals for minority groups ... [and] would ... contrast with the independence scripts that characterize the cultural roots of Euro-American socialization and development goals.

Greenfield and Cocking (1994, p. 8) also noted that:

> value judgements concerning the superiority of the independent individual became reified ... [hence] respect for elders and the socialization practices that support it have been given a negative evaluation in developmental psychology as lack of initiative and authoritarian childrearing (cf. Baumrind, 1980).

They have not been considered as simply derivatives of a contrasting value system – an interdependence developmental script (Greenfield and Cocking, 1994; Greenfield et al., 2003). However, Greenfield and Cocking (1994) argued that a value that is adaptive for socialisation under one set of societal conditions becomes maladaptive under another. In a comparative study of Korean parental strictness in Korea, the USA and Canada, Kim et al. (1994) found that a collectivistic child-rearing practice such as strictness can become maladaptive under new societal conditions.

Because people from collectivistic cultures view interdependence as important, they foster it through children's socialisation process (Brislin and Yoshida, 1994). While cultures tend predominantly to be either individualistic or collectivistic, both exist in all cultures. Individualism has been central to the life of western industrialised societies such as the USA and the UK (Hofstede, 1984). Collectivism is particularly high among Asian and African societies. However, diversity within each country is very possible. In the USA, for instance, Hispanics and Asians tend to be more collectivistic than other ethnic groups (Triandis, 1990, 2001), and in the UK, Asians and African Caribbeans tend to be more collectivist than white people. Dwivedi (2002, p. 47) noted that:

> in western culture, 'independence' is viewed as the cherished ideal and 'dependence' is seen as a despicable state ... professionals working with their clients consider that fostering independence is the most important aspect of their work.

Cultures vary in their styles of discipline. Boushel (2000, p. 74) stated: 'Childrearing approaches to control and discipline are closely related to the values and goals of socialisation.' Kagitcibasi (1996, p. 21) indicated that 'in general, higher levels of control are common wherever childrearing does not stress the development of individualistic independence in the child'. It is common for some cultures, for example, to include physical punishment as part of their disciplinary repertoire (Fontes, 2005). Stricter parental control is more valued in African, African American and Asian cultures than it is among Euro-Americans (Carlson and Harwood, 2003).

In an article on the overrepresentation of black children in the child protection system, Chand (2000, p. 72) pointed out that 'the issue of punishment is one of the most controversial areas relating to black families, child abuse and social work intervention'. He argued that social workers may be confused about 'the reasons why punishment is employed in certain situations'. Social workers, therefore, need to have some knowledge and understanding about acceptable and unacceptable behaviours within the service user's culture, since it seems that the severity of the punishment needs somehow to match the severity of the 'crime' in order for it to be more acceptable (Chand, 2000). A leading authority on the cultural aspects of child abuse, Korbin (1987, 1997) exposed the weaknesses of the child abuse knowledge basis in working with cultural minorities since it was based almost entirely on research and clinical experience in western nations. Korbin (1987) pointed out that a particular behaviour may be viewed by one cultural group as abusive but as a mode of discipline by another cultural group.

The child abuse inquiry reports of Jasmine Beckford (Blom-Cooper, 1985) and Tyra Henry (London Borough of Lambeth, 1987) noted that:

> abusive behaviours were interpreted as aspects of culture and that the workers ... had no right to criticise the supposedly cultural (child abusing) practices of others. This gives rise to the concepts of cultural relativism and the rule of optimism. (O'Hagan, 2001, p. 114)

> [Cultural relativism] provides one explanation for incompetence ... Instead of an exposure of the behaviours which have been wrongfully interpreted as culture, and the ineffectual response to such behaviours, cultural relativism speaks of those interpretations as if they are fact. (O'Hagan, 1999, p. 278)

I agree with Segal's (1999, p. 41) statement that: 'Ethnocentrism must be avoided, but extreme cultural relativism may justify acceptance of physically, socially and emotionally damaging practices.'

Chand (2000, p. 67) argues that black children and their families may 'be more or less likely to be subjected to child abuse investigations by social work agencies'. This may be due to the pathologisation of black families or cultural relativism. Thus, the potential consequences of either approach for black families will be unnecessary investigation or there will not be appropriate intervention for black children at risk. Practitioners must be able to assess when the cultural norm of physical punishment becomes abusive and dangerous (Brophy et al., 2003). Culturally sensitive social work practice:

> does not mean accepting inhumane acts as 'normal' in any culture ... Social workers will have to exercise their judgement over contentious issues and not use 'culture' as an excuse for not doing so. Not spotting child abuse in black families because they are perceived as disciplinarian is one example. (Dominelli, 2008, p. 33)

In his article, Chand (2000, p. 75) concluded that:

> overall cultural differences in the way families rear their children should be acknowledged and respected, but where child abuse does occur it should be understood that this particular family has gone beyond what is acceptable not only in the British culture, but also in their own ... Hence, causing significant harm to a child physically, emotionally, sexually or through neglect is not acceptable in any culture.

According to Straus and Donnelly (2001), an important distinction between corporal punishment and abuse is whether the child is psychologically damaged. Thoburn et al. (2005, p. 84) discussed Brophy et al.'s (2003) research, which stresses 'the importance of differentiating between "normal" childcare practices and deviant ... behaviours that are [unacceptable] in any community'. Abuse is not condoned by any ethnic group. Children need to be protected. To work effectively and assess whether abuse is taking place, we need to understand the context. Gopaul-McNicol (1999, p. 79) noted that:

> Researchers in the Caribbean [and Britain] should focus on eluci-dating the differences in disciplinary practices in various subcultures, so that advocates for children do not erroneously diagnose a parent as abusive when he or she is, in the eyes of that culture, merely disci-plining the child.

The Race Relations Act has 'not really been able to make the necessary link between the quality of social work for black children and their families and the equality in social work with black children and their families' (Ahmad, 1991, p. 20).

There is a need to understand child-rearing and socialisation practices among BME parents in Scotland. Services are still dominated by white norms (Dalrymple and Burke, 2008). Social workers need to assess black families in the context of a racist society. They need to be aware that BME families face many issues, including personal and institutional racism and the impact of immigration, nationality laws and separated families (O'Neale, 2000).

The key principles of the British Association of Social Workers include that social workers have a duty to 'recognise and respect ethnic and cultural identity and diversity' (BASW, 2002, p. 4). Social workers should respect the cultural differences in the way families discipline their children but they must also be able to assess when the cultural norm of physical punishment becomes abusive and dangerous.

The Children (Scotland) Act 1995 states that the race, culture, language and religion of children and young people must be addressed in the provi-sion of services. As noted above, the Race Relations (Amendment) Act 2000 provides a statutory duty to promote race equality and therefore an obligation to deliver appropriate services. Anti-discriminatory practice 'needs to incorporate sociological, political and economic concerns above and beyond narrow legal requirements' (Thompson, 2001).

Research studies in the UK asking BME communities about access and the services they have received have revealed the sense of frustration of service users about the lack of progress towards equality and the need for action (Butt and Dhaliwal, 2005). Some of the barriers identified by Butt and Dhaliwal (2005) to promoting anti-discriminatory practice are a lack of appropriate services, social workers without the experience and skills needed to work with diverse communities, and direct and institutional discrimination.

Social workers in Scotland need more training in working with black families and children. They need to be aware, for example, that individualism–collectivism differences between countries and cultures are associated with differences in socialisation practices. Research knowledge and information from a cross-cultural perspective on BME family life, BME children and young people are vital to the social work profession. But there is a dearth of cross-cultural perspectives in the social work research literature in the UK (Williams and Soydan, 2005). Knowledge about child-rearing values, attitudes and behaviours among BME parents in Scotland is limited. As a result of this gap, there is a lack of professional knowledge about patterns of family life in BME communities and the impact of discrimination generally.

I would like to conclude with this quote from Gardiner and Kosmitzki (2005, p. 72):

Cross-cultural study of development frequently resembles a confused mosaic of often contradictory findings. Yet therein lies the promise and excitement of future endeavours ... Much more needs to be done, and as the cross-cultural perspective reveals, discovery of similarities and dissimilarities in human behaviour will make our understanding both easier and more difficult.

References

Abbas, T. (2005) *Muslim Britain: Communities under Pressure*, London, Zed Books.

Ahmad, B. (1991) *Black Perspectives in Social Work*, Birmingham, Venture Press.

Ball, C. and MacDonald, A. (2002) *Law for Social Workers*, Aldershot, Ashgate.

Barn, R. (2002) '"Race", ethnicity and child welfare', in B. Mason and A. Sawyer (eds) *Exploring the Unsaid*, London, Karmac.

BASW (British Association of Social Workers) (2002) *The Code of Ethics for Social Workers*, Birmingham, BASW.

Baumrind, D. (1980) 'New directions in socialization research', *Psychological Bulletin*, 35: 639–52.

Blom-Cooper, L. (1985) *A Child In Trust: The Report of the Panel of Inquiry into the Circumstances Surrounding the Death of Jasmine Beckford*, London, London Borough of Brent.

Boushel, M. (2000) 'What kind of people are we? "Race", anti-racism and social welfare research', *British Journal of Social Work*, 30: 71–89.

Bowes, A.M. and Dar, N. (2000) *Family Support and Community Care: A Study of South Asian Older People*, Edinburgh, Scottish Executive Research Unit.

Brislin R.W. and Yoshida, T. (1994) *Improving Intercultural Interactions: Modules for Cross-cultural Training Programs*, Thousand Oaks, CA, Sage.

Brophy, J., Jhutti-Johal, J. and Owen, C. (2003) 'Assessing and documenting child ill treatment in ethnic minority households', *Family Law*, 33: 756–64.

Butt, J. and Dhaliwal, S. (2005) *Different Paths: Challenging Services*, London, Habinteg Housing Association.

Carlson, V. and Harwood, R. (2003) 'Attachment, culture and the care-giving system: the cultural patterning of everyday experiences among Anglo and Puerto Rican mother-infant pairs', *Infant Mental Health Journal*, 24: 53–73.

Chand, A. (2000) 'The over-representation of Black children in the child protection system: possible causes, consequences and solutions', *Child and Family Social Work*, 5: 67–77.

Dalrymple, J. and Burke, B. (2008) *Anti-oppressive Practice: Social Care and the Law*, Milton Keynes, Open University Press.

Dominelli, L. (2008) *Anti-racist Social Work*, Basingstoke, Palgrave Macmillan.

Dwivedi, K. (2002) *Meeting the Needs of Ethnic Minority Children*, London, Jessica Kingsley.

Fontes, L.A. (2005) *Child Abuse and Culture*, New York, Guildford Press.

Gardiner, H. and Kosmitzki, C. (2005) *Lives Across Cultures*, Boston, MA, Allyn & Bacon.

Gopaul-McNicol, S.A. (1999) 'Ethnocultural perspectives on childrearing practices in the Caribbean', *International Social Work*, 42(1): 79–86.

Gordon, D., Graham, L., Robinson, M. and Taulbut, M. (2010) *Dimensions of Diversity: Population Differences and Health Improvement Opportunities*, Glasgow, NHS Health Scotland.

Greenfield, P.M. and Cocking, R.R. (1994) *Cross-cultural Roots of Minority Child Development*, Hillsdale, NJ, Lawrence Erlbaum.

Greenfield, P.M., Keller, H., Fuligni, A. and Maynard, A. (2003) 'Cultural pathways through universal development', *Annual Review of Psychology*, 54: 461–90.

Gudykunst, W.B. (2003) *Bridging Differences: Effective Intergroup Communication*, London, Sage.

Hall, S., Critcher, C. Jefferson, T. et al. (1978) *Policing the Crisis*, London, Macmillan.

Hofstede, G. (1984) *Culture's Consequences: International Differences in Work-related Values*, Newbury Park, CA, Sage.

Home Office (2002) *Secure Borders, Safe Havens: Integration with Diversity in Modern Britain*, London, Home Office.

Hui, C.H. and Triandis, H.C. (1986) 'Individualism-collectivism: a study of cross-cultural researchers', *Journal of Cross-cultural Psychology*, 17: 225–48.

Kagitcibasi, I. (1996) *Family and Human Development Across Cultures: A View from the Other Side*, Hillsdale, NJ, Lawrence Erlbaum.

Kim, U., Triandis, H.C., Kagitcibasi, C. et al. (1994) *Individualism and Collectivism: Theory, Method and Application*, Thousand Oaks, CA, Sage.

Korbin, J.E. (1987) 'Child abuse and neglect: the cultural context', in M.E. Helfer and R.S. Kempe (eds) *The Battered Child* (4th edn), Chicago, University of Chicago Press.

Korbin, J.E. (1997) 'Culture and child maltreatment', in M.E. Helfer, R.S. Kempe and R.D. Krugman (eds) *The Battered Child* (5th edn), Chicago, University of Chicago Press.

LeVine, R.A. (1974) 'Parental goals: a cross-cultural view', *Teachers College Record*, 76(2): 226–39.

London Borough of Lambeth (1987) *Whose Child? The Report of the Public Enquiry into the Death of Tyra Henry*, London, London Borough of Lambeth.

Macpherson, W. (1999) *The Stephen Lawrence Inquiry: Report of an Inquiry by Sir William MacPherson of Cluny*, Cm 4261-1, London, TSO.

Netto, G. (2006) 'Vulnerability to homelessness, use of homelessness services and BME communities', *Housing Studies*, 21(4): 581–603.

Netto, G., Arshad, P., de Lima. P. et al. (2001) *An Audit of Minority Ethnic Issues from a 'Race Perspective'*, Edinburgh, Scottish Executive.

NHS Greater Glasgow (2006) *Black and Minority Ethnic Health in Glasgow*, available online at www.nhsgg.org.uk/publications/reports [accessed 28 August 2010].

O'Hagan, K. (1999) 'Culture, cultural identity, and cultural sensitivity in child family and family social work', *Child and Family Social Work*, 4: 269–81.

O'Hagan, K. (2001) *Cultural Competence in the Caring Professions*, London, Jessica Kingsley.

O'Neale, V. (2000) *Excellence not Excuses: Inspection of Services for Ethnic Minority Children and Families*, London, Social Services Inspectorate.

ONS (Office for National Statistics) (2001) *Census 2001*, available online at www.statistics.gov.uk/census2001/census2001.asp [accessed 8 July 2010].

REAF (Race Equality Advisory Forum) (2001) *An Action Plan for Race Equality*, Edinburgh, Scottish Executive.

Richards, A. and Ince, L. (2000) *Overcoming the Obstacles: Looked after Children – Quality Services for Black and Minority Ethnic Children and their Families*, London, Family Rights Group.

Robinson, L. (2008) *Psychology for Social Workers: Black Perspectives*, London, Routledge.

Schuster, L. and Solomos, J. (2003) 'Race, immigration and asylum: New Labour's agenda and its consequences', *Ethnicities*, 4: 267–300.

Segal, U.A. (1999) 'Children are abused in eastern countries', *International Social Work*, 42(1): 39–52.

Shaffer, D.R. (1999) *Developmental Psychology: Childhood and Adolescence* (5th edn), Pacific Grove, CA, Brook Cole.

Straus, M.A. and Donnelly, D.A. (2001) *Beating the Devil out of Them: Corporal Punishment in American Families and its Effects on Children* (2nd edn), New York, Lexington Books.

Thoburn, J., Chand, A. and Procter, J. (2005) *Child Welfare Services for Minority Ethnic Families*, London, Jessica Kingsley.

Thompson, N. (2001) *Anti-discriminatory Practice*, Basingstoke, Palgrave – now Palgrave Macmillan.

Triandis, H.C. (1990) 'Toward cross-cultural studies of individualism and collectivism in Latin-America', *Revista Interamericana de Psicologia*, 24: 199–210.

Triandis, H.C. (2001) 'Individualism and collectivism: past, present and future', in D. Matsumto (ed.) *The Handbook of Culture and Psychology*, Oxford, Oxford University Press.

Whiting, B.B. and Edwards, C.P. (1992) *Children of Different Worlds: The Formation of Social Behaviour*, Cambridge, MA, Harvard University Press.

Williams, C. and Soydan, H. (2005) 'When and how does ethnicity matter? A cross-national study of social work responses to ethnicity in child protection cases', *British Journal of Social Work*, **35**(6): 901–20.

Williams, C. and de Lima, P. (2008) 'Devolution, multicultural citizenship and race equality: from laissez-faire to nationally responsible policies', *Critical Social Policy*, **26**(3): 498–522.

Wren, K. (2007) 'Supporting asylum-seekers and refuges in Glasgow: the role of multi-agency networks', *Journal of Refugee Studies*, **20**(3): 391–413.

Chapter 6

Children's Hearings in Scotland: Balancing Rights and Welfare

JANICE McGHEE

Introduction

The children's hearings tribunal system is the primary decision-making forum for child welfare in Scotland. It is distinctive, in that decisions regarding the need for compulsory intervention for children in trouble with the law and those in need of care and protection remain integrated within a unitary system of lay tribunals. The origins of the system lie in the Kilbrandon Report (1964), which reviewed the legal framework addressing juvenile offending, children in need of care and protection and those regarded as beyond parental control following public concern about a postwar rise in delinquency. At the same time, professional concerns highlighted the restricted development of the Scottish juvenile court system (Cowperthwaite, 1988).

The Kilbrandon proposals represented a radical alternative to court-based systems to address the behaviour and needs of children who offend and those in need of care and protection. The committee considered the adversarial forum of the court inappropriate for addressing the welfare needs of child offenders. Similar principles of intervention based on prevention and procedures enabling decisions to be informed by full assessment of background and family circumstances were seen as necessary for child offenders. This reflected the criterion and procedure under the Children and Young Persons (Scotland) Act 1937, which, in Kilbrandon's (1964) view, embodied an 'implicit recognition of the "preventive principle"' (para. 59, p. 30). The Kilbrandon Committee (1964, para. 13, p. 12) regarded the legal classification of the child into offender or non-offender as of limited 'practical significance' when the underlying circumstances of children were examined. A unitary tribunal system supported by high-quality services to assist parents and meet the needs of children, some of whom were likely to need compulsory intervention, was envisaged.

The hearings system was established in 1971 and the central welfare philosophy of integrated decision making and intervention based on the need for compulsory intervention, irrespective of the formal reason for referral, remains unchanged. This stands in sharp contrast to many jurisdictions that have moved towards greater separation of children who offend from those in need of care and protection (Murray and Hill, 1991; Hallett, 2000). The welfare principle is set out in s. 16(1) of the Children (Scotland) Act 1995, emphasising welfare 'throughout ... childhood' as the 'paramount consideration' in decision making. Courts are only involved where there the child and/or relevant person contests the facts (whether grounds of referral exist) or appeals. This separation of adjudication of facts from decisions about compulsory measures in the child's best interests has been regarded as the 'genius' of the hearings system (Lord President Hope, *Sloan* v *B*).[1]

The hearings system places a strong emphasis on community participation in child welfare decision making. Lay volunteers are selected and trained annually. At the hearing, the child and family meet together with three lay tribunal members who, following discussion, come to a decision about the need for compulsory measures of supervision in respect of the child. This decision is also informed by the principle of minimum intervention, the 'no order' principle (s. 16(3) of the 1995 Act), to ensure compulsory measures are not imposed unnecessarily and will be of benefit to the child.

Participation by children and parents[2] is central and specific provisions ensure that children have the right to attend the hearing and that their views are taken into account (s. 16(2) of the 1995 Act). Notwithstanding the informal and wide-ranging nature of discussion permissible within hearings, it remains a quasi-judicial tribunal with formal procedures embedded within the process and with the power to make decisions that may significantly affect the lives of children and their families.

Continuity and change

Despite the continuing centrality of the welfare philosophy and relative stability in structure and functioning, the hearings system has evolved in response to internal and external influences. The United Nations Convention on the Rights of the Child (1991) influenced the Children (Scotland) Act 1995, embedding the importance of participation by the child. The incorporation of the European Convention on Human Rights (ECHR) within UK domestic law with the Human Rights Act 1998 has brought more robust challenges, further testing the system against long-standing human rights obligations.

Growing numbers of referrals have been a key trend until relatively recently. This sits alongside a changing balance in referrals, with a greater proportion on care and protection grounds. As a system primarily established to address the needs of child offenders, although drawing on child welfare principles, this brings further challenges for policy and practice. Hallett et al. (1998) found professionals positive about the ability of the hearings to deal with childcare and protection cases, although a minority expressed some disquiet. At the same time, there has been concern about the effectiveness of the hearings in addressing the needs of young people who persistently commit offences.

These factors, together with policy developments supporting the integration of service responses for children and their families, have been key drivers in a series of governmental reviews and consultations regarding the hearings system since 2005. The most recent consultation *Strengthening for the Future* (Scottish Government, 2008a), and subsequent extensive consultation on a redrafted Bill, has resulted in the presentation of a Children's Hearings (Scotland) Bill to the Scottish Parliament. The intention is to retain the core principles and philosophy of the hearings, while ensuring that the system is best placed to confront challenges including high levels of referrals and human rights obligations. A key proposal is the creation of a national Children's Hearings Service to coordinate recruitment and training of panel members, in the context of a national children's panel, and to provide independent advice to children's hearings (Scottish Parliament, 2010a).

Social work in children's hearings

Social workers within the hearings system have a range of legal and practice responsibilities and duties. Local authorities have a duty to provide information to the reporter and the hearing (ss. 53(1), 56(2)(7) of the 1995 Act), testing the assessment skills of social workers and other practitioners who provide such information. High-quality social background reports offer valuable assistance to the deliberations of hearings. Local authorities hold responsibility to implement supervision requirements, necessitating sound planning, coordinated across agencies, to address children's needs and to support parents in safeguarding and maintaining their child's wellbeing. Articles 6 (right to a fair hearing) and 8 (right to respect for private and family life) of the ECHR respectively demand fair procedures and proportionate decision making that respects family life. These should be seen as reinforcing well-established social work principles and practice that underpin balanced and transparent decision making within the boundaries of relevant legal frameworks.

Families may have little knowledge about hearings until their child is referred and social workers are therefore well placed, alongside formal processes, to provide information about the philosophy, procedures and decision-making powers of the hearings to children and their parents, including their rights at different stages of the process. A national survey of 398 adults and 232 children and young people attending hearing centres found that social workers were the group most commonly consulted in advance of a hearing (SCRA, 2009a).

Reporters, referrals and decisions

The children's reporter is the gatekeeper to the hearings system, investigating referrals and making decisions about the need for compulsory measures of supervision. Police are the primary agency referring children to the reporter on both offence and care and protection grounds (88.4% of all referrals, and 83.3% of care and protection referrals in 2008/09), followed by social work (6.2% of all referrals) and education (3.9% of all referrals) in the same year (SCRA, 2009b, p. 4). Principles and guidance aim to provide consistency and transparency in reporter decision making (SCRA, 2006). At this stage, social workers and practitioners in education and/or health may be asked to provide information to assist the reporter's deliberations. This may be limited, for example, to recorded information or may require more detailed assessment and direct contact with families. A key professional skill is the timely transmission of accurate and relevant information. Regular liaison with the reporter in relation to potential referrals and ongoing cases can be beneficial in ensuring that only children who require compulsory measures are dealt with in the hearings.

There has been growing demand on the children's hearings, reaching a high point in 2006/07 when 56,199 children were referred (SCRA, 2007, p. 23). In the following two years, a consistent reduction has been observed, with 47,178 children referred in 2008/09 (SCRA, 2009c, p. 3). This decrease primarily related to fewer children referred on offence grounds (a decrease of 18.6%) compared to a smaller decrease of 2.5% on care and protection grounds (SRCA, 2009b, p. 3). However, these numbers continue to represent a significant proportion of the child population in Scotland: 5.2% of all children under 16 years (SCRA, 2009c, p. 3).

Since the inception of the hearings in 1971, there has been a striking shift in the balance between offence and non-offence referrals. In a major research study early in the development of the hearings (Martin et al., 1981), 73% of first grounds of referral were for child offending contrasted with 5% due to parental neglect or an offence committed against a child. By the twenty-first century, an almost complete reversal can be observed. In 2008/09, 69% of referrals were on care and protection grounds and 31% on offence grounds (SCRA, 2009b, p. 15).[3] This changing balance creates increasingly complex demands on decision making in children's hearings and requires great skill in mediating between the conflicting interests and rights of parents and children.

Vulnerable children: social disadvantage

Patterns of social and economic disadvantage have been identified as common features in the lives of children in the hearings (Waterhouse et al., 2000; Murray et al., 2002; Wallace and Henderson, 2004). In a sample of 1,155 children referred in 1995, Waterhouse et al. (2000) found dependence on state benefits (55% of families) and housing tenure primarily located in local authorities (72% of families). Lone parenting (46%) was higher than comparable national proportions and is recognised as closely associated with poverty (Townsend, 1996). Family structure appears to have remained unchanged, with just under half (47.9%) of children referred in 2008/09 living in a lone-parent household (SCRA, 2009c, p. 6). These patterns of social disadvantage have been found more widely in the backgrounds of children drawn into public child welfare and youth justice systems (Bebbington and Miles, 1989; Gibbons et al., 1990; Goldson, 2000).

Social and economic adversity is not a causal explanation of either offending or child maltreatment but suggests that broader welfare needs require consideration in assessment and planning. The long-term outcomes for children living in poverty are well established, including the impact on psychological development (Dearing, 2007) and educational outcomes (Wilkinson and Pickett, 2009). Moreover, when aligned with personal adversity located, for example, in parental difficulties (such as mental health problems, parental substance misuse), health and/or behavioral difficulties, social disadvantage can be seen to create additional hazards in the lives of children referred (McGhee and Waterhouse, 2007). The presence of social and economic adversity reinforces the importance of the ecological approach to assessment outlined in the National Practice Model developed as part of the Scottish Government's *Getting it right for every child* programme (see Chapter 4). This aims to improve wellbeing and outcomes for all children and young people in Scotland, coordinating the necessary support through agencies working together, whether universal or more specialist, and whether primarily child and/or adult focused.

Assessment and reports

Social workers have a central role in the provision of detailed social background reports to the hearings, including recommendations about the need for compulsory measures of supervision. This increasingly takes place in the context of the *Getting it right for every child* programme (Scottish Government, 2008b), requiring liaison with other agencies, primarily education and health. Social workers need to be clear about the basis for their assessment and the reasons for their recommendations. Hallett et al. (1998, p. 57) observed 60 hearings and found that in 84%, the lay panel's decision matched the social worker's recommendation. Accurate and accessible reports may support children and their families to be better prepared to participate in the hearing and to effectively engage in the process. Good practice suggests that social workers should discuss the contents of their reports and their recommendations with parents and children, taking account of the child's age and maturity. This is especially important where either may have a learning disability, a communication difficulty, or where English may not be their first language. This direct contact also facilitates the provision of information to children and families about their right to discuss the referral with the reporter and to consider seeking legal advice.

Relevant persons have had access to all hearings papers, including social background reports, following the judgment of the European Court of Human Rights in the case of *McMichael* v *United Kingdom*,[4] which found that the failure to do so was a breach of Article 6 of the ECHR. A balance has to be struck between openness and confidentiality, as the hearing requires full information to make a decision. Difficulties can arise between relevant persons, for example parents who have been divorced for a long time may be unhappy with ex-spouses becoming aware of the presence of, for example, mental health problems. Children may not wish to express their concerns about parental difficulties or their desire to remain in current fostering arrangements in written form. Children do not have a legal right to receive all hearings papers including copies of reports. However, following the case of *S* v *Miller*,[5] the Scottish Children's Reporter Administration (SCRA) introduced a system to provide children with hearing papers: children and young people aged 12 years and older will generally receive hearings papers, but there are specific restrictions where significant harm or distress may be caused to the child and/or relevant person; children aged between 8 and 12 years can receive hearing papers on request by themselves or their adult representative, or where receipt would be in the child's best interests in the view of the report writer, subject to the same restrictions (SCRA, 2003).

This balances the rights of the child to information against potential risks to their welfare. Report writers should be alert to identifying such concerns for reporters.

Parents have expressed concern about the potential breach of their privacy when their children receive copies of reports and the potential adverse effect that information about parents (especially 'past' experiences) may have on parent–child relationships (SCRA, 2009a). This illustrates the tension between children's right to information and their parents' right to manage information about their previous and current private life. The Children's Hearings (Scotland) Bill proposes a statutory right of access to papers for children to be fully defined within secondary legislation and this is likely to function is a similar way to the present system (Scottish Parliament, 2010a).

Well-balanced reports rooted in thorough and accurate assessment should support sound decision making. This is particularly relevant in more complex cases where childcare and protection concerns are present and where the lay decision makers have to arbitrate between the conflicting rights and interests of children and their parents. In 2008/09, two grounds were the most common basis of referral to reporters, s. 52(2)(d) 'victim of a schedule 1 offence' (18,621 children) and s. 52(2)(c) 'lack of parental care' (15,320 children) (SCRA, 2009c, p. 10). Cases of child abuse and neglect are the starkest situations where Article 8 of the ECHR is engaged and children's hearings can make decisions that may profoundly affect the lives of children and their families. Well-founded reports are essential to ensure that families and their representatives are better placed to contest or provide alternative views to social workers and other practitioners' views in the hearing, supporting effective participation and rights under Article 6 of the ECHR. The preparatory role can be complex where there is divergence between practitioners and the child and/or parents' views about the need for compulsory state intervention. This emphasises the importance of building relationships of confidence and trust that may serve to accommodate differing perspectives when they arise.

Children's hearings

The hearings system is predicated on a straightforward, non-adversarial forum where participation by children and their families is central to decision making. The lay tribunal lies at the heart of the system and functions as the independent decision maker about the need for compulsory state intervention in a child's life. Three panel members meet together with the child, their parents (and potentially other family members) in the presence of the reporter, social worker and, in some instances, other practitioners involved in the child's life. The intention is to provide an opportunity for discussion about difficulties and potential resolutions. The reporter maintains a record of the proceedings but they do not act as an adviser to the panel members or the hearing. SCRA (2009d) guidance ensures that reporter practice is aligned with Article 6 of the ECHR, the right to a fair hearing before an independent tribunal: reporters may point out matters regarding fairness of the process to the hearing but panel members/hearing are not required to accept these views. Moreover, reporters may not have substantive discussions about the case with panel members and contact outwith the presence of the child and relevant persons should be minimal. This serves to preserve the independence of the lay tribunal in decision making. The Children's Hearings (Scotland) Bill will reinforce this independence through the proposed appointment of a National Convenor of Children's Hearings Scotland with inter alia responsibility to provide independent advice to panels, including legal advice (Scottish Parliament, 2010a).

Participation

Participation by children and parents therefore lies at the heart of the hearings system. The hearing is required to take account of the views of children (s. 16(2) of the 1995 Act; Rule 15 of the Children's Hearings (Scotland) Rules 1996).[6] Social workers and other professionals have an important role in supporting children and their families to fully participate. Preparation by social workers for attendance at hearings is an aspect of the social work role appreciated by children and families (Hallett et al., 1998; SCRA, 2009a). However, evidence suggests that participation is not always easy to achieve (Hallet et al., 1998; Waterhouse et al., 2000). Hallett et al. (1998, p. ii) observed 60 children's hearings and noted that children and young people frequently had limited involvement in the discussion and the majority of responses were 'monosyllabic' or fewer than 12 words. However, these somewhat limited contributions could be vital in accessing the child's views.

Studies have highlighted children and young people's views about difficulties in communicating and expressing their views within hearings in ways that they felt heard (Griffiths and Kandel, 2000; McGhee, 2004). The introduction of the user-friendly 'Having Your Say' form offers children the opportunity to provide their views in advance of hearings. However, only 36% of children and young people surveyed had used it, although most found it helpful when they did so (SCRA, 2009a). More positively, adults and young people who considered they had 'things to say' at their hearings were positive about conveying their views and confident they would be attended to by panel members (SCRA, 2009a).

Privacy, confidentiality and exclusion

Children and relevant persons have a right and an obligation to attend the hearing, although both can be released from this obligation in specific circumstances (s. 45 of the 1995 Act). This may be appropriate, for example, where a child is 16 years old and living with family carers and there is no parental contact. In this case, it may be proper that a parent, who is a relevant person, be released from the obligation to attend. Competing interests between children and parents do arise and are especially testing where there are concerns about the parental care of a child. The increase in care and protection referrals where child abuse and neglect may be present raises complex issues for the decision-making process as well as the substantive decision about the imposition of compulsory supervision measures. Children may feel inhibited, through fear, conflicting loyalties or unwillingness to expose parental shortcomings, to fully express their views in the hearing (Griffiths and Kandel, 2000; McGhee, 2004).

In an attempt to ensure that a child's view can be heard in circumstances where there may be undue influence by a relevant person, or the presence of the person may cause significant distress, for example where a relevant person has harmed or neglected the child, there is a provision to exclude the person from parts of the hearing (s. 46 of the 1995 Act). This provides an opportunity for the child to speak directly to the hearing. However, it does not provide confidentiality, in that the substance of the discussion must be disclosed to the excluded person (s. 46(2) of the 1995 Act). This contrasts with provisions in family actions in the Sheriff Court, where the views of the child may be sealed in an envelope and kept confidential to the sheriff (Sheriff Courts (Scotland) Act 1907, Ordinary Cause Rules 33 (20(2)(b))). However, the provision provides a balance between encouraging participation by the child while upholding the parents' right to a fair hearing.

Griffiths and Kandel (2006) found varied use of this exclusionary power among a group of 34 panel members interviewed. They identified three broad patterns of approach to the requirement to disclose:

1. *literalists:* panel members who interpreted the provision as providing all 'substantive information'
2. *gisters:* those who provided 'the gist', a broad 'summary discussion'

3. *loopholers:* who focused discussion more generally on the child's feelings and wishes, disclosing these in vague terms, hoping to encourage parents to reveal difficulties themselves.

This suggests some exercise of discretion in balancing the autonomy of the child with parents' due process rights. The Children's Hearings (Scotland) Bill outlines a limited right of privacy to the child where disclosure would be 'significantly against the interests of the child' (s. 171) (Scottish Parliament 2010b).

While child abuse and neglect raise specific concerns, evidence from a wider study of child protection cases in England suggested that children do benefit from parental involvement in decision-making processes, and that there are relatively few cases where the severity of difficulties precludes participation (Thoburn et al., 1995). Moreover, children can be supported in complex situations, such as child protection case conferences, to take part in the discussion (Schofield and Thoburn, 1996).

Representation and advocacy

Relevant persons and children have a right to bring a representative to a hearing and this may be a friend, voluntary advocate, children's rights officer, or solicitor (Rule 11, Children's Hearings (Scotland) Rules 1996). However, civil legal aid is not available for legal representation at a hearing. This was considered incompatible, in some circumstances, with Article 6 of the ECHR in *S* v *Miller* (see above), although, taken as a whole, the procedural framework of the hearings was deemed compliant with the ECHR. The child's hearing is intended to facilitate discussion; however, there are formal aspects of the process to address: the child and/or relevant person may decide to contest the grounds of referral and all hold appeal and review rights. The Children's Hearings (Legal Representation) (Scotland) Rules 2002[7] created provision for a hearing or business meeting to appoint a legally qualified safeguarder or curator ad litem to a child in two circumstances: first, where this would enable effective participation by the child and, second, where a supervision requirement is to be made (or continued) that includes provision for the child to reside in a named residential unit and the child fits the criteria for secure accommodation, essentially where placement in secure accommodation is being considered (Rule 3, 2002 Rules).

Ormston and Marryat (2009, p. 3) found mixed views of the legal representation scheme among professionals: legal representatives could aid calm discussion, or help to focus on key legal matters but at times discussion could be 'bogged down in legal jargon'. In their interviews with 23 young people from four secure units, they found varied views:

some young people found legal representation helpful in putting forward their views; others preferred to speak directly to the panel; others considered representatives failed to transmit their views effectively. Young people with no contact (or very limited contact) with their lawyer in advance of the hearing appeared to be more 'dissatisfied' with the experience of legal involvement (p. 2).

In 2009, responding to the legal challenge presented in the case *SK* v *Paterson*,[8] the 2002 Rules were amended to permit state-funded legal representation of some relevant persons to support effective participation in certain circumstances (primarily where parent–child separation and/or regulation of contact may arise or parental rights affected). These provisions recognise that some parents need additional support, beyond the current entitlement to bring a representative, to challenge information or present their views. A national scheme for state-funded legal representation at children's hearings is proposed in the Children's Hearings (Scotland) Bill. It remains to be seen whether more routine involvement of lawyers in children's hearings will arise and how this may come to affect the future operation of the system.

Supervision: compulsory state intervention

There are growing numbers of children subject to compulsory measures: at 31 March 2009, 13,523 children were subject to supervision requirements (SCRA, 2009b, p. 19). The majority remained in the care of parents/relevant persons (53%) or with relatives or friends (15%) (SCRA, 2009b, p. 19).[9] The duty to implement supervision requirements lies with local authorities and social workers generally have the key role in coordinating with other professionals, in addition to engaging in direct work with children and their families. There is some evidence to suggest that social workers are less skilled in assessing and supporting parents with learning disabilities (Tymchuk and Andron, 1990) and therefore links with adult services may be particularly important for such parents.

The imposition of compulsory measures of supervision on a child opens private family life to scrutiny by practitioners. Parents retain their parental responsibilities and rights but cannot exercise these in ways that are inconsistent with the supervision requirement (s. 3(4) of the 1995 Act). Parents are not under any direct legal compulsion when their child is under supervision; however, they are, in practice, required to cooperate with practitioners, including the expectation that they address those personal difficulties that may adversely affect the welfare of their child. Kilbrandon (1964) did not consider that parents should be subject to punitive fines for the actions of their children but that advice and assistance should be offered. Parental civil and criminal liability for harms caused by children is present in other jurisdictions such as the USA (Sutherland, 2004). Tensions, embedded in the power imbalance present with compulsory state intervention, inevitably arise between parents and practitioners, so practitioners need to be able to empathise with parents while keeping the child's welfare to the fore.

Partnership working is fundamental to effective practice and requires good communication skills alongside the capacity to build trusting relationships with children and families across diverse social and ethnic backgrounds. Moreover, clarity about the basis for decisions, promoting understanding of the decision-making processes and effective inclusion of families and children are crucial (Waterhouse and McGhee, 2002). Forrester et al. (2007) studied social workers' interaction with simulated clients (actors) where child protection concerns were present and found many had more interrogatory styles of communication. In contrast, those with more empathic approaches elicited greater information disclosure and cooperation with parents. Building positive relationships with children and families is crucial for practice but can be inhibited by high staff turnover and non-allocation of cases, a feature identified by Murray et al. (2002).

Troubled and troubling children

Despite declining numbers of offenders, political and public concern about young people who commit offences was a central feature of many countries in the 1990s (Roberts, 2004). Hallett et al. (1998) reported professional and panel members' concerns about the effectiveness of the hearings in dealing with persistent young offenders. Audit Scotland (2002) identified deficiencies in specialist services and a need for improved training for social workers in addressing the behaviour and needs of young people who offend. As part of a wider strategy, the Scottish Executive funded a pilot to fast-track decision making for young people identified as persistent offenders within the hearings. This sat alongside improved assessment and access to appropriate intervention (Hill et al., 2007). Despite improved processing times, better assessment, and access to relevant resources, a reduction in offending was less than in selected comparison sites and the programme was not extended (Hill et al., 2007). Current government policy is focused on prevention and early intervention that is holistic and effective in addressing children's broader social and educational needs alongside offending behaviour. This approach draws on the principles of the *Getting it right for every child* programme and, in addition, recognises the importance of developing effective interventions for children who may present a greater risk of harm to themselves or others (Scottish Government, 2008c).

Many young people who offend have had prior contact with social services (Hagell and Newburn, 1994; Goldson, 2000). Moreover, as Kilbrandon (1964) contended, there is evidence to suggest the presence of common underlying circumstances in children's lives, and that they move between categories of referral over time (Waterhouse et al., 2004). In an analysis of the referral patterns for a group of children with prior involvement in the hearings, it was apparent that for two-thirds of the children, movement between offence and non-offence grounds was not uncommon over time, although the remaining third tended to have consistent referrals solely on either offence or care and protection grounds (Waterhouse et al., 2004). This points to the importance of addressing 'needs' as well as 'deeds' for young people who are referred on offence grounds. It also suggests that more focused intervention may be necessary for children who solely have offence or care and protection referrals over time.

Human rights and children's hearings

The children's hearings system holds the welfare of the child at the centre. At the same time, the rights of children and their parents within the hearings must be upheld. Participation is central yet there are tensions in balancing autonomy and welfare for children especially where concerns about child abuse and neglect are foremost. Article 6 of the ECHR requires a fair hearing before an independent and impartial tribunal. Practitioners need to be mindful of this in working within the hearings, emphasising the importance of clarity in communication in discussion of reports and recommendations, and in recognising the role they may serve in preparing and supporting children and their families within the hearings system. Prevention and early intervention should restrict the need for compulsory measures and ensure that this is only invoked, for some children, when necessary, reflecting the provisions of Article 8 of the ECHR. Practitioners operating within the legal framework of the hearings system need to draw on well-established social work principles and high-level practice skills to ensure that they are effectively equipped to promote the welfare of children while respecting the rights of children and their families.

References

Audit Scotland (2002) *Dealing with Offending by Young People*, Edinburgh, Auditor General/Accounts Commission.

Bebbington, A. and Miles, J. (1989) 'The background of children who enter local authority care', *British Journal of Social Work*, 19: 349–68.

Cowperthwaite, D.J. (1988) *The Emergence of the Scottish Children's Hearings System: An Administrative/Political Study of the Establishment of Novel Arrangements in Scotland for Dealing with Juvenile Offenders*, Southampton, University of Southampton.

Dearing, E. (2007) 'Psychological costs of growing up poor', *Annals of the New York Academy of Sciences*, 1136: 324–32.

Forrester, D., Kershaw, S., Moss, H. and Hughes. L. (2007) 'Communication skills in child protection: how do social workers talk to parents?', *Child and Family Social Work*, 13: 41–51.

Gibbons, J. with Thorpe, S. and Wilkinson, P. (1990) *Family Support and Prevention: Studies in Local Areas*, London, HMSO.

Goldson, B. (2000) '"Children in need" or "young offenders"? Hardening ideology, organizational change and new challenges for social work with children in trouble', *Child and Family Social Work*, 5: 255–65.

Griffiths, A. and Kandel, R.F. (2000) 'Hearing children in children's hearings', *Child and Family Law Quarterly*, **12**(3): 283–99.

Griffiths, A. and Kandel, R.F. (2006) 'Children's confidentiality at the crossroad: challenges for the Scottish children's hearings system', *Journal of Social Welfare and Family Law*, **28**(2): 137–52.

Hagell, A. and Newburn, T. (1994) *The Persistent Offender*, London, Policy Studies Institute.

Hallett, C. (2000) 'Ahead of the game or behind the times? The Scottish children's hearings system in international context', *International Journal of Law, Policy and the Family*, 14: 31–44.

Hallett, C. and Murray, C. with Jamieson, J. and Veitch, B. (1998) *The Evaluation of Children's Hearings in Scotland,* vol. 1, *Deciding in Children's Interests,* Edinburgh, Scottish Office Central Research Unit.

Hill, M., Walker, M., Moodie, K. et al. (2007) 'More haste, less speed? An evaluation of fast track policies to tackle persistent youth offending in Scotland', *Youth Justice*, **7**(2): 121–38.

Kilbrandon, L. (1964) *Report of the Committee on Children and Young Persons, Scotland*, Cmnd 2306, Edinburgh, Scottish Office, HMSO.

McGhee, J. (2004) 'Young people's views of the Scottish children's hearings system', in J. McGhee, M. Mellone and B. Whyte (eds) *Meeting Needs, Addressing Deeds: Working with Young People who Offend*, Glasgow, NCH Scotland.

McGhee, J. and Waterhouse, L. (2007) 'Care and protection in Scottish child welfare: evidence of double jeopardy?' *European Journal of Social Work*, **10**(2): 145–60.

Martin, F.M., Fox Sanford, J. and Murray, K. (1981) *Children out of Court*, Edinburgh, Scottish Academic Press.

Murray, C., Hallett, C., McMillan, N. and Watson, J. (2002) *Home Supervision Scotland's Children, Children (Scotland) Act 1995*, Research Findings, No. 4, Edinburgh, Scottish Executive.

Murray, K. and Hill, M. (1991) 'The recent history of Scottish child welfare', *Children & Society*, **5**(3): 266–81.

Ormston, R. and Marryat, L. (2009) *Review of the Children's Legal Representation Grant Scheme: Research Report*, available online at www.scotland.gov.uk/Publications/2009/06/30092403/0 [accessed 26 April 2010].

Roberts, J.V. (2004) 'Public opinion and youth justice', in M. Tonry and A.N. Doob (eds) *Youth Crime and Youth Justice: Comparative and Cross-national Perspectives*, London, University of Chicago Press.

Schofield, G. and Thoburn, J. (1996) *Child Protection: The Voice of the Child in Decision Making*, London, Institute for Public Policy Research.

Scottish Government (2008a) *Strengthening for the Future: A Consultation on the Reform of the Children's Hearings System*, available online at www.scotland.gov.uk/Publications/2008/08/01110537/0 [accessed 31 March 2010].

Scottish Government (2008b) *The Guide to Getting it right for every child*, available online at www.scotland.gov.uk/Publications/2008/09/22091734/0 [accessed 6 July 2010].

Scottish Government (2008c) *Preventing Offending by Young People: A Framework for Action*, available online at www.scotland.gov.uk/Publications/2008/06/17093513/0 [accessed 26 April 2010].

Scottish Parliament (2010a) *Children's Hearings (Scotland) Bill: Policy Memorandum*, available online at www.scottish.parliament.uk/s3/bills/41-ChildrensHearing/index.htm [accessed 8 March 2010].

Scottish Parliament (2010b) *Children's Hearings (Scotland) Bill*, available online at www.scottish.parliament.uk/s3/bills/41-ChildrensHearing/index.htm [accessed 8 March 2010].

SCRA (Scottish Children's Reporter Administration) (2003) *Practice Instruction Note 24: Papers for Children*, Stirling, SCRA.

SCRA (Scottish Children's Reporter Administration) (2006) *Framework for Decision Making by Reporters*, available online at www.scra.gov.uk/cms_resources/Framework%20for%20Decision%20Making%20by%20Reporters.pdf [accessed 6 July 2010].

SCRA (Scottish Children's Reporter Administration) (2007) *Annual Report 2006/07*, available online at http://www.scra.gov.uk/publications/annual_report.cfm [accessed 2 April 2010].

SCRA (Scottish Children's Reporter Administration) (2009a) *The Views and Experiences of Children and Families Involved in the Children's Hearings System in Scotland*, available online at www.scra.gov.uk/home/children_and_families_survey_report.cfm [accessed 6 April 2010].

SCRA (Scottish Children's Reporter Administration) (2009b) *Annual Report 2008/09*, available online at www.scra.gov.uk/cms_resources/FINAL%20Annual%20Report%2008%2009%20web.pdf [accessed 31 March 2010].

SCRA (Scottish Children's Reporter Administration) (2009c) *Online Statistics 2008/09*, available online at www.scra.gov.uk/cms_resources/Online%20Stats%20v1.3%20Final.pdf [accessed 6 July 2010].

SCRA (Scottish Children's Reporter Administration) (2009d) *Practice Instruction Note 1: The Role of the Reporter at the Children's Hearing*, Stirling, SCRA.

Sutherland, E.E. (2004) 'Parenting orders: a culturally alien response of questionable efficacy', *Juridical Review*, 49: 105–32.

Thoburn, J., Lewis, A. and Shemmings, D. (1995) 'Paternalism or partnership? Family involvement in the child protection process', in Department of Health, *Child Protection, Messages from Research*, London, HMSO.

Townsend, P. (1996) *A Poor Future: Can we Counter Growing Poverty in Britain and Across the World?*, London, Lemos and Crane.

Tymchuk, A. and Andron, L. (1990) 'Mothers with mental retardation who do or do not abuse or neglect their children', *Child Abuse and Neglect*, **14**(3): 313–23.

Wallace, K. and Henderson, G. (2004) *Social Backgrounds of Children Referred to the Reporter: A Pilot Study*, Stirling, SCRA.

Waterhouse, L. and McGhee, J. (2002) 'Social work with children and families', in R. Adams, L. Dominelli and M. Payne (eds) *Social Work: Themes, Issues and Critical Debates* (2nd edn), Basingstoke, Palgrave Macmillan.

Waterhouse, L., McGhee, J. and Loucks, N. (2004) 'Disentangling offenders and non-offenders in the Scottish children's hearings: a clear divide?', *Howard Journal of Criminal Justice*, **43**(2): 164–79.

Waterhouse, L., McGhee, J., Whyte, B. et al. (2000) *The Evaluation of Children's Hearings in Scotland*, vol. 3, *Children in Focus*, Edinburgh, TSO.

Wilkinson, R. and Pickett, K. (2009) *The Spirit Level: Why More Equal Societies Almost Always Do Better*, London, Allen Lane, Penguin Books.

Notes

1. *Sloan* (Reporter: Children's Hearings) v *B* (A Parent), 1991, SC 412; 1991 SLT 530, IH (1 Div).
2. The 1995 Act refers to relevant persons, which includes a wider range of people/carers with rights to attend hearings etc. other than parents, and indeed some parents may be excluded from this definition. However, for the purposes of this chapter, references will be to children and parents for ease of discussion of professional practice issues but should be seen as an inclusive term.
3. Calculated from the breakdown of referrals in 2008/09: 83,742 referrals.
4. *McMichael* v *United Kingdom* (A/308) (1995) 20 EHRR 205.
5. *S* v *Miller* (No. 1); sub nom *S* v *Principal Reporter* (No. 1) 2001 SC 977; 2001 SLT 531, (IH) (1 Div).
6. Children's Hearings (Scotland) Rules 1996, SI 1996, No. 3261.
7. Children's Hearings (Legal Representation) (Scotland) Rules 2002, SI 2002, No. 63.
8. *SK* v *Paterson* [2009] CSIH 76 XA25/09; sub nom *K* v *Authority Reporter*, 2009 SLT 1019.
9. Calculated from the breakdown of types of supervision requirements in Table 5, p. 19 for the 13,523 children.

Chapter 7

The Voice of the Child

KATHLEEN MARSHALL

Introduction

This chapter explores how children's voices are heard in children's hearings and court proceedings, covering both 'private' (mostly family) law and 'public' (childcare and protection) law. A historical survey covers the period up to the Social Work (Scotland) Act 1968, adjustments introduced by the Children Act 1975, and the attempt by the Children (Scotland) Act 1995 to take account of the 1989 UN Convention on the Rights of the Child (UNCRC) and the European Convention on Human Rights (ECHR). It discusses the UNCRC and shows that, while it did not invent the principle of listening to children, it gave it a boost, ensuring a more focused approach to hearing children's voices. The chapter is structured around four questions:

- Why should we listen to children?
- When do we listen to children?
- How do we listen to children?
- Who has the job of listening to children?

The conclusion considers current steps towards a more strategic approach to child advocacy.

Why should we listen to children?

The traditional Scottish approach

Historically, the justification for listening to children was their legal status, based on the stages of childhood that were understood to involve different levels of maturity. 'Infancy' lasted from birth to 7 and its passing was assumed to herald the ability to tell right from wrong. Seven was the legal age of criminal responsibility until 1932, when it was raised to 8. The next threshold was puberty (known legally as 'minority'), entailing the right to make decisions about your person, for example medical decisions, getting married, leaving home. Puberty was assumed to occur at 12 for girls and 14 for boys. When you reached the age of majority at 21, you were an adult and had full capacity to make what were regarded as more complex decisions about your property. This was reduced to 18 by the Age of Majority (Scotland) Act 1969.

Further changes include:

- The age of consent to medical treatment was changed by the Age of Legal Capacity (Scotland) Act 1991. This says that young people aged 16 and over have a general capacity to make decisions about medical procedures. Section 2(4) says that children under 16 have capacity where a medical practitioner believes that they understand the nature and possible consequences of the treatment or procedure proposed.
- The age of marriage was raised to 16 in 1929 and is now regulated by s. 1 of the Marriage (Scotland) Act 1977.
- The law on the right to leave home was affected by the Custody of Children Act 1939, referred to below, which allowed courts to make custody orders up to the age of 16.

The UN Convention on the Rights of the Child

The biggest catalyst for change in recent decades has been the UNCRC. The year 1979 was the International Year of the Child, and the United Nations decided to mark it by starting work on a Convention on the Rights of the Child. There had been a series of international statements of children's rights since 1924 when the League of Nations adopted the Geneva Declaration of the Rights of the Child. However, these had been mere exhortations with no legal effect or monitoring mechanisms. A convention is a piece of international law that individual states are invited to ratify. It took 10 years to draft a convention that the UN's member states were happy with. It was adopted by the UN General Assembly on 20 November 1989 and ratified in the UK in 1991. By 2010, it had been ratified by 195 states, the two exceptions being the USA and Somalia.

The UNCRC had a rationale for listening to children that was different from the traditional Scottish approach. Children were to be listened to because it was a fundamental right, and because it led to better informed decisions that were more likely to promote the child's interests. The threshold for the right to express views was 'the ability to form a view', which can happen at a very young age. There was no lower threshold and it was not linked to formal stages of childhood. Age and maturity were relevant only in deciding what weight to give to the view the child had expressed.

Thus, Article 12.1 of the UNCRC says:

> States Parties shall assure to the child who is capable of forming his
> or her own views the right to express those views freely in all matters
> affecting the child, the views of the child being given due weight in
> accordance with the age and maturity of the child.

Article 12.2 insists that this be embedded into legal processes:

> For this purpose, the child shall in particular be provided the opportunity
> to be heard in any judicial and administrative proceedings affecting the
> child, either directly, or through a representative or an appropriate body,
> in a manner consistent with the procedural rules of national law.

However, the UNCRC does not insist on the autonomy of the child.
Article 3.1 embraces the child's interests:

> In all actions concerning children, whether undertaken by public or
> private social welfare institutions, courts of law, administrative
> authorities or legislative bodies, the best interests of the child shall be
> a primary consideration.

Earlier drafts of the UNCRC made an explicit connection between views
and interests. What is now Article 12.2 used to follow on from Article 3.1;
listening to a child was part of promoting their interests. Something was lost
when the text was tidied up into an article based on views and an article
based on interests, but the insight remains valid: how can any decision
maker claim to be acting in the interests of a child if the child has views on
the matter and the decision maker does not know what they are?

Ratification of the UNCRC committed the UK government to
bringing law, policy and practice into line with it. Progress in achieving
this is monitored by the UN Committee on the Rights of the Child,
which calls governments to account two years after ratification and
every five years thereafter.

The Children (Scotland) Act 1995

The Children (Scotland) Act 1995 was the earliest and most comprehensive attempt to bring Scottish law into line with the UNCRC. The
government White Paper (Scottish Office, 1993) that set out plans for
the Act made it clear that it was to be built on the twin pillars of the
UNCRC and the ECHR. Three principles run throughout the Act:

1. The best interests of children are to be paramount when decisions
   are made about them.

2. Children should be invited to express their views and these should be taken into account in accordance with age and maturity.
3. Children's lives should not be overregulated by court orders. Courts should make decisions about children only when having a court order will be better than not having one. This is sometimes referred to as the 'minimum intervention' principle, but is more accurately described as the 'no order' principle. It is important that practitioners be aware that sometimes a court order is necessary. The idea of 'minimum intervention' should not be perceived as a barrier to appropriate action.

These principles are restated at different points in the 1995 Act and it is important to become acquainted with the structure of the Act to make sure that you are referring to the correct section of it.

Part I of the Act deals with 'private' law – family matters that do not generally entail state interference or concern about the child's upbringing. The principles for Part I are set out in s. 11(7). Parts II and III of the Act deal with childcare and protection. The principles for courts and children's hearings are set out in ss. 16(1) to (3) and the principles for local authorities are set out in ss.17(1), (3) and (4).

The permanency provisions of Part IV of the 1995 Act have been replaced by the Adoption and Children (Scotland) Act 2007. Sections 14 and 28 of this Act set out the principles in relation to adoption, and s. 84 does so for permanence orders.

When do we listen to children?

We should always listen to children when they are trying to express concerns or make comment about their lives because this leads to better decisions. For parents, s. 6 of the 1995 Act requires that they consult their children in all 'major' decisions, although these are largely undefined. For children looked after by local authorities, the requirement to listen to children is set out in ss. 17(3) and (4) of the 1995 Act. This is a core function of social workers acting on behalf of the local authority. Scottish law requires that listening to children should be integrated into everyday practice, not just formal processes such as courts and children's hearings, which are more specifically regulated. We will look here at the voice of the child in family law, adoption, children's hearings and criminal law processes.

Family law

Historically, Scottish family law insisted that 'minor' children (girls of 12 and above, boys of 14 and above) had rights, not only to be heard, but to make significant decisions. They could get married and, in the absence of a father (mothers had very few rights), could decide on residence, education and medical treatment.

In 1939, the Custody of Children Act allowed courts to award custody of minors below the age of 16, not to restrict their autonomy, but to protect them from the need to make difficult decisions about which parent to live with.[1] They were still entitled to be heard by the court and sometimes to be cited as respondents.[2] This principle got lost in later practice. It had always been possible for children's interests to be separately represented in court through appointment of a 'curator ad litem', but this was not standard practice. This kind of curator is an officer of the court rather than the representative of the child and is usually a solicitor.

Adoption

Minor children could be adopted only if the child consented. In 1991, s. 2(3)(a) of the Age of Legal Capacity (Scotland) Act standardised this age at 12 for boys and girls. Curators also played a role. This is discussed further below.

Children's hearings

The principle of listening to children was at the heart of the children's hearing system, introduced by the 1968 Act as a mechanism for dealing with children who needed compulsory measures of care on a number of possible grounds, including offences by the child, certain offences against the child, and neglect or abuse by parents or carers. The Kilbrandon Report (1964) first suggested this system and emphasised the involvement of parents and child. This can be problematic where the parent is suspected of abusing or neglecting the child, as it can be difficult for the child's voice to be heard with the parent present. The report said (para. 108) it might sometimes be appropriate for the child and parents to be seen separately, but it did not explain this and there was no provision for this in the 1968 Act. Nevertheless, it sometimes happened in practice with the agreement of the parents. Section 46 of the 1995 Act put this on a more formal footing by allowing hearings to exclude parents to avoid significant distress to the child or allow the hearing to obtain the child's views. However, the hearing had to tell the excluded person 'the substance of what had taken place in his absence'. The child did not have an explicit right to attend the hearing until this was introduced by s. 45(1)(a) of the 1995 Act, although some think this was implied (Kearney, 1987, pp. 78–9).

The Kilbrandon Report (para. 9) thought children's hearings would deal largely with child offenders and that cases of abuse or neglect would be few. However, as an increased number of neglect and abuse cases came to light, it became clear the system needed rebalancing in favour of children. A public inquiry into the death of seven-year-old Maria Colwell (DHSS, 1974) concluded that current systems could not cope adequately with a conflict of interest between the parent and child. Although this was an English case, there were lessons for Scotland, necessitating a reappraisal of the assumptions built into the children's hearing system. This led to the 1975 Children Act's introduction of the 'safeguarder'. It amended the 1968 Act so that, if the hearing felt there was a conflict of interest between the parent and child, it could appoint a person 'for the purpose of safeguarding the interests of the child in the proceedings' (Social Work (Scotland) Act 1968, s. 34A). Despite the urgency referred to in parliamentary debates, the 'safeguarder' provisions were not implemented until 1985.[3] They were little used at first but experience led to acceptance (Hill et al., 2002). The 1995 Act widened the role by removing the criterion of a conflict of interest between the parent and the child and allowed the hearing to appoint a safeguarder where it considered this necessary to safeguard the interest of the child in the proceedings.

The 1975 Act also amended s. 20(1) of the 1968 Act to require local authorities to consider the views of children in care when making decisions about them. In the author's experience, this provision was generally unknown and disregarded until its stronger formulation appeared in the 1995 Act.

Criminal law

The setting in which children's voices were expected to be heard, often unrealistically, was the criminal court. In Scotland, the age of criminal responsibility is 8 – one of the lowest in the world. Until recently this meant that a child of 8 could be tried in an adult court. This assumes that the child is capable of fighting their prosecutors with an 'equality of arms' (a concept created by the European Court of Human Rights in the context of Article 8 – the right to a fair trial – that neither party in either civil or criminal trials should be procedurally disadvantaged). It is unrealistic to expect a young child to understand the situation and instruct a defence. In practice, very few children appear in Scottish criminal courts. Most are diverted to the children's hearing system. However, the possibility of prosecution remains, although the Criminal Justice and Licensing (Scotland) Act, which received royal assent on 6 August 2010, has raised the age of prosecution to 12. Children aged 8 to 11 who commit offences will now all be dealt with through the children's hearing system.

Listening to children is not a notion foreign to Scotland. In the decades preceding the UNCRC, it was a core principle of the children's hearing system, it was central to the criminal justice system, but it had lost currency in family law proceedings.

How do we listen to children?

Social workers have a particular role as the ears of the local authority with regard to children looked after by them. However, the pressures of work can make it difficult to make time for this. This can lead to children and young people feeling neglected and not having the information they need to participate in decision making or to understand decisions (Who Cares? Scotland, 2009). In 2004, the Scottish Executive published the Children's Charter, developed with the insights of children and young people 'who have experienced the need to be protected and supported' (Scottish Executive, 2004). The messages they wished to convey to adults charged with helping them were:

- Get to know us
- Speak with us
- Listen to us
- Take us seriously
- Involve us
- Respect our privacy
- Be responsible to us
- Think about our lives as a whole
- Think carefully about how you use information about us
- Put us in touch with the right people
- Use your power to help
- Make things happen when they should
- Help us be safe.

These simple messages may sound self-evident, but it can be instructive to reflect on whether social workers are truly allowed the time to 'get to know' their young clients and listen to them. It may seem difficult to justify giving priority to relationship-building contact and activities that facilitate effective listening when there is so much else to do, but the central thesis of this chapter, and of the UNCRC, is that listening to children and young people is an essential part of making good decisions and achieving good outcomes, so it has to be a priority.

Family law

Section 11(7) of the 1995 Act restated the principle of the paramountcy of the child's welfare and introduced a requirement about the child's views. The wording is complex and has been debated in important legal cases. The Act requires the court to find out whether an affected child wants to express a view and, if so, to ascertain that view. It refers to the child's 'age and maturity' as a threshold, but it is not clear from the wording what parts of the process this applies to. Children aged 12 and over are 'presumed to be of sufficient age and maturity to form a view'. Some courts have used this age as a more significant threshold than was intended and have held back from inviting children under 12 to indicate whether they wish to express their views. This practice was challenged in 2002 in the case of *Cunningham* v *Shields*.[4] The lower court decided in favour of the mother without inviting the 7-year-old boy to express a view. The Court of Session decided this was wrong. It adopted an interpretation of the 1995 Act that took account of the wording of Article 12 of the UNCRC. The child's age and maturity should be taken into account only to determine what weight should be given to the child's views and not to decide whether those views should be invited. Courts should not use the fact that a child was under 12 as a reason to avoid inviting expression of their views.

There are a number of ways in which children's views can be introduced into family law processes. A form F9 can be sent to children to alert them to the fact that the court is being asked to make a decision about them and invite them to express their views.[5] It points the child in the direction of the Scottish Child Law Centre for help in understanding or completing it. The sheriff may also instruct a local authority or other person to prepare a report on the child's circumstances. Some sheriffs invite children to talk to them privately in chambers, while others feel uncomfortable about this.

The Rules (Act of Sederunt (Sheriff Court Ordinary Cause Rules) 1993) say that, where a child has indicated a wish to express views, the sheriff is not to grant an order unless the child has had an opportunity to do this, and the sheriff must give due weight to those views, having regard to the child's age and maturity. The Rules allow the sheriff to keep the child's views confidential. However, some concerns have been raised about the human rights of the parents who may be faced with a decision that was based on information to which they have not had access. This is a subject that still needs informed debate, because Article 12 speaks of the child's right to express views 'freely'. Children can be inhibited through love or fear: they may be afraid of hurting the feelings of parents they love, or they may be afraid of incurring the wrath of parents they fear.

Adoption

As indicated above, s. 32(1) of the Adoption and Children (Scotland) Act 2007 says that 'an adoption order may not be made in respect of a child who is aged twelve or over unless the child consents'. Section 32(2) allows the court to dispense with the child's consent where it is satisfied that the child is incapable of consenting. The same applies to a 'permanence order' that falls short of adoption (ss. 84(1) and (2) of the Adoption and Children (Scotland) Act 2007). Section 84 of that Act also includes a duty to take account of the child's view, with a presumption of maturity at age 12.

Even for younger children, there are procedures for ascertaining views where adoption or permanence orders are being sought. Section 108 of the Adoption and Children (Scotland) Act 2007 identifies two roles, but they can be carried out by one person where that seems appropriate:

1. A curator ad litem – to safeguard the interests of the child
2. A reporting officer to witness agreements.

Details are set out in the Act of Sederunt (Sheriff Court Rules Amendment) (Adoption and Children (Scotland) Act 2007) 2009. Rules 11–17 deal with adoption and Rules 32 and 42–47 are about permanence orders.

Although the curator's primary role relates to the child's interests, Rule 12(3)(u) of the Act of Sederunt (Sheriff Court Rules Amendment) (Adoption and Children (Scotland) Act 2007) 2009 says that they must also 'ascertain from the child whether he wishes to express a view and, where the child indicates his wish to express a view, ascertain that view'. The curator must submit a written report to the sheriff but is allowed to give the child's views orally if the curator thinks that is appropriate. These Rules provide that the sheriff can also take other steps to ascertain the child's views and can order that these, and any views expressed to the curator, should be kept confidential.

Children's hearings

The 1995 Act gives children a right to attend their hearing. They also have a duty to attend, but the hearing can absolve them from that duty in some circumstances, for example where they believe that attendance might be detrimental to the child's interests. However, because the child has a right, the child can insist on attending even if the hearing members believe it would be better for the child not to be there (s. 45, Children (Scotland) Act 1995).

In recent years, children's rights officers (appointed by many local authorities and some voluntary organisations), advocacy organisations like Who Cares? Scotland (for young people in care), and supporters of various descriptions have developed ways of helping children to get their views across, including through writing their own reports, and this has often been found to be helpful. However, concern for the human rights of parents has led to reports written by children being copied to parents. In 2010, the Children's Hearings (Scotland) Bill is before the Scottish Parliament, which proposes allowing the hearing to withhold information about a child if disclosure would be significantly against the child's interests.

The children's hearing was designed to be informal. It was supposed to be a forum in which ordinary people – children and adults – could speak for themselves. There was no provision for publicly funded legal representation. Parents and children could bring a 'representative' to assist in the discussion and this could be a person of their choosing (Rule 11, Children's Hearings (Scotland) Rules 1996). It could be a friend or relative or, for children, a children's rights officer or a worker from Who Cares? Scotland. Some families choose to bring a lawyer who they pay for themselves. For others that is not an option. The situation changed a little through a human rights challenge. The case of *S* v *Principal Reporter and the Lord Advocate* (2001)[6] involved a 15-year-old who was before the children's hearing for an alleged serious assault. He had received legal advice but was not represented at the hearing, which could have resulted in a decision to place him in secure (locked up) accommodation. The Court of Session decided that, as the children's hearing had the power to interfere with the young person's civil right to liberty of the person, it had to comply with the 'fair trial' provision of Article 6.1 of the ECHR. In some cases, this would be difficult to achieve without legal representation. This led to the introduction of publicly funded legal representation for children at hearings where a recommendation of secure accommodation was likely, or where the members of the hearing felt the child needed legal representation to allow effective participation. The legal representatives are drawn from panels maintained by local authorities. A qualitative study of the scheme gave it a mixed reception, with suggestions for improving it (Ormston and Marryat, 2009).

As indicated above, the role of safeguarders has increased and developed since their introduction in 1985.

Criminal law

Criminal law has witnessed significant developments in support for child witnesses, including the child accused. The Vulnerable Witnesses (Scotland) Act 2004 strengthened the special measures available to lessen children's distress. These include live television links so that the child does not have to appear in court, screens to hide the witness from the accused (or co-accused) and the use of supporters for the child. Research showed that the new provisions were gradually being translated into practice, even though the proper procedures for flagging up the involvement of a child through a child witness notice were not always observed (Morris Richards Ltd, 2008). While these developments are welcome, a critical question remains about the extent to which the rights of accused children can be respected in criminal courts.

Instructing a solicitor

The 1995 Act also clarified the child's right to instruct a solicitor and to raise or defend civil actions. It inserted the following sections to the Age of Legal Capacity (Scotland) Act 1991:

> 2(4A): A person under the age of sixteen years shall have legal capacity to instruct a solicitor, in connection with any civil matter, where that person has a general understanding of what it means to do so; and without prejudice to the generality of this subsection a person twelve years of age or more shall be presumed to be of sufficient age and maturity to have such understanding.
>
> (4B): A person who by virtue of subsection (4A) above has legal capacity to instruct a solicitor shall also have legal capacity to sue, or to defend, in any civil proceedings.
>
> (4C): Subsections (4A) and (4B) above are without prejudice to any question of legal capacity arising in connection with any criminal matter.

It is interesting to note that subsection (4C) is careful to safeguard the position in criminal law. The criminal law system could not fairly prosecute children unless they were presumed to have capacity to understand and to instruct their defence. So the criminal system basically presumes understanding from the age of 12, which is at least an improvement on the earlier age of 8.

Who has the job of listening to children?

The mechanisms for taking account of children's views have increased in recent years. However, the way this is done varies considerably. There is an expectation that some of those charged with reporting on a child's interests will also take account of the child's views and reflect them in their reports or conclusions. Table 7.1 identifies some of the individuals with roles focusing on the views and/or the interests of children in proceedings.

Table 7.1　Representation of children's interests and views

Name	Processes	Focus on interests	Focus on views	Training/ qualifications
Legal representative	If privately funded – any case. Otherwise dependent on legal aid	Not specifically but see comments in next column	Yes, but a solicitor who feels these go against child's interests can withdraw from the case[7]	Prescribed by Law Society of Scotland
Curator ad litem (general power at common law) (Scottish Executive, 2006)	Any civil action	Protect and safeguard interests in a legal process		Not specified. Usually solicitors acting as officers of the court
Reporter (Rule 33.21, Act of Sederunt (Sheriff Court Ordinary Cause Rules) 1993)	Family action	Report on 'the arrangements for future care and upbringing of children … or otherwise to investigate and report to the court on the circumstances of a child and on proposed arrangements for the care and upbringing of the child'	No requirement for the report to focus on views of the child but the sheriff could order this	A local authority or 'other person' – no training or qualifications specified. Often a social worker or solicitor (Scottish Executive, 2006, para. 9.11)
Curator ad litem	Adoption and permanence orders	Safeguard the interests of the child	As part of that duty – find out whether the child wishes to express a view and, if so, ascertain that view and report it to the sheriff	May or may not be drawn from a specially appointed panel. Local authority can determine qualifications or experience
Reporting officer	Adoption and permanence orders		To witness the consent to an adoption or permanence order of children aged 12 or over	May or may not be drawn from a specially appointed panel. Local authority can determine qualifications or experience

Name	Processes	Focus on interests	Focus on views	Training/ qualifications
Safeguarder	Children's hearings and associated court processes	To safeguard the interest of the child in the proceedings	An expectation that the safeguarder will help the child to express their views (Scottish Executive, 2003)	None specified. Local authorities can determine at point of recruitment. Often solicitors or social workers (Scottish Safeguarders Association, n.d.)
'Representative' at children's hearing (see Rule 11, Children's Hearings (Scotland) Rules 1996)	Children's hearings		To assist the child in the discussion of the case	None. Could be a friend, family member or professional, including a lawyer
Children's rights officer[8]	Could be at a children's hearing as a 'representative' or in administrative processes		Normal role would be to support the child to express their views	Specified by employers
Independent advocate	Could be at a children's hearing as a 'representative' or in administrative processes		Help child to express their views	Specified by employers
Sheriff	Family proceedings and children's hearing-related cases	Decisions will take interests as paramount	Required also to invite views and consider them as part of determining interests	Legally qualified

Social workers feature in this list in the context of some specific roles but, more broadly, they are often the main point of contact between the child and the social welfare or legal system and often see themselves as advocates for the child in a broad sense. As employees of the local authority, they will act in accordance with the local authority's duties to promote the welfare of 'looked after' children and also to take account of their views (s. 17, Children (Scotland) Act 1995). They will often act as a link with other agencies and help prepare the child for decision-making forums. However, there can be a tension in the social worker's role where they attend a children's hearing as the bearer of the local authority's recommendation, which may be at odds with the wishes of the child.

A strategic approach?

Arrangements for hearing the voices of children have grown up piece-meal, with no real reflection on how the system can best accommodate representation of the child's interests and views, who should undertake the primary role in ascertaining these, what qualifications and experience these people should have and how a person charged with both roles should carry out this complex task while being faithful to both principles. Following comment by the UN Committee on the Rights of the Child, the Scottish Government published a response to its observations (Scottish Government, 2009):

> No coherent national plan exists for the provision of advocacy support and the Scottish Government has commissioned initial scoping work to identify what gaps there are and how we might look to make improvements.

In January 2010, the report of this study concluded that there was a diverse range of well-regarded child advocacy services in Scotland, but a lack of a consistent approach and a lack of provision in some geographical areas. Significant gaps existed for some groups of children (Elsely, 2010, p. 6). It concluded in favour of a more strategic approach, informed by the views and experiences of children and young people.

Already, at a strategic level, the Scottish Government has manifested a commitment to respect the rights of the child through the establishment of the office of Scotland's Commissioner for Children and Young People, a post held by the author from 2004 to 2009. The basic function of the commissioner is to promote and safeguard the rights of children and young people. The commissioner is required to review law, policy and practice for their adequacy and effectiveness in respecting these rights and must also 'have regard to, and encourage others to have regard to, the views of children and young people on all matters affecting them, due allowance being made for age and maturity' (s. 5(3)(b) of the Commissioner for Children and Young People (Scotland) Act 2003). The commissioner involves children and young people in identifying the priority areas the office should address. In 2010, Tam Baillie, the current commissioner, is prioritising awareness and understanding of the UNCRC and the participation of children and young people in matters that affect them.

What's missing?

The fact that the commissioner's remit extends to practice as well as law and policy is important. Many a well-intentioned principle falls foul of lack of time, resources, expertise and even insight.

If we want to devise a system that allows children's voices to be heard, we need to ensure that their perspectives and experiences shape it. We need to embed into our practice the messages of the Scottish Executive's Children's Charter (Scottish Executive, 2004).

The quality of the personal relationship between child and adult is central to making the right things happen. Only if workers have the time and space to 'get to know' children and young people will they be able to gain their trust, hear their voices, understand them, inform them and use their power to help them. It is not good enough for a legal representative to be introduced to a child just before a children's hearing takes place. It is not good enough for a social worker to maintain brief and sporadic contact and then write a report. It is not good enough for the family law system to rely on printed forms to encourage children to get involved. What children and young people tell us is that they need and value personal relationships – people who are interested in them, who listen to them, and who are willing and able to embark on the adventure of seeing the world, its problems and opportunities, from the child's perspective. This presents a challenge in our bureaucratic world, dominated by systems, procedures and papers that have often been introduced for good reason but which threaten to overwhelm the very real human needs of the child – and often, too, the wishes of the workers who chose their profession out of a desire to engage with children and to help make life better for them. This is the challenge of the day.

References

DHSS (Department of Health and Social Security) (1974) *Report of the Inquiry into the Care and Supervision Provided in Relation to Maria Colwell*, London, HMSO.

Elsley, S. (2010) *Advocacy Makes you Feel Brave: Advocacy Support for Children and Young People in Scotland*, available online at www.scotland.gov.uk/Publications/2010/01/07144331/0 [accessed 23 April 2010].

Hill, M., Lockyer, A., Morton, P. et al. (2002) *The Role of Safeguarders in Scotland*, available online at www.scotland.gov.uk/Resource/Doc/46905/0024042.pdf [accessed 23 April 2010].

Kearney, B. (1987) *Children's Hearings and the Sheriff Court*, Edinburgh, Butterworths.

Kilbrandon, L. (1964) *Children and Young Persons, Scotland*, Cmnd 2306, Edinburgh, HMSO.

Morris Richards Ltd (2008) *Turning up the Volume: The Vulnerable Witnesses (Scotland) Act 2004*, available online at www.scotland.gov.uk/ Publications/2008/07/25160344/0 [accessed 23 April 2010].

Ormston, R. and Marryat, L., Scottish Centre for Social Research (ScotCen) (2009) *Review of the Children's Legal Representation Grant Scheme: Research Report*, available online at www.scotland.gov.uk/Publications/ 2009/06/30092403/0 [accessed 23 April 2010].

Scottish Executive (2003) *Safeguarder Training: Design, Content and Evaluation*, available online at www.scotland.gov.uk/Publications/2003/12/ 18589/29795 [accessed 23 April 2010].

Scottish Executive (2004) *Protecting Children and Young People: The Charter*, available online at www.scotland.gov.uk/Publications/2004/04/ 19082/34410 [accessed 23 April 2010].

Scottish Executive (2006) *Report by the Research Working Group on the Legal Services Market in Scotland*, available online at www.scotland.gov. uk/Resource/Doc/111789/0027239.pdf [accessed 19 April 2010].

Scottish Government (2009) *Do the Right Thing: For People who Work with Children or Work on their Behalf. A Scottish Government Action Plan in Response to the UN Committee 2008 Concluding Observations*, available online at www.scotland.gov.uk/Publications/2009/08/27111754/0 [accessed 21 May 2010].

Scottish Office (1993) *Scotland's Children: Proposals for Child Care Policy and Law*, Edinburgh, HMSO.

Scottish Safeguarders' Association (n.d.) *Notes re Panels of Persons to Safeguard the Interests of Children*, available online at http://www.chscotland. gov.uk/article.asp?ID=14 [accessed 23 April 2010].

Who Cares? Scotland (2009) *Reaching Higher: Annual Review 2008/2009*, available online at www.whocaresscotland.org/pdf/WCS_AR_2009_low_ res.pdf [accessed 6 July 2010].

Notes

1. Hansard (HC) vol 342, cols 1557–8 (9 December 1938) and vol 893, col 1836 (20 June 1975).
2. See the case of Morrison Petr., 1943 SC 481.
3. Hansard (HC) vol 893, col 1836 (20 June 1975).
4. *Cunningham* v *Shields* 2002 SC 246, also available at http://www.scotcourts. gov.uk/opinions/XA165_01.html (accessed 23 April 2010).
5. Form F9 can be accessed on the Scottish courts website at www.scotcourts. gov.uk, where it is listed in an appendix to the Act of Sederunt (Sheriff Court Ordinary Cause Rules) 1993. Chapter 33 of the Rules sets out the procedure for family actions. See in particular Rules 33.19–33.23 for provisions relating to children.

6. *S* v *Principal Reporter and Lord Advocate*, http://www.scotcourts.gov.uk/
   opinions/A2730_00.html (accessed 23 April 2010). Also reported as *S* v *Miller*
   2001 SLT 531.
7. This is a complex area. In 2004, the Law Society of Scotland issued Child
   Protection and Representation Principles for Children's Lawyers. See the
   article 'Born to instruct' by Morag Driscoll in the *Law Society Journal
   Online*, 13 December 2004 at www.journalonline.co.uk/Magazine/49-12/
   1001308.aspx (accessed 23 April 2010).
8. Non-statutory role. Many local authorities have appointed children's
   rights officers, mostly to promote the rights of looked after children (see
   Elsley, 2010).

Chapter 8

Community Care and the Promotion of Independence

ALISON PETCH

Introduction

The development of community-based support and the promotion of
independent living can be characterised as a series of shifting priorities
over the decades. In the 1970s, for example, strategies to promote the
resettlement of people with learning disabilities or mental ill health from
the long-stay hospitals started to accelerate. In the 1980s, the voices of
the disability movement started to be heard more strongly and the initial
principles of independent living were set out: accessible environment
and transport; barrier-free housing; peer support and peer advocacy;
personal assistance; income; employment and health. The 1990s saw the
advent of the community care assessment process, while the 2000s saw
an increasing emphasis on the voice of service users and the development of user-led organisations. As we move further into the twenty-first
century, there is a major emphasis on the transformation of support
through personalisation, mechanisms such as personal budgets and
co-production.

The changing policy emphasis has been paralleled by shifts of terminology and concepts. Throughout, legal structures and processes have
tended to provide a shadowy backcloth, in comparison to, for example,
childcare or formal mental health interventions. Particularly in Scotland,
there have been few legal challenges, by way of judicial review at the
Court of Session, restricting the amount of case law and diluting further
day-to-day familiarity with legal implications. This chapter will highlight the emergence of assessment as a key driver and will plot the trajec-
tory from 'service led' to 'needs led' to the current focus on outcomes. It
will explore the emergence of direct payments and their role in the wider
personalisation agenda, providing an appropriate comparison with
developments under the *Putting People First* (HM Government, 2007)
initiative in England. Finally, the challenges introduced by a focus on
eligibility criteria will be outlined.

The emergence of assessment

Prior to the introduction of formal assessment processes, the response for individuals requiring some element of support was very much dictated by available services. There was little capacity to identify and respond to the nature of the individual and what might be most effective for their particular situation; at best there might be a crude characterisation on the basis of age or perceived severity of impairment. The historical legacy of service provision endured from year to year and people were slotted into these available services. This had dictated the confinement, over decades, of many with learning or physical disabilities or mental ill health to institutional settings, while for older people, the absence of more intensive home support had often accelerated entry into long-stay care.

A key staging post on this evolving journey was the introduction of a requirement for the needs of an individual seeking publicly funded community care services to be assessed. This was in major part a response to the exponential rise in public expenditure on places in residential and nursing home care, which had occurred over the 1980s subsequent to the then Department of Health and Social Security meeting the full costs of such care for individuals on lower incomes (in receipt of what was known as 'supplementary benefit'). In addition to the financial demands, the availability of this funding created a perverse incentive, favouring care homes at a time when policy was ostensibly seeking to maximise support within the community. The legislative route to constraining this expenditure was the NHS and Community Care Act 1990, which, through the addition of s. 12A into the Social Work (Scotland) Act 1968, created a duty to assess the needs of any individual who it appears may require community care services that the local authority has a duty or power to provide or secure. This milestone is often referred to as the shift from service-led to needs-led provision.

The circular *Guidance on Assessment and Care Management* (Scottish Executive, 1991) detailed the key features of this new assessment process:

- there was to be an initial screening process
- the service user and any carer were to be active participants in the process
- the assessment was to encompass physical, mental and social functioning
- a clear decision on the services required was to be made
- review procedures and the name of a contact person were to be detailed
- information was to be provided about the complaints procedure.

Further specification of the procedures for older people was provided in *Community Care Needs of Frail People: Integrating Professional Assessments and Care Arrangements* (Scottish Office, 1998). The Community Care and Health (Scotland) Act 2002 subsequently amended s. 12A of the 1968 Act to make it a legal requirement that the views of both the person being assessed and any carer are taken into account in deciding what services to provide.

Carers

An enduring debate over the decades in respect of community care and the provision of support is, of course, the role of unpaid carers. Following the *Report of the Scottish Carers' Legislation Working Group* (Scottish Executive, 2001a), Scotland has increasingly taken a distinctive stance on how carers are framed. Rather than a potential user of services with needs to be met, they are considered to be a resource, a partner to the formal sector in providing support. Any needs that arise are a product of their caring role and are more appropriately regarded as the needs of the cared-for person. The Community Care and Health (Scotland) Act 2002 provided a legal right for carers providing a 'substantial amount of care on a regular basis' to have a carer's assessment. The purpose of this is to establish the level of care they are willing and able to provide and what assistance they need in their caring role. The right was also extended to carers of disabled children and to young carers under 16.

Guidance on the implementation of support to carers was provided in the circular *Community Care and Health (Scotland) Act 2002: New Statutory Rights for Carers* (Scottish Executive, 2003). The Act also placed a duty on local authorities to inform eligible carers of their right to an assessment, and gave the Scottish Executive the power to require NHS boards to draw up care information strategies informing people of their right. This was subsequently put in place through *NHS Carer Information Strategies* (Scottish Executive, 2006). This set out minimum requirements for NHS carer information strategies, including an obligation to submit a strategy by the end of October 2006, and guidance for their implementation. Boards are required to ensure that staff are trained to signpost carers to sources of support and advice and to inform them of their right to an assessment, and to develop plans for training carers, including 'expert carer' programmes. In 2010, *Caring Together: The Carers Strategy for Scotland 2010–2015* (Scottish Government/COSLA, 2010) was published, outlining support for carers and young carers for the next five years. Carers Scotland worked closely with the Scottish Government in developing this new strategy.

Single shared assessment

Scotland has been distinctive in the emphasis given to partnership working across health, housing and social care (Petch, 2008), manifest in the report and recommendations from the Joint Future Group (Scottish Executive, 2000) and in the activities of the Joint Improvement Team.[1] A key component of partnership working was seen as the development of the single shared assessment (SSA), a lead professional taking responsibility for ensuring a holistic assessment to be shared across agencies. Although there had always been a requirement in undertaking a community care assessment to notify health or housing if it was thought such services might be needed, individuals often experienced multiple visits from different professionals undertaking not dissimilar assessments. Moreover, this could be from within a single agency – social worker, occupational therapist, homecare organiser. Underpinning the introduction of the SSA were a number of principles:

- a single point of entry for community care services
- less bureaucracy, duplication and delay, leading to faster access to support
- appropriate information sharing between professionals and agencies
- acceptance of the assessment results by all professionals.

Also it is expected that individuals and carers should be actively involved, and that the type of assessment should be appropriate to the person's needs: simple, comprehensive, specialist or self-assessment.

The expectation of SSA was introduced for older people from April 2003 and for all community care groups from April 2004. *Guidance on Single Shared Assessment* (Scottish Executive, 2001b) had laid out the requirements, setting in train a lengthy debate about the desirability of a common assessment model and an integrated IT system, manifest in continuing activity to develop a universal tool such as CARENAP, the Care Needs Assessment Package, which was originally developed for joint health and social work assessment of people with dementia but subsequently extended to other groups. As with many policy initiatives, there can be different perspectives on the appropriate balance between local discretion and central control. The concordat between the Scottish Government and the local authorities, signed in November 2007, for the three years 2008–2011, setting out a new relationship based on mutual respect and partnership, reduces the degree of central intervention. SSA should not, of course, be seen in isolation and it was paralleled by attempts to promote joint resourcing and joint management (Scottish Executive, 2001c). There has also been the development in parallel of the Indicator of Relative Need (IoRN), formerly known as the Resource Use Measure (RUM) and initially developed in the context of free personal care. This places individuals in bands of relative levels of need and seeks to introduce an element of comparability and equity. Further guidance can be found in *Single Shared Assessment – Indicator of Relative Need: Operational Guidance* (Scottish Executive, 2004).

There are differing accounts of the extent to which SSA has been achieved. Exploration in the initial years highlighted a number of classic barriers (MacNamara, 2006; Eccles, 2008):

- stereotypes of other professionals and reluctance to validate their judgement
- incompatible IT systems
- lack of a common language
- frustration with the constraints imposed by assessment pro formas
- issues of consent and duplication.

A number of measures relating to SSA have been included in the local improvement targets for local partnerships. These include:

- the waiting times for assessment
- the time taken for assessment to be completed
- the time taken for the first elements of the care package to be delivered
- the increase in the number of carer assessments
- the levels of satisfaction among users and carers with SSA.

For many, such targets can sit uncomfortably with a person-centred approach, in which assessment and the negotiation of an appropriate package of support may well be conceived as an ongoing process. There has also been the introduction of *National Minimum Standards for Assessment and Care Planning for Adults* (Scottish Executive, 2008). These standards relate to assessment, shared care and support plans, review and carers' assessment and support. They seek to standardise the content of assessment and support the National Outcomes Framework for Community Care (Gooday and Stewart, 2009).

An outcomes focus

Most recently, there has been a significant shift of emphasis, preoccupied less with the front end of assessment and more with the outcomes that support is seeking to achieve for the individual, in effect, from a needs-led to an outcomes-based system (Scottish Executive, 2006). The Joint Improvement Team has adopted the Talking Points framework, building on research projects that have highlighted the outcomes sought by people who use services and carers (Table 8.1).

Table 8.1 Outcomes important to service users

Quality of life	Process	Change
Feeling safe	Listened to	Improved confidence and skills
Having things to do	Having a say	Improved mobility
Seeing people	Treated as an individual	Reduced symptoms
Staying well	Responsiveness	
Living life as you want	Reliability	
Dealing with stigma		

Source: Adapted from Joint Improvement Team, 2009

The challenge for an outcomes-based approach is to prioritise the outcomes for the specific individual, to identify the support most likely to assist with achieving these outcomes, and to monitor and review on the basis of the extent of progress made towards these outcomes. Examples of outcomes-focused assessment tools for both service users and carers developed by early adopters can be accessed on the Joint Improvement Team website.[2]

The shift to an outcomes focus is part of the broader personalisation agenda, promoted in England through the three-year *Putting People First* transformation programme (Newman, 2009; Carr, 2010). Backed by a £520m Social Care Reform Grant, the Department of Health programme south of the border requires all local authorities to have at least 30% of those eligible for publicly funded adult social care accessing a personal budget by the end of the three-year period in March 2011 (IBSEN, 2008). Around a third of local authorities aim to have everyone they support receiving a personal budget. The programme is often characterised as having this emphasis on co-production (active input by people who use services as well as the traditional provider), self-directed support and the use of personal budgets. Its vision, however, is more wide-reaching, with four distinct elements: early intervention and prevention, choice and control, social capital, and universal services. The English programme is perceived as having raised a number of interesting legal questions, in respect of the principle of self-assessment (not yet widely developed in Scotland) and more generally in terms of fulfilling the overarching duty of care.

In response to these uncertainties, the Association of Directors of Adult Social Services (the parallel body to the Association of Directors of Social Work in Scotland) has produced a briefing paper (ADASS, 2009). This confirms that:

- the duty of care can be properly met within a personalised system

- universal services can be used to respond to needs that fall below a local authority's eligibility criteria
- support planning can be as minimal or as detailed as the user's needs or preferences suggest
- self-assessment per se is not lawful but self-directed assessment is.

This last statement may require some elaboration. It is designed to meet the challenge that the determination of eligibility is reserved to the local authority:

> The process should not be seen as self-assessment. It should be called 'person-' or 'user-led' or 'centred' or 'self directed' assessment, and the person must be asked to do it according to FACS ... and the LA must still make a judgment as to eligibility across each domain which has been explored. (ADASS, 2009, p. 8)

In England, a personal budget can be offered through two main routes, either as a direct payment or through a variety of contractual arrangements between local authority and provider. The emerging picture in Scotland, however, looks somewhat different.

Direct payments in Scotland

The opportunity for local authorities to offer an individual a direct payment rather than direct service provision in response to assessed need was first introduced in the Community Care (Direct Payments) Act 1996. Initially, the power was discretionary, local authorities being able, should they choose, to offer a scheme of direct payments to people with disabilities aged 18–64 from April 1997. A number of subsequent amendments extended the range of individuals eligible for direct payments and from June 2003 the duty to offer a direct payment became mandatory under the Community Care and Health (Scotland) Act 2002.

The following are those entitled at May 2010 to ask for a direct payment in Scotland:

- Disabled adults assessed as requiring community care services, including housing support services
- Disabled 16- and 17-year-olds assessed as requiring community care services, including housing support services
- Disabled adults and 16- and 17-year-olds to purchase housing support services

- Disabled people with parental responsibility purchasing the children's services their children have been assessed as needing
- Parents and people with parental responsibility for a child in need (under the age of 16) who has been assessed as requiring children's services
- Parents and people with parental responsibility for children whose health or development may be impaired or below a reasonable standard without services from the local authority
- Older people aged 65 years and over who are assessed as needing community care services due to infirmity or age.

A direct payment can be used by the individual to purchase services or to pay for the support of a personal assistant; it cannot be used to pay for long-term residential care but can be used for short stays of up to four weeks in any twelve months. Individuals of 65 or over who are accessing free personal and nursing care (see below) can arrange for the personal care element to be made as a direct payment. People who lack capacity to consent and have guardianship arrangements in place can receive a direct payment through an attorney or guardian as defined by the Adults with Incapacity (Scotland) Act 2000. In Scotland, unlike England, there is no positive power to provide direct payments to carers – they can only receive a direct payment if they meet one or more of the eligibility criteria in their own right, for example the need for community care services.

The initial guidance on direct payments from June 2003 was replaced in July 2007 by new guidance on self-directed support (Scottish Executive, 2007a), and a subtle change in terminology. The emphasis was on putting the principles of independent living into practice and enabling people to be active citizens in their communities. Designed to increase take-up and to respond to stakeholder commentary, local authorities were required to provide a range of initiatives. These included:

- a local support service, preferably independent and user led
- early involvement of individuals with the local support service to assist with self-assessment and care planning
- training for individuals on self-directed support and training of personal assistants (PAs)
- designated self-directed support lead officers or teams within each local authority
- training on self-directed support for care managers, finance managers and local authority directors
- legal support for PA employers where appropriate, for example indemnity insurance
- packages during PA employers' short stays in hospital, where appropriate.

Within the guidance, individual chapters focus on direct payments for ethnic minority communities, and on self-directed support for users of children's services and users of mental health provisions. An update to the guidance in November 2007 (Scottish Executive, 2007b) allows close relatives to be employed through direct payments where a local authority is satisfied that it is necessary to meet the beneficiary's need for that service or in order to safeguard or promote the welfare of a child in need.

A number of studies have documented the continuing endeavour to enhance the use of direct payments in particular and self-directed support more generally (Pearson, 2006; Riddell et al., 2006; Priestley et al., 2007). The latter provides a comparison of implementation across the different countries of the UK. Rates of uptake across England are typically at least twice that of the other countries (the most recent figures available for Scotland suggest a figure of just over 3,000 compared to 86,000 in England). A number of potential explanations are offered for this variation:

- more systematic investment in staffing, training and publicity in England
- the impact of mandatory duties and targets in tackling local resistance and local discretion
- variation in local disability activism and user-led support schemes.

Most importantly for social justice, the question of whether devolution has led to differential opportunities and inequities for disabled people is raised.

The pursuit of direct payments should not detract from the broader aims of the independent living movement (see for example Hurstfield et al., 2007). In Scotland, this has recently been given voice in the form of Independent Living in Scotland,[3] a project hosted by the Equality and Human Rights Commission and led by disabled people funded by the Scottish Government until March 2011. ILIS (2009) sets out the priorities necessary in each of the key areas to make independent living a reality, and also highlights some of the existing barriers. It builds on the context provided in a scoping study commissioned by the Disability Rights Commission (2007).

The need to respond to priorities for independent living was strengthened by the Disability Equality Duty, which came into effect in 2006. The Duty is designed to ensure that all public bodies pay 'due regard' to the promotion of equality for disabled people in every area of their work. All public authorities are required to produce a Disability Equality Scheme and action plan, involving disabled people in the development. Schemes can last for three years before a new scheme has to be prepared. An accompanying code of practice has been provided by the Disability Rights Commission, together with guides on impact assessments, evidence gathering, involving disabled people, and a disabled people toolkit.[4]

Self-directed support

In 2010, major changes are in the pipeline in Scotland with respect to direct payments in particular and the personalisation agenda more generally (ADSW, 2009; Etherington et al., 2009). The Scottish Government has sought responses to two consultations, a strategy for self-directed support (Scottish Government, 2010a), and proposals to consolidate and extend the legislation relating to direct payments and to introduce legislative provision for self-directed support (Scottish Government, 2010b).

Self-directed Support: A National Strategy for Scotland (Scottish Government, 2010a) sets out a 10-year plan for the personalisation of health and social care services in Scotland. It builds on a review of developments by Homer and Gilder (2008) and of workforce issues by Reid Howie Associates (2010), and against a backcloth of current pilot projects in Glasgow (with people with learning disabilities), Dumfries and Galloway and Highland. These pilots are focusing on three themes: bridging finance, cutting red tape, and leadership and training. The evaluation will report in early 2011. There is also a pilot with health services in Lothian and with Alzheimer Scotland for people with dementia. The strategy builds on a commitment to independent living as one of four areas set as priorities for coordination of activity across the public sector. The vision is one in which, 'based on the core principles of choice, control, freedom and dignity, disabled people across Scotland will have equality of opportunity at home and work, in education and in the social and civic life of the community' (Scottish Government, 2010a, p. 11).

A number of key issues are highlighted in the consultation paper. These include:

- the essential role of leadership in promoting change and a commitment to co-production
- the importance of universal services
- the contribution of health services
- the focus on outcomes
- a policy on risk enablement rather than aversion
- the need for transparent resource allocation systems
- management of the social care market.

The strategy sets out 26 recommendations for consultation. These include:

- clarification on the use of eligibility criteria (see below)
- development of social capital and local area coordination by community planning leads
- consideration of the need to develop a national organisation to support PAs and strategies for accessing training
- greater flexibility in allowing the employment of a family members as PAs where circumstance dictates
- the development of provider networks in each area.

The proposed legislation, a Self-directed Support (Scotland) Bill, seeks to introduce legislative provision for self-directed support and the personalisation of services and to extend the provisions relating to direct payments. In part, it is a response to the comparatively poor take-up of direct payments in Scotland, and in part a desire to consolidate the scattered provisions in respect of direct payments into a single statute. It is suggested that the guiding principles for the new legislation should focus on:

- better outcomes for individuals
- choice
- participation
- mutuality – family carers affirmed as partners rather than recipients of care
- equality.

Moreover, it is suggested that the term 'self-directed support' should be introduced and defined in statute, together with a specification of the various forms of self-directed support that are available following assessment.

There is no plan in the proposed Bill to extend self-directed support to other funding streams, unlike in England where legislation allows individualised budgets for services provided by the NHS, local authorities and Jobcentre Plus. The consultation indicates, however, that experiences such as the Right to Control Trailblazers in England[5] will be monitored, and the Bill will be framed 'in such a way as to create the legislative basis for potential future developments in self-directed support through social care' (Scottish Government, 2010b, p. 11). This could allow for further legislation to amend current social care provision in the future, and could set the parameters to allow for the combining of social and healthcare and other budgets into one direct payment or individual budget.

The proposed Bill does, however, suggest a radical change from an opt-in model for accessing direct payments to an opt-out model that would assume a direct payment as the default position:

> A change from opt in to opt out would not remove the right of individuals to refuse a direct payment but it would ensure that clients were presented with this option as a matter of course and it would embed self-directed support into the assessment process. (Scottish Government, 2010b, p. 12)

The consultation on the Bill also seeks responses to the proposal to extend the access to direct payments by removing the requirement for a guardianship order or a power of attorney before someone can receive a direct payment on behalf of an adult with incapacity. Local authorities would themselves make the decision as to whether an individual would be permitted to manage the direct payment on behalf of the person requiring support.

The consultation also seeks views on extending eligibility for direct payments to:

- include people with mental health problems who are subject to certain compulsory treatment orders
- remove the exclusion on the use of direct payments for the purchase of residential care
- allow carers to obtain certain forms of support in their own right.

The practice implications of personalisation and self-directed support are further discussed in Chapter 10.

Free personal and nursing care

One of the first major results of devolution in Scotland was the decision of the Scottish Parliament in January 2001 to endorse the recommendation from the Royal Commission on Long Term Care (1999), the Sutherland Report, to provide free personal and nursing care on the basis of assessed need to older people. This has been available since July 2002, the legislation put in place through the Community Care and Health (Scotland) Act 2002. The implementation of this policy in practice has been the focus of considerable scrutiny (Bell and Bowes, 2006; Bell et al., 2006, 2007; Vestri, 2007). In 2007, Lord Sutherland was asked by the new SNP Scottish Government to undertake an *Independent Review of Free Personal and Nursing Care in Scotland* (Sutherland Review,

Scottish Government, 2008). Among the key recommendations from a 12-point plan were:

- a clear entitlement for those assessed as needing personal and nursing care, analogous with the NHS
- a standard eligibility framework
- common assessment processes
- clearly stated target waiting times.

The interpretation of eligibility criteria is critical, whether in respect of free personal and nursing care or more broadly. Following the Sutherland Review, the Scottish Government produced guidance on eligibility criteria to be implemented by December 2009 (Scottish Government, 2009). This specifies:

- a common standard eligibility framework for older people, which categorises the needs of individuals and which is applied by all local authorities
- a common commitment to deliver personal and nursing care services to older people within a maximum period of six weeks following the identification of need, identified as being at critical or substantial risk as regards their independent living or wellbeing
- the application of the SSA model, and associated tools, by local authorities and their partners as a key element in ensuring consistent processes for individual needs assessment
- appropriate management and review arrangements for responding to the needs of individuals assessed as having less intensive care needs, including preventive services.

The guidance identifies four risk bands:

- *critical:* major risks to an individual's independent living or health and wellbeing likely to call for immediate (one to two weeks) or imminent (within six weeks) provision of social care services
- *substantial:* significant risks
- *moderate:* some risks
- *low:* some quality of life issues but low risks.

Examples are provided of the different definitions of risk in respect of neglect or physical or mental health; personal care/domestic routines/ home environment; participation in community life; and carers. The guidance also sets out maximum six-week waiting time for those assessed as being at critical or substantial risk. Additional funding of £40m was also provided from 2009/10 in response to the pressures identified in the Sutherland Review. Although focused on older people, local authorities may choose to apply the funding across community care groups.

The guidance sought to re-enforce the central role of assessment in determining access to social care services and the responsibility of local authorities for determining local provision. In defining eligibility criteria, the aim was to promote fairness, consistency and transparency. The guidance also indicates that:

> the prioritisation process should target resources towards responding to people at critical or substantial risk as regards independent living or well-being, whilst not excluding consideration of the benefits of preventative support and less intensive care services for people at less risk. (Scottish Government, 2009, p. 2)

It is interesting that Scotland is formalising eligibility criteria at a time when England is subjecting their use to increasing scrutiny (CSCI, 2008; DH, 2010; SCIE, 2010). In part, this reflects an enduring tension between eligibility criteria and preventive agendas; the desire to intervene early in order to avert crisis as against priority for service accorded to those already at substantial or critical risk. The Fair Access to Care Services (FACS) criteria were introduced in England in 2003 (DH, 2003), in an attempt to provide a single process to determine eligibility for social care support, based on risks to independence over time. The aim was to ensure allocation of social care resources 'fairly, transparently and consistently' (SCIE, 2010, p. 1). The focus on the personalisation agenda and *Putting People First*, with its emphasis on universal services, early intervention and prevention, choice and control, and social capital, has revived the debate on the extent to which there are conflicting policy drivers. The argument presented is that development of readily accessible universal services should provide the wider basis for the promotion of independence and wellbeing.

> Councils should ensure that in applying eligibility criteria to prioritise individual need, they are not neglecting the needs of their wider population. Eligibility criteria should be explicitly placed within a much broader context whereby public services in general are well placed to offer all individuals some level of support. For example, people who do not meet the eligibility threshold should still be able to expect adequate signposting to alternative sources of support. (Department of Health (2010, p. 9)

Both north and south of the border, the strategies through which the balance between eligibility criteria and earlier, preventive support is managed will be critical. For England, the Social Care Institute for Excellence (SCIE, 2010) has detailed the change in emphasis between the original criteria and the current approach. Reflecting features evident above, this is characterised as a shift from needs-based assessments and reviews to outcomes-based assessments and reviews, from preventive approaches to preventive strategies, and from care planning to personalisation and support planning. This document offers a 'top 10 tips', which are likely to resonate also in the Scottish context. They include:

- assessment and support planning are focused on ways to achieve agreed outcomes, not driven by needs or impairments
- think prevention, early intervention, wellbeing and safeguarding: they can prevent or delay needs escalating
- think self-directed support, direct payments, personal budgets and co-production as the means to achieve more flexible, personalised solutions.

Whatever the detail, as the evolution of strategies and priorities continues, the changing nature of support provision has major implications for the workforce at all levels. A focus on reablement, for example, as part of the early intervention and prevention agenda requires that care staff traditionally trained in the provision of support have to adopt the very different approach of encouraging individuals to do things for themselves. More fundamentally, a focus on self-directed support requires a shift in the traditional relationship between worker and support user from one of authority and dependency to one based much more on principles of co-production and mutuality. Successful management of this change process for staff is one of the features critical to the achievement of the personalisation agenda. Those involved in assessment and planning have to adopt new ways of working, which focus on the achievement of outcomes rather than the delineation of needs, and respect the rights of the individual to determine the ways in which these outcomes are achieved. An understanding of underpinning principles, a commitment to positive risk-taking, and support from senior management are all essential components for the workforce in this transformation of social care.

References

ADASS (Association of Directors of Adult Social Services) (2009) *Personalisation and the Law: Implementing Putting People First in the Current Legal Framework*, available online at www.dhcarenetworks.org.uk/_library/

Resources/Personalisation/Personalisation_advice/ADASS_Personalisation_ and_the_law_12.10.09.pdf [accessed 7 July 2010].

ADSW (Association of Directors of Social Work) (2009) *Personalisation: Principles, Challenges and a New Approach*, available online at www.adsw.org. uk/Our-Work/Publications/ [accessed 7 July 2010].

Bell, D. and Bowes, A. (2006) *Lessons from the Funding of Long-term Care in Scotland*, York, Joseph Rowntree Foundation.

Bell, D., Bowes, A. and Dawson, A. (2007) *Free Personal Care in Scotland: Recent Developments*, York, Joseph Rowntree Foundation.

Bell, D., Bowes, A., Dawson, A. and Roberts, E. (2006) *Establishing the Evidence Base for an Evaluation of Free Personal Care in Scotland*, Edinburgh, Scottish Executive Social Research.

Carr, S. (2010) *Personalisation: A Rough Guide*, London, SCIE.

CSCI (Commission for Social Care Inspection) (2008) *Cutting the Cake Fairly: CSCI Review of Eligibility Criteria for Social Care*, available online at www. cqc.org.uk/_db/_documents/FACS_2008_03.pdf [accessed 17 May 2010].

DH (Department of Health) (2003) *Fair Access to Care Services: Guidance on Eligibility Criteria for Adult Social Care*, London, TSO.

DH (Department of Health) (2010) *Prioritising Need in the Context of Putting People First: A Whole System Approach to Eligibility for Social Care – Guidance on Eligibility Criteria for Adult Social Care*, London, TSO.

Disability Rights Commission (2007) *Independent Living in Scotland: A Policy Scoping Study*, Burntisland, Reid Howie Associates.

Eccles, A. (2008) 'Single shared assessment: the limits to "quick fix" implementation', *Journal of Integrated Care*, **27**(1): 22–30.

Etherington, K., Hatton, C. and Waters, J. (2009) *Way Ahead: Our Early Experience in North Lanarkshire of Demonstrating the Impact of the In Control Approach*, available online at www.in-control.org.uk/site/INCO/ Templates/General.aspx?pageid=1336&cc=GB [accessed 7 July 2010].

Gooday, K. and Stewart, A. (2009) 'Community care and the Single Outcome Agreement in Scotland: driver or barrier to better outcomes?' *Journal of Integrated Care*, **17**(5): 31–7.

HM Government (2007) *Putting People First: A Shared Vision and Commitment to the Transformation of Adult Social Care*, London: HM Government.

Homer, T. and Gilder, P. (2008) *A Review of Self-directed Support in Scotland*, Edinburgh, Scottish Government Social Research.

Hurstfield, J., Parashar, U. and Schofield, K. (2007) *The Costs and Benefits of Independent Living*, available online at www.officefordisability.gov.uk/docs/ res/il/costs-benefits-summary.pdf [accessed 7 July 2010].

IBSEN (2008) *Evaluation of the Individual Budget Pilot Programme*, available online at www.york.ac.uk/inst/spru/pubs/pdf/IBSEN.pdf [accessed 7 July 2010].

ILIS (2009) *Ready for Action: Key Issues and Disabled People's Priorities for Independent Living*, Burntisland, Reid Howie Associates.

Joint Improvement Team (2009) *Explaining Outcomes to Service Users and Carers (the UDSET)*, available online at http://www.jitscotland.org.uk/ [accessed 7 July 2010].

MacNamara, G. (2006) 'The implementation of Single Shared Assessment in Meadowbank, Falkirk: a joint future', *Journal of Integrated Care*, **14**(4): 38–44.

Newman, S. (ed.) (2009) *Personalisation: Practical Thoughts and Ideas from People Making it Happen*, Brighton, OLM-Pavilion.

Pearson, C. (ed.) (2006) *Direct Payments and Personalisation of Care*, Edinburgh, Dunedin Academic Press.

Petch, A. (2008) *Health and Social Care: Establishing a Joint Future?* Edinburgh, Dunedin Academic Press.

Priestley, M., Jolly, D., Pearson, C. et al. (2007) 'Direct payments and disabled people in the UK: supply, demand and devolution', *British Journal of Social Work*, **37**(7): 1189–204.

Reid Howie Associates (2010) *Study of the Workforce and Employment Issues Surrounding Self-directed Support*, Edinburgh, Scottish Government Social Research.

Riddell, S., Ahlgren, L., Pearson, C. et al. (2006) *The Implementation of Direct Payments for People who Use Care Services*, Report SP Paper 624, Edinburgh, Scottish Parliament Health Committee.

Royal Commission on Long Term Care (1999) *With Respect to Old Age: Long Term Care – Rights and Responsibilities* (Sutherland Report), London, TSO.

SCIE (Social Care Institute for Excellence) (2010) *Facts about FACS 2010: A Guide to Fair Access to Care Services*, available online at www.scie.org.uk/publications/guides/guide33/index.asp [accessed 7 July 2010].

Scottish Executive (1991) *Guidance on Assessment and Care Management* (SWSG 11/91), Edinburgh, Scottish Executive.

Scottish Executive (2000) *Report of the Joint Future Group*, available online at www.scotland.gov.uk/Resource/Doc/1095/0013865.pdf [accessed 7 July 2010].

Scottish Executive (2001a) *Report of the Scottish Carers' Legislation Working Group*, available online at www.scotland.gov.uk/health/carerslaw/wglthc-00.asp.[accessed 7 July 2010].

Scottish Executive (2001b) *Guidance on Single Shared Assessment* (CCD 8/2001), available online at http://www.sehd.scot.nhs.uk/publications/DC20011129CCD8single.pdf [accessed 7 July 2010].

Scottish Executive (2001c) *Joint Resourcing and Joint Management of Community Care Services* (CCD 7/2001), available online at www.scotland.gov.uk/Resource/Doc/924/0036464.pdf [accessed 7 July 2010].

Scottish Executive (2003) *Community Care and Health (Scotland) Act 2002: New Statutory Rights for Carers* (CCD 2/2003), available online at www.sehd.scot.nhs.uk/publications/cc2003_02full.pdf [accessed 7 July 2010].

Scottish Executive (2004) *Single Shared Assessment – Indicator of Relative Need: Operational Guidance* (CCD 5/2004), available online at www.sehd.scot.nhs.uk/publications/CC2004_05.pdf [accessed 7 July 2010].

Scottish Executive (2006) *NHS Carer Information Strategies: Minimum Requirements and Guidance on Implementation*, NHS Circular HDL(2006)22, available online at http://www.sehd.scot.nhs.uk/mels/HDL2006_22.pdf [accessed 7 July 2010].

Scottish Government (2007a) *Self-directed Support: New National Guidance* (CCD 7/2007), available online at www.scotland.gov.uk/Resource/Doc/181224/0051499.pdf [accessed 7 July 2010].

Scottish Government (2007b) *Change to Guidance on Employing Close Relatives Under Self-directed Support Schemes*, available online at http://www.carerscotland.org/Policyandpractice/Keylegislationandpolicy/SelfDirected-CareDirectPayments [accessed 7 July 2010].

Scottish Government (2008) *Independent Review of Free Personal and Nursing Care in Scotland*, available online at www.scotland.gov.uk/Resource/Doc/221214/0059486.pdf [accessed 7 July 2010].

Scottish Government (2009) *National Standard Eligibility Criteria and Waiting Times for the Personal and Nursing Care of Older People (Guidance)*, available online at www.scotland.gov.uk/Topics/Health/care/17655/research/NewPage/guidancedoc [accessed 7 July 2010].

Scottish Government (2010a) *Self-directed Support: A National Strategy for Scotland*, available online at www.scotland.gov.uk/Resource/Doc/301424/0094007.pdf [accessed 7 July 2010].

Scottish Government (2010b) *Proposals for a Self-Directed Support (Scotland) Bill – Consultation*, available online at www.scotland.gov.uk/Resource/Doc/307325/0096619.pdf [accessed 7 July 2010].

Scottish Government/COSLA (Convention of Scottish Local Authorities) (2010) *Caring Together: The Carers Strategy for Scotland 2010–2015*, available online at www.scotland.gov.uk/Publications/2010/07/23153304/0 [accessed 20 August 2010].

Scottish Office (1998) *Community Care Needs of Frail People: Integrating Professional Assessments and Care Arrangements*, SWSG, 10/98, Edinburgh, Scottish Office.

Vestri, P. (2007) *Evaluation of the Operation and Impact of Free Personal Care*, Edinburgh, Scottish Executive Social Research.

Notes

1. Further details about the Joint Improvement Team can be found at www.jitscotland.org.uk.
2. See the Joint Improvement Team website, www.jitscotland.org.uk.
3. The website address for Independent Living in Scotland is www.ilis.co.uk.
4. This toolkit is available at www.dotheduty.org.
5. Further details about Right to Control can be found on the website of the Office for Disability Issues, www.odi.gov.uk/working/right-to-control.php.

Chapter 9

Vulnerability, Autonomy, Capacity and Consent

KATHRYN MACKAY

Introduction

Adults (people over 16) are assumed in law to be able to make their own decisions unless proven otherwise. This chapter addresses three civil statutes that give social work practitioners authority to intervene in the lives of adults. These include people who have been diagnosed as having a mental disorder, adults who lack capacity to make decisions and, most recently, adults at risk of harm. Patrick and Smith (2009, p. 169) highlighted the key challenge in this area of work:

> Those involved in adult protection must be very aware of the need to balance their duty to investigate and protect adults at risk with the need to respect the autonomy of the person.

The Scottish Parliament and public authorities are required to uphold the European Convention on Human Rights (ECHR), which includes the right to individual liberty for adults but also denotes occasions when the duty to act outweighs an individual's right to autonomy (see also Chapter 3). There are a few other examples where the law allows intervention in the lives of adults: the control of infectious diseases, immigration and the Children (Scotland) Act 1995 in relation to 16- to 18-years-olds. These will not be considered in this chapter.

There was limited scope to impose intervention on adults prior to 2000 unless they had a mental disorder or lacked capacity. Mental health law had not kept pace with changes in community care and treatment, incapacity was an all-or-nothing affair, and there were limited safeguards for the people concerned. The Scottish Parliament has modernised this area of law to make it more flexible, to improve the accountability of professionals, and to improve the rights of people. The Scottish legal framework for adult support and protection contains three statutes: the Adult Support and Protection (Scotland) Act 2007 (ASPA), the Adults with Incapacity (Scotland) Act 2000 (AwIA) and the Mental Health (Care and Treatment) (Scotland) Act 2003 (MHA). The MHA also applies to children. The word 'support' should not be dropped because law is concerned with more than just protection: there is now an enhanced legal basis for offering and providing support to adults to promote their independence and welfare. Each statute underlines local authorities' and practitioners' responsibilities to support and promote a person's humans rights where they may not have the ability, permanently or temporarily, to do so themselves.

These statutes are complex and much of the work by local authorities is undertaken either by mental health officers (MHOs – social workers who have undertaken specialist training) or experienced social workers, under advice from local authority solicitors. It requires a high level of skill due to the requirements of reports, legal applications, giving evidence in court, working quickly and effectively across agencies, often under pressure of time, and sometimes against the opposing views of the person in question and, occasionally, other professionals. At the heart of it lies the challenge of determining at what point a person's right to place themselves at risk is overridden by the duties given under these statutes to intervene.

The aim here is to give readers a brief overview of these statutes' purpose, principles and powers so they understand what types of action might taken, with whom and when. Readers are advised to refer to the codes of practice for each statute to gain detailed explanation (Scottish Executive 2005; Scottish Government 2009a, 2009b). First, I will explore the contexts of vulnerability and then I will use a pyramid of intervention (Mackay, 2008) to demonstrate how the powers in the statutes place increasing levels of restrictions on a person's autonomy. I will then explore what capacity and consent mean in practice. Finally, I will highlight the safeguards for people who may be subject to these statutes and how practitioners can support their legal rights.

Contexts of vulnerability

We are all more or less vulnerable at different points in our lives due to the myriad of events we experience: illness, bereavement, unemployment and so on. However, some adults, for a combination of reasons, are more vulnerable to harm and this section provides a brief overview. A literature review of research into abuse and protection identifies four spheres of factors that appear in various models of protection: the individual, others in close contact with the individual, environmental factors, and cultural and societal factors (Johnson et al., 2010). Therefore assessments undertaken by practitioners often have to be comprehensive and cover all four spheres.

The individual

Factors such as ill health, disability and cognitive impairment might make someone more vulnerable. However, people also have personal resources, linked to life experience such as education and employment, that reduce their vulnerability. They may have financial security and a wide circle of friends. They may be more confident when dealing with situations of potential harm and be more likely to involve the police or other agencies where appropriate. Therefore a whole range of factors can make people more or less vulnerable. This demonstrates the need to understand the person and their world from their viewpoint and not to make assumptions about an adult's vulnerability.

People in close contact

The emotional and practical support of family and friends is a key protective factor in everyone's life: interdependency is a natural part of living. A person's vulnerability might increase where they have no such support system or where existing relationships become strained, for example due to the stress of caring and being cared for. Hence there is a need to get away from the overly simplistic idea of abused and abuser. Sometimes there is reliance on someone who, to some extent, will take advantage, but there may seem to be little alternative. Financial abuse, for example, can occur when an older disabled person becomes increasingly housebound and gives their son or daughter access to their bank account. This might take the form of excessive cash withdrawals or loans taken out in the parent's name. Older people might put up with such abuse for several reasons, including the fear that the son or daughter will stop helping them or visiting with the grandchildren.

Environmental factors

Having one's own home is a protective factor and homelessness increases a person's risk of harm. In extreme cases, serious neglect of the home itself might prove to be a hazard. Institutional care can also make people more vulnerable as they have less control over their immediate environment. Harm within hospitals or care homes can take many forms, from rough handling, lack of help with eating and drinking, to lack of stimulation, poor understanding of care needs to the more extreme forms of physical or sexual violence (Collins, 2010). A fatal accident inquiry into the death of a man with learning disability and dementia within a care home determined that this was due, in part, to a lack of knowledge and understanding as to how the AwIA 2000 could have been used to ensure

that the man received r   ient (Patrick and
Smith, 2007). Abusive   ̶esources, training
and leadership and a ⌐   ; in long-term care
facilities, but the cu⌐   ital disregard for a
person's humanity (⌐   should be noted that
such harm is not li⌐   also to care provided
within people's ow

Societal and cul̷

Johnson et al. (201   may devalue one section of
the population cc   ildren, for example, have
received statutory ,   ars. In contrast, the Scottish
Law Commission produc̶̶   vhich included specimen Bills,
one on incapable adults (1995) ana a̶̶   ̶er on vulnerable adults (1997),
which would have modernised legislation much earlier. Political and
public interest in this area of welfare has since increased due to pressure
groups and high-profile inquiries into the neglect by services of people in
dangerous and abusive situations (Atkinson, 2006). There are also other
structural factors such as poverty and social deprivation that might
increase vulnerability.

Scottish legal framework for adult support and protection

It can be difficult to see how the three statutes, AwIA 2000, MHA 2003
and ASPA 2007, 'fit' together. The pyramid of intervention (Figure 9.1)
(Mackay, 2008) places the different powers for adults at risk of harm,
across the three statutes, into one hierarchical framework. At the lowest
level, human rights are assumed but the further up the pyramid you go,
the more they may be compromised, and the more reliant the person is
upon the law and professional practice for their rights to be upheld. The
pyramid shape underlines the fact that many more people may be subject
to lower levels of intervention such as initial inquiries and assessments.
There should be very few people who are placed in an environment that
routinely restricts their liberty at the apex of the pyramid. The Scottish
Government (2009c) has produced a detailed table that tracks the differences and commonalities across the three statutes, which will complement this chapter. The three statutes have some common powers and
practitioners may have to decide which statute is the best one to use (see
Table 9.1) (Mackay, 2008).

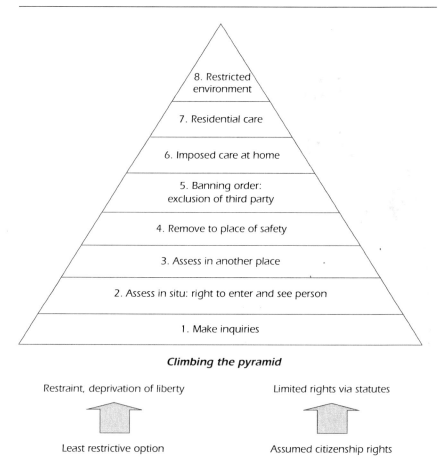

Climbing the pyramid

Restraint, deprivation of liberty

Least restrictive option

Limited rights via statutes

Assumed citizenship rights

Figure 9.1 Pyramid of statutory intervention: from minimum to maximum compulsion when adults are at risk of harm
Source: First published in the *Journal of Adult Protection*, 10(4): 28, November 2008

Table 9.1 Powers in the different statutes

Levels of power	Statutes
8 Restricted environment	MHA
7 Imposed residential care	AwIA, MHA
6 Imposed care at home	AwIA, MHA
5 Banning order: exclusion of third party	ASPA
4 Removal to place of safety	MHA, ASPA
3 Assess (take to another place)	MHA, ASPA
2 Assess in situ: right to enter and see person	MHSA, ASPA
1 Make inquiries	AwIA, MHA, ASPA

Source: Adapted from the one first published in the *Journal of Adult Protection*, **10**(4): 28, November 2008

A move from one level of intervention to the next allows control to be exercised over the person. The ASPA 2007 inhabits the first five levels only and 'banning orders' for excluding a third person have been placed at level five because it is the only long-term option available. From level six upwards, a person will have to meet the criteria for the AwIA 2000 as an adult with incapacity or the MHA 2003 as a person with a mental disorder.

Figure 9.1 and Table 9.1 focus on welfare options. There are a number of financial measures that can be used under the AwIA 2000 to manage a person's financial and wider estate where they have lost the capacity to do so. They form their own pyramid, with options that the person can put in place before they lose capacity, such as setting up a joint bank account or appointing a power of attorney to manage their affairs once they become incapable. Once capacity is lost, the authority to intromit with funds provides a straightforward way of accessing funds. Any third party can apply to the Office of the Public Guardian to gain access to the adult's bank account. The application requires explicit details of what the money was needed for and then a specified fixed sum transferred to a new account managed by the third party. Where management of the person's entire estate is required, then a financial guardianship order can be granted by the Sheriff Court. Single large transactions can be taken by an intervention order. These measures can be used in conjunction with the options noted below where there is concern about financial abuse, or where inability to manage financial affairs is causing a person problems in other areas of their life.

Who is the focus of each statute?

Each statute defines who may be subject to the measures within it. The Adult Support and Protection (Scotland) Act 2007 covers potentially the largest population. It has a three-part definition of an adult at risk of harm and all three must be met:

1. The person is unable to safeguard their own wellbeing, property, rights or other interests
2. The person is at risk of harm
3. The person is more vulnerable because they have a disability, mental disorder, illness or physical or mental infirmity.

Harm, likely or actual, might be caused by another person or the person may be causing the harm themselves. There are categories of harm: physical, neglect, emotional, financial or sexual, but what constitutes harm in specific situations will vary (Scottish Government, 2009a).

One factor that does increase vulnerability is the incapacity to make decisions and act upon them. This could be due to mental disorder or an inability to communicate because of physical disability, but it does not include people who may be able to communicate by other means. The Adults with Incapacity (Scotland) Act 2000 defines incapacity as being incapable of:

- acting; or
- making decisions; or
- communicating decisions; or
- understanding decisions; or
- retaining the memory of decisions.

The new MHA 2003 defines mental disorder as a mental illness, personality disorder, or learning disability. Three of the core aspects to establishing the grounds for compulsory intervention whether in hospital or in the community are the existence of a mental disorder, evidence that the person is placing themselves and or others at risk, and that because of the mental disorder, the patient's ability to make decisions about the intervention is significantly impaired. *The Code of Practice* (Scottish Executive, 2005, vol. 2) provides full details of application processes.

It is quite possible for someone to meet all three definitions. The question then becomes which statute is the best one to proceed under. The answer lies in the nature of the presenting concern and what action, meeting the least restrictive principle, might need to be taken.

Legal principles

All three statutes have a statement of principles at the beginning that should be a guide to practitioners working under it. The following principles appear in each statute:

- Any intervention should be the least restrictive
- It should benefit the person
- Regard for the wishes of the individual person, current and past
- Promote the person's participation in decision making
- Regard for the diversity of the individual
- Seek the views of relatives, carers or other relevant people.

There are also principles that are unique to each statute. Within the ASPA 2007, the adult at risk of harm should not treated 'without justification, any less favourably than the way in which a person who is not an "adult at risk, would be treated in a comparable situation"' (Scottish Government, 2009a, p. 12). This is intended to address the value judgements people might make, based on a person's disability, rather than their capacity to take risks or make what other people might view as bad decisions.

The MHA 2003 and AwIA 2000 have principles that aim to address the long-term nature of mental disorder and incapacity, and the ongoing power that might be exercised over a person. The MHA 2003 has a principle of reciprocity, defined in s. 6, as having 'regard to the importance of the provision of appropriate services to the person who is, or has been, subject to the certificate or order concerned'. Therefore, reciprocity acknowledges that compulsory intervention and hospitalisation, as well as a mental disorder itself, can adversely affect a person's wider circumstances, and so, for example lead to social exclusion (Rogers and Pilgrim, 2003). Therefore, the statute has also given the local authority a general duty to promote wellbeing, to minimise the effect of the mental disorder, and give people the opportunity to lead lives that are as normal as possible. The AwIA's unique principles include using all means necessary to communicate with the person and to maintain and develop areas where a person can make decisions for themselves.

Inquiries

All three statutes place a duty on the local authority to make inquiries about a person's wellbeing, property or financial affairs if it knows or believes that a person is an adult at risk. The ASPA 2007 gives a council officer (who need not be but will most likely be a social worker) the right to enter any place and to interview the person in private. Where appropriate, there is also the right for a health professional to undertake a medical examination in private. It is essential that the person is informed of their right to refuse to answer any questions and a medical examination. There are also powers in the ASPA 2007 and the MHA 2003 to request and examine records to assist inquiries.

Purely financial concerns can be pursued under the AwIA 2000 because there are reciprocal duties for the Office of the Public Guardian, a national legal body, to investigate financial matters, and to register and oversee people who have been appointed to manage the financial affairs of adults with incapacity. The Mental Welfare Commission, another national body with responsibility under the MHA 2003 and the AwIA 2000, also has powers of inquiry. There is a duty on these public authorities to liaise with each other.

Assessment orders

The assessment of an adult who might be at risk of harm seeks to gain the perspective of that person of their current situation, to identify factors that might be placing them at risk and what action might be taken to reduce it. In doing so, the views of other relevant people and workers might be sought. The majority of assessments and ensuing actions will be undertaken on a voluntary basis. However, there are powers available within the ASPA 2007 and the MHA 2003 to proceed with an assessment when either the person does not wish to be interviewed or someone else is preventing access. Under the ASPA 2007, the assessment order is the first of three orders that are known as 'protection orders'. These have a higher threshold requirement of risk of serious harm, because action will be taken, to some extent, against the will of another person. A council officer applies to the Sheriff Court for an assessment order, to allow them to take that person to another place for interview and, if necessary, a medical examination. It only gives the power to take them to a designated place and cannot be used to keep them there. The council officer has to show that there is reasonable cause to believe the person is at risk of serious harm, that the order is required to establish whether this is the case, and that the proposed location for assessment is suitable.

There is a requirement that the person must agree to the order or if they do not, the council officer has to prove that they would have done but for undue pressure by a third party. This notion of undue pressure and whether someone with incapacity can be subject to ASPA protection orders is a contested area and there are doubts as to whether it is fully compatible with the ECHR (see Patrick and Smith, 2007). If it is doubtful that the council officer will be granted access to the person, a warrant of entry can be gained at the same time and this would be enforced by the police.

The MHA 2003 has a number of allied provisions that essentially give an MHO, medical practitioner and police officer the right to enter premises to assess a person's mental health and to remove them to hospital. There is an emergency detention order that lasts up to 72 hours and a short-term detention order that lasts up to 28 days. These are used to take someone to hospital after they have been assessed by a medical practitioner and with the consent of the MHO. Warrants and removal orders are granted by a sheriff but these detention orders do not require such approval. Additionally, the police have the power to remove someone from a public place if they believe they have a mental disorder and to take them for assessment by a medical practitioner.

Removal order to a place of safety

A removal order to a place of safety is available under the ASPA 2007 and the MHA 2003. It is the second protection order under the ASPA and has the same requirements as the assessment order. While a person cannot be kept in a place of safety against their will, it is possible to specify who may or may not have contact with the adult at risk of harm during that time. Where physical harm has taken place, that person may be admitted to hospital but a non-hospital environment is mainly envisaged. The MHA 2003 allows a person to be taken to a place of safety and detained there for up to seven days, again underlying the greater powers in the MHA 2003.

Banning orders

Banning orders, the third protection order under the ASPA 2007, replicate those that can be gained in domestic violence situations. The subject of the order can be banned from an address and its vicinity, ejected from that place and a power of arrest can be attached to the order. Banning orders can last up to six months and can be used where a person's wellbeing or property can be better safeguarded by banning another person from a place occupied by the adult than by moving the adult from that place. Temporary banning orders are an option to keep a person safe while preparing an application for a full order.

Intervention and guardianship orders

Intervention and guardianship orders are similar in terms of duration (up to three years) and consist of powers specified by a sheriff. Intervention orders are seen as more discrete and limited in duration. Guardianship is for more complex, ongoing situations. It has most commonly been used to place someone in a care facility, although it can be used to provide care and support within a person's own home. Patrick's (2005) discussion paper reviewed the intention of the AwIA 2000 and the view given in the Muldoon judgment (Glasgow Sheriff Court, W37/04) that anyone, whether they are objecting to a move into a care home or not, should be subject to guardianship in order to uphold their human rights. Such applications, however, incurred expense, led to delays in a person's admission to a care home, and were arguably not in line with the principle of least restrictive option (Patrick, 2005).

As a result, the ASPA 2007 introduced amendments to the Social Work (Scotland) Act 1968 to allow a local authority to provide community care services (including a move to a care home), where they are needed to improve the welfare of an adult with incapacity. The local authority has to take the principles of the AwIA 2000 into account. If the adult in question or an appropriate third person objects to this, then an application under AwIA would be called for. Consideration would have to be given as to whether the new environment was restrictive in such a way that would also warrant legal safeguards.

Compulsory treatment orders

Compulsory treatment orders (CTOs) are available under the MHA 2003 and there are two types: hospital or community CTOs. Hospital CTOs are a means by which people can be placed or continued to be kept in hospital for care and treatment for their mental disorder, following on from a short-term detention order. They can last up to six months initially. They are granted by the Mental Health Tribunal for Scotland, the legal decision-making forum for CTOs.

Community-based CTOs were seen as the most controversial aspect of the MHA 2003, due to the potential invasion of privacy and the allied power of community-based personnel responsible for the person's care plan (Ferguson, 2003). The alternative view is that they allow people to live in the community who might otherwise become subject to long-term hospital care. They are intended only for those people with a history of avoiding treatment and hospital admissions. They can be applied for in their own right or the Mental Health Tribunal can grant a variation if the person is already on a hospital-based CTO.

When a community-based CTO is applied for, the MHO has to detail a care plan, which includes social care as well as medical treatment and supervision. This might include a requirement to live in a form of residential care (supported accommodation or care home) or to accept support within their own home. Medical treatment will often include taking medication and attending outpatient clinics. However, medical treatment cannot be forced upon a person on a community-based CTO.

The apex of the pyramid of intervention (see Figure 9.1) should only be occupied by people who are subject to CTOs because they continue to pose a risk to themselves or others and have to be placed within a restricted environment. This may include people in a care facility in the community, which has locked doors or a staffing regime that monitors and restricts the person's actions. There are also people who continue to be subject to hospital-based CTOs and are within secure NHS facilities. There is a complex debate evolving around the need for someone to be protected by law when they are within a restrictive environment, when guardianship can be used and when a CTO offers better protection. It is very much linked to the ECHR and aims to determine what is, sometimes, a fine line between what is a restriction and what is deprivation of liberty (see Patrick, 2008).

Capacity, consent and the deprivation of liberties

This section will look in more depth at capacity and consent. Capacity is the ability to make reasoned decisions and take actions unless it is proven otherwise. As we have seen, the ASPA 2007 limits what action can be taken in the short term to minimise the extent to which a person's explicit views might be overruled. Consent cannot be automatically dispensed within the ASPA. Equally, the AwIA 2000 stresses that incapacity is not all or nothing and has to be specific to the decision(s) in hand. The MHA 2003 requires evidence of impaired decision making by the person about the treatment proposed before dispensing with consent. Even when people are subject to the AwIA and the MHA, they have not had all their rights waived, only those specified in the order. There is still a general requirement that people should have the right to continue to exercise as much control as they can (see Mandelstam, 2009, who details case law to highlight how courts have approached the variable nature of consent and capacity).

The assessment of incapacity is not straightforward. In Scotland, a medical certificate of incapacity is required before local authorities can apply to the court for action under the AwIA 2000. This is often by way of a 'mini mental state examination', which is seen as limiting in terms of understanding the nature of a person's capacity to make the wide range of decisions associated with everyday life (Horton-Deutsch et al., 2007). Determining the extent of someone's capacity to make informed decisions is therefore more a process than an event. Guidance by the Scottish Government (2008) provides useful advice for social work practitioners about how to assess capacity in relation to the AwIA 2000. It emphasises how important it is for workers to develop good communication skills, to take time with people and to resist pressures from others to do a 'quick assessment'. The more time spent, the more you will understand that person and therefore empower them by giving them a voice that might otherwise go unheard.

First, there is a need to take account of the environment and the general health of the person. Hospitals can exacerbate confusion in people with dementia due to noise, unfamiliarity and lack of sleep. Infections, pain and medication can all increase confusion. Second, the practitioner should try to maximise communication between them and the person. The AwIA requirement to gain the views of the person by any means of communication has positively influenced practice (Killeen et al., 2004). This has included seeking the assistance of speech therapists and spending more time in observing the person and how others communicate with them.

Capacity and informed consent require a degree of understanding. Understanding has two aspects: grasp of the facts and ability to weigh up options and foresee different outcomes (Scottish Government, 2008). This entails seeking the person's views of the presenting concern, for example how they are coping at home on their own, and then comparing this to the views of people who know the person well and other evidence such as the condition of the house and their own physical condition. Coping at home is such a wide issue that it should be broken down into discrete parts of day-to-day living. For example, a person with dementia might be able to make themselves something to eat and drink but have no appreciation of money and be unable to find their way to the shops.

Care homes with locked doors provide an obvious example of the challenges around capacity and consent. While the locked door is not a deprivation of liberty per se, preventing someone who is trying leave might be. Patrick (2008) advises that we need to consider the frequency of the occurrence and the person's reasons for wishing to leave. For example, if a person wishes to go for a walk to get some exercise and fresh air, and there is no evidence that this would create unacceptable risk, then to constantly refuse this is a deprivation of liberty even if a guardianship order is in place. It is also the case that regular physical restraint by staff or by medication is also considered a deprivation of liberty (Patrick, 2008). Such situations, she argues, warrant the use of the MHA 2003 because CTOs afford greater safeguards for the person and, indeed, the staff.

Rights and representation

There are a number ways in which the rights of people who may be subject to compulsory intervention are promoted within the statutes. The AwIA 2000 and the ASPA 2007 both have the Sheriff Court as the legal decision-making forum where there is scrutiny of the evidence for the requested order. It is interesting that the MHA 20003 established the Mental Health Tribunal for this purpose and took such decision making away from the Sheriff Court. The tribunal hearings are preferred by all who have used the system: it is seen to be less daunting and holds professionals to account much more (Mental Welfare Commission, 2008). However, the tribunal system is not perfect and is under review because interim orders now outnumber agreed CTOs. The Scottish Government has yet to propose changes in the law. Interim orders have the effect of keeping a person subject to detention for longer before the application is fully heard.

The person subject to any proposed order has the right to attend any hearing regarding them unless it can be proven that this would not be in their best interests. All three statutes support the use of advocacy and practitioners should advise the person about this and support access to this service if they wish. The person also has the right to instruct a solicitor and they can apply for legal aid to cover the cost of this. There is evidence from MHA research that independent advocacy has been effective in giving the person's viewpoint and asking questions of those presenting evidence at hearings, although the quality of legal representation has been variable (Dawson et al., 2009).

There are also rights to appeal for the following orders: short-term detention, banning, intervention, guardianship orders and CTOs. Again, practitioners need to be aware of the extent of such rights, be able to communicate them to the person and support them to take action if they wish. If they are concerned about how an appointed person is carrying out orders under the AwIA 2000, then the local authority, the Office of the Public Guardian and the Mental Welfare Commission all have powers of investigation.

There are statutory duties to inform the nearest relative and carer where a local authority proposes to take action under these statutes. This is seen as a protective factor. However, there is the facility under the MHA 2003 to nominate a 'named person' in their place. This provision was created as a direct response to concerns about the abuse of powers vested in nearest relatives under the old Act (Atkinson, 2006). An adult can nominate a named person who then has a number of rights when they become subject to the Act: to attend hearings, request a review of an order and express *their* views. Where there is no named person, the carer or nearest relative becomes the default named person. The MHA 2003 also created advance statements, so that people could record how they would like to be treated if they become subject to compulsion under the Act. For example, this could include whether they wished to avoid certain types of medication. Professionals have to take the advance statement into account but can overrule it. These two new methods of improving representation highlight the fact that any such measures to support a person's rights do need to be actively promoted as there has been a low take-up of each.

It is a key role of all social workers to ensure that people understand legal processes and are aware of their rights. This framework of legislation is complex, so information has to be given in a way that makes sense to people receiving it and time taken to explain and answer questions. The aims should always be to support the person to make informed decisions, to ensure that their views are heard, and that they are helped to access a solicitor or advocacy worker if they wish one.

Conclusion

This chapter has provided an introduction into law that allows local authorities and their practitioners to intervene in the lives of adults.

Each of the three statutes is complex in the way it aims to provide a balance between the rights to autonomy on the one hand and the duty to protect on the other. While the statutes deal with what can be seen, at first sight, as different groups of people, people with a mental disorder, adults with incapacity and adults at risk of harm, there are common approaches and principles to be found. There are also contradictions that cannot be covered here. For example, the MHA 2003 allows short-term detention without recourse to a legal decision-making forum and yet, under the ASPA 2007, an application has to be made to the court to gain a removal to place of safety order, which does not include the right to keep a person at the designated place once they have been moved there.

However, the reader should have gained an insight into the law in this area, be aware of the need to uphold the statutes' principles in their work and how important it is to understand what the law can or cannot do in terms of protecting adults. This, along with further reading, will help readers not only to consider their duty to protect but also their duty to support adults to maintain their autonomy, improve their welfare, and make full use of their rights to participation in decision making when they become subject to these statutes.

References

Atkinson, J. (2006) *Private and Public Protection: Civil Mental Health Legislation*, Edinburgh, Dunedin Academic Press.

Collins, M. (2010) 'Thresholds in adult protection', *Journal of Adult Protection*, **12**(1): 4–12.

Dawson, A., Ferguson, I., Maxwell, M. and Mackay, K. (2009) *An Assessment of the Operation of the Named Person Role and its Interaction with Other Forms of Patient Representation under the New Mental Health Act*, Edinburgh, Scottish Government.

Ferguson, I. (2003) 'Mental health and social work', in D. Baillie, K. Cameron, L.A. Cull et al. (eds) *Social Work and the Law in Scotland*, Basingstoke, Palgrave Macmillan/Open University Press.

Horton-Deutsch, S., Twigg, P. and Evans, R. (2007) 'Health care decision-making of persons with dementia', *Dementia*, **6**(1): 105–20.

Johnson, F., Hogg, J. and Daniel, B. (2010) 'Abuse and protection issues across the lifespan: reviewing the literature', *Social Policy and Society*, **9**(2): 291–304.

Kelly, F. (2010) 'Abusive interactions: research in locked wards for people with dementia', *Social Policy and Society*, **9**(2): 267–77.

Killeen, J., Myers, F. and MacDonald, F. (2004) *The Adults with Incapacity (Scotland) Act 2000: Implementation, Monitoring and Research*, Edinburgh, Scottish Executive.

Mackay, K. (2008) 'The Scottish adult support and protection legal framework', *Journal of Adult Protection*, **10**(4): 25–36.

Mandelstam, M. (2009) *Safeguarding Vulnerable Adults and the Law*, London, Jessica Kingsley.

Mental Welfare Commission (2008) *Annual Report 2007–2008*, Edinburgh, Mental Welfare Commission.

Parley, F. (2010) 'The understanding that care staff bring to abuse', *Journal of Adult Protection*, **12**(1): 13–26.

Patrick, H. (2005) *Adult with Incapacity Act: When to Invoke the Act*, Edinburgh, Mental Welfare Commission.

Patrick, H. (2008) *Autonomy, Benefit and Protection*, Edinburgh, Mental Welfare Commission.

Patrick, H. and Smith, N. (2007) 'An avoidable death: reflections on the fatal accident inquiry into the death of Roderick Dinnet', *Scottish Legal Action Group Journal*, 360: 222–5.

Patrick, H. and Smith, N. (2009) *Adult Protection and the Law in Scotland*, Haywards Heath, Bloomsbury.

Rogers, A. and Pilgrim, D. (2003) *Mental Health and Inequality*, Basingstoke, Palgrave Macmillan.

Scottish Executive (2005) *The Code of Practice for the Mental Health (Care and Treatment) (Scotland) Act 2003*, vols 1 and 2, Edinburgh, Scottish Executive.

Scottish Government (2008) *Communication and Assessing Capacity: A Guide for Social Work and Health Care Staff*, Edinburgh, Scottish Government.

Scottish Government (2009a) *Adult Support and Protection (Scotland) Act 2007: Code of Practice*, Edinburgh, Scottish Government.

Scottish Government (2009b) *Adults with Incapacity (Scotland) Act 2000: Code of Practice: For Local Authorities Exercising Functions under the 2000 Act*, Edinburgh, Scottish Government.

Scottish Government (2009c) *Short Comparison of the Adult Support and Protection Act, the Adults with Incapacity (Scotland) Act 2000 and the Mental Health (Care and Treatment)(Scotland) Act 2003*, Edinburgh, Scottish Government.

Scottish Law Commission (1995) *Incapable Adults Report 151*, Edinburgh, Scottish Law Commission.

Scottish Law Commission (1997) *Vulnerable Adults Report 158*, Edinburgh, Scottish Law Commission.

Chapter 10

Working with Adults who Use Services and Carers

KIRSTEN STALKER AND LISA CURTICE

Introduction

There are common principles that should inform practice with adults who need support in order to live full, safe and healthy lives, despite the very many differences in circumstances and needs among people who use adult social care services. There has been a shift in thinking about services for adults from a focus on satisfying needs to an emphasis on protecting and promoting rights. The responsibility to promote and protect rights is the first standard of practice required under the code of practice for Scottish social service workers (SSSC, 2009). It is acknowledged that people who use social work services are citizens who share the same rights and should have the same opportunities and responsibilities as other citizens (Duffy, 2006). These responsibilities include being able to make a contribution to society, for example through employment, offering peer support to others, or using their experience to influence the way services are designed and delivered for the benefit of others (Changing Lives User and Carer Forum, 2008).

While social work values have always referenced the principles of human dignity and social justice (BASW, 2002), there is an increasing emphasis on enabling self-determination by people who use services and carers. Therefore the practitioner will be called upon not only to arrange or deliver services, but to support an individual to identify their needs and develop the capacity for choice. Supporting someone to have more control over their life and services and to have a say in decisions about their support is particularly challenging where the person is an involuntary user of services. However, the principles of maximising choice and control apply even when the person has limited capacity or is subject to restrictions for the safety of themselves and others. The Adults with Incapacity (Scotland) Act 2000, the Mental Health (Care and Treatment) (Scotland) Act 2003 and the Adult Support and Protection (Scotland) Act 2007 set out common principles in this respect (see Chapter 9), based on Article 12 of the UN Convention on the Rights of Persons with Disabilities.

Linked to the principle of enabling greater choice and control is the principle that services should enable people to enjoy as much independence as possible. While the relevant approaches are known by different terms, there is a common emphasis on improving quality of life and reducing dependency in the principles of independent living (disabled people), recovery (mental health, addictions) and re-enablement (older people). These principles have significant implications for practice with adults and carers. The practitioner has a role to build the capacity of the individual and their family so that they can avoid crisis situations and live more independent lives. Independent living does not mean people doing without support, but rather having access to the specific support that will enable them to access the same opportunities as others (Equality and Human Rights Commission, n.d.). The focus of practice must be the difference that can be made to a person's life. It follows that respect and attention must be given to listening to the individual or the carer about what they value and the outcomes they expect.

The range of people who may receive support from adult care services includes older people, people with mental health problems, people with learning disabilities and brain injury, people with sensory impairments (sight and/or hearing), people with physical impairments, people with drug and/or alcohol problems, people with HIV/Aids and people requiring palliative care. Support for carers is also the remit of adult care services. However such a list is not comprehensive, as new needs emerge or achieve recognition over time. For example, as the life expectancy of people with Down's syndrome increases, there is more awareness of their increased risk of dementia which creates a requirement for specific staff training, housing and support strategies. A person with mental health problems may also be a carer for a disabled child or adult. Age, gender, ethnicity and sexuality are cross-cutting identities and it is important to avoid stereotypes. Men may be subject to domestic violence, black and minority ethnic carers may be particularly isolated, people with learning disabilities may be gay or in a relationship and need support with parenting (Ward and Tarleton, 2007).

The range of services available to adults with support needs is changing and becoming more flexible, as the focus of support shifts from delivering services to supporting better lives. Over half of employment in social work services is now in the independent (private plus voluntary) rather than the public sector, although these figures include those employed in early years services (Scottish Executive National Workforce Group, 2004). In addition to provision such as resource centres, support at home with personal care or domestic tasks, care homes and equipment and adaptations, social care assistance may take the form of supporting someone into employment or enabling them to access their local leisure centre. A social worker, who formerly might have been looking for a resource centre place for a young disabled person leaving school, may now be assisting their transition to work or further training, for example by contacting a supported employment service to find a job in an ordinary workplace that would match their skills and abilities (Scottish Government, 2010). Scottish legislation recognises that the local authority as a whole has a role to play in improving mental health by ensuring that its own services promote wellbeing and that community facilities, which provide the opportunity for people to meet others and pursue their interests, are accessible to all (Scottish Government, 2007a). Local area coordinators, whose role is to enable a disabled person to become more included in their community, have demonstrated how a person-centred approach can enable a person with learning disabilities to make new connections in their local community (Stalker et al., 2008).

Anti-discriminatory practice

Discrimination is a major barrier that prevents people from accessing their rights to equal treatment in society. Access is a complex process that involves physical access, knowledge, power, relationships and communication, advocacy, participation and quality of life (Seale and Nind, 2010). Through the Disability Equality Duty, implemented in 2006, those working in the public sector and their organisations have a responsibility to promote the rights of disabled people and actively to engage with them as well as to ensure that disabled people are not discriminated against on grounds of their disability (Disability Rights Commission, 2006). It is therefore the responsibility of a worker in social care services to ensure that their own practice is inclusive, but also to challenge barriers that the people they support may encounter in their daily lives. Discrimination can take many forms, including indifference or overt hostility, resulting in harassment and hate crime (Higgins, 2006).

A subtle form of discrimination can occur in failing to meet people's communication needs. A communication need is defined as a problem in expressing oneself, understanding information or social interaction. Such needs can often be hidden, for example multiple sclerosis or epilepsy may affect a person's ability to process information and respond to others. Support for communication is an important part of enabling people to take an active part in decision making. *The Same As You?* review of services for people with learning disabilities made the point that accessible information, advocacy and communication support are all important in enabling people to have 'better choices, stronger voices' (Scottish Executive, 2000). Bath and North East Somerset Council has a helpful website giving information about a range of accessible formats, including Braille, audio tapes, DVDs and type talk. It is obviously important to select the format that best suits the individual.[1] An online toolkit is also available to enable people to engage more effectively with anyone with a communication need (Communication Forum Scotland, n.d.). Some organisations have signed websites, for example the Royal National Institute for Deaf People.[2]

There are also principles that can be applied to engage with people with complex communication needs, including paying close attention, responding to the way the person themselves communicates, and respecting and listening to explanations by someone who knows the person well (Nind and Hewett, 2001). It is important to note that, even where a person does not have a communication need, it is still part of the role of a social care worker to signpost them to useful knowledge and information to enable them to make informed choices about their support (NES/IRISS, 2010).

Self-directed support

Changing Lives: Report of the 21st Century Social Work Review concluded that 'more of the same won't work' and recommended that personalised, flexible support, tailored to the person and their family, was likely to deliver much better outcomes (Scottish Executive, 2006). In their introduction to the review, written for other people who use services and carers, the User and Carer Panel explained that this meant that in future people should expect services to start from 'where you are at', to better match your needs and wishes, to enable you to have more say over your assessment and more control over your services (Scottish Executive, 2006). Self-directed support is one of the main mechanisms by which these changes are expected to occur. It is premised on the assumption that giving people more control, in particular control over how the funding for their service is spent, will result in services providing better value and making a greater difference to people's lives (Scottish Executive, 2007). There are different ways in which self-directed support can be offered. The best known is through a direct payment by which the person (or their appointee) themselves receives the funding to meet the need for which they have been assessed and can spend it to achieve that support, often by directly employing personal assistants. Other ways of accessing self-directed support are through an individual budget, where you know the amount of funding allocated to you, but choose to use a support provider or the local authority to deliver a service to you.

Self-directed support represents a transformation both in culture and in systems. It requires those working in services to hand over some power to those receiving them and for individuals and families to take more responsibility for decisions and for the management of their support, although it is possible to use a service to deal with the employment responsibilities of having personal assistants. Both commissioning authorities and service providers have to change their systems to work out what they can spend on each person and to administer funding on an individual basis. Self-directed support can enable more imaginative use of funding to enable someone to improve their health and quality of life. For example, rather than using a short break service, an older person might choose to go on holiday with a friend. More controversially, an individual might purchase a season ticket to their local football club in preference to having a mental health befriender, on the grounds that this will enable them to maintain their interests and meet others. Thus self-directed support is intended to improve the delivery of social care, to make it meet individual needs more effectively, and to make better use of informal supports.

Critics of self-directed support have portrayed it as an extension of privatisation, with the risks, costs and responsibilities of care being transferred from the public sector to the individual. However, evaluation of the early experience of self-directed support in North Lanarkshire, and of individual budgets in England using the In Control model, has provided evidence of efficiencies and of better outcomes and satisfaction (Etherington et al., 2009; Tyson et al., 2010). Moreover, for its success, self-directed support depends not just on monetary resources, but on positive attitudes and contributions from others. Evaluation of Partners for Inclusion, an organisation that supports people with learning disabilities and mental health problems, has shown how a provider can use an individualised model of support to enable people to live in their own homes and build significant connections in their community (MacIntyre, 2009, p. 19). For example, a support worker explained:

> At first when we started talking about a job I wondered if it was just about ticking a box somewhere but ... it has really cemented her role in the community ... now people know her and she is an accepted member of the community.

These new developments in social care do not necessarily represent a challenge to professional competence, but can be seen as a partnership model of care. For example, the Changing Lives User and Carer Forum (2008) has stressed that the changes it wants to see, through Citizen Leadership, involve working alongside social work staff, whom they wish to see more empowered. Engaging people who use services and carers in staff training can enable them to use their expertise in a way that can improve staff competence and increase mutual understanding. At the University of Dundee, social work and nursing students have the opportunity for a 24-hour placement in the family of a person with profound and multiple learning disabilities where they can experience the challenges that the family faces (Social Services Learning Networks West and Southeast, 2009).

Supporting people to access advocacy

The importance of advocacy is increasingly recognised in legislative and policy frameworks. The Mental Health (Care and Treatment) (Scotland) Act 2003 gives anyone with a 'mental disorder', meaning mental illness, learning disabilities, personality disorder, dementia or acquired brain injury, the right to access advocacy services (Patrick and Smith, 2009). Both the *National Guidance on Self-directed Support* (Scottish Executive, 2007) and *The Same as You? A Review of Services to People with Learning Disabilities* (Scottish Executive, 2000) highlight the importance of enabling people to access advocacy.

It is often stressed that advocacy should be independent, meaning that the advocate must represent only the individual's interests, having no formal connection with any services the person is using nor indeed with their family. There are various forms of independent advocacy:

- *Professional advocacy* involves a paid professional from an independent advocacy agency working with an individual, usually on a short-term, task-centred basis.
- *Citizen advocacy* is a longer term process where a volunteer advocate builds up a relationship with an individual over time, often with the aim of promoting social inclusion as well as supporting the person to speak up.
- *Self-advocacy*, which refers to a group activity, means people speak up for themselves about common concerns.

The advocate does not make decisions for the person or tell them what to do. However, some people will not be able to speak up for themselves, including those most likely to experience difficulty and possibly discrimination in accessing services. Here the advocate must argue for the individual's best interests so far as these can be reasonably judged by an independent person: this is called 'non-instructed advocacy'.

Nevertheless, to some extent and in some circumstances, social workers can and should act as advocates for adults using social care services. There are various tasks associated with advocacy that do not necessarily fall into the remit of an independent advocate (Scottish Executive, 2004). These include helping the person get to grips with large amounts of information about services, benefits or health conditions, helping those with low literacy to complete forms, and accompanying the person to meetings with other agencies. However, social workers must recognise when there is a potential or actual conflict of interest between the individual's interests and their own employer's interests or requirements and here an independent advocate should be brought in. The social worker should see this as a positive support for the individual rather than a threat to their own professional standing. They need to know where and how to access advocacy services and should pass on information about them in a format accessible to each person.

There is increasing recognition of the benefits of advocacy for marginalised groups including substance misusers and homeless people (Scottish Executive, 2004). For example, drug users may be unaware of the generic and specialist services that are available and can face barriers in accessing them, including low self-esteem. Drug users in one study identified 'personal treatment', such as accessing GP services and negotiating changes in treatment programmes, as the main area where they wanted advocacy. Service providers reported that drug users required advocacy to cope with financial, health, occupational and childcare issues (Scottish Executive, 2004, p. 17). One person described his experience of advocacy:

> It was useful ... I needed stuff sorted with the housing and I saw my worker dealing with it. It was really helpful to see how they went about it, seeing what they said and how they said it; this really gave me a lot of confidence to do it myself.

Supporting unpaid carers

It is estimated there are over 650,000 unpaid carers in Scotland, representing 1 in 8 of the population (Scottish Executive, 2003a). With numbers of older people growing, so unpaid caring will increase. While the stereotypical carer may be a white, middle-aged, non-disabled woman looking after an ageing parent, in reality a very wide range of individuals act as carers at some point in their lives, supporting a broad range of people. Carers may be men or women, children or adults, gay or straight, of any ethnic background and may have impairments of their own, for example when adults with learning disabilities take on caring tasks for elderly parents. As that example implies, the informal caring relationship can be fluid, complex and interdependent, and each has its own history and dynamics that social workers must take into account when working with families.

All carers in Scotland are entitled to information about support and help, such as carers' groups and benefits, and to advocacy and training. While the NHS has responsibilities here, so too do social workers who should pass on information in a variety of formats and languages. If it seems likely that a carer is providing 'a substantial amount of care on a regular basis' (Scottish Executive, 2003b, p. 10), the social worker should inform them that they are entitled to an assessment. Assessment should be holistic and user friendly, taking account of the carer's views. There can be an element of self-assessment. The social worker will consider whether the carer is able and willing to continue caring and, if so, at what level and with what support.

Alternatively, carers' needs can be considered alongside those of the person they support, as part of their assessment. However, it is advisable for both parties to have an opportunity to talk to the social worker alone. They may have different views about the caring relationship; carers may be reluctant to discuss their own needs or feelings of stress in front of their relative or, at worst, there may be elements of abuse on either side.

It is important that assessments lead to positive outcomes. The Scottish Government (2008) has identified factors contributing to good outcomes from carers' assessments, including identifying current and potential risks to the carer's health and wellbeing, and what resources are needed to enable them to have 'a life of their own'. A policy distinction is made between the *support and resources* needed to enable carers to continue caring and the *services* required by the person with community care needs (Scottish Executive, 2003b). This is based on a view of the carer as a care provider who is only eligible for community care services if they have needs of their own, independent of the person supported. This may sometimes be a tricky distinction for social workers to make in practice. However, services intended to provide a positive experience for the person with community care needs, such as short breaks, have the potential to offer huge support to carers. Indeed, carers consistently identify short-term care as their top priority.

So far as possible, the support offered to carers and the services provided to their relatives should be integrated and personalised. Although this partly depends on what is available within specific local authorities, social workers can aid the process by involving partner agencies in the assessment process, by ensuring information is shared as required and appropriate, and that planning is well coordinated, and by offering families a range of options drawing on voluntary and statutory sources. Carers and their relatives should be given as much choice as possible and services provided in a flexible manner tailored to individual need. Drawing on carers' expert knowledge of their relative will enable more personalised services to be put in place as will attention to religious and cultural needs. Carers will derive most benefit from care arrangements they have confidence in, which free them up to pursue other interests and make the most of their lives (Scottish Executive, 2003c).

Young carers

There are an estimated 100,000 or more young carers in Scotland. These are young people under 18 with caring responsibilities for another person, often a disabled, chronically ill or substance misusing parent, although it may be a grandparent, sibling or other person. 'Young carers' is a contested concept which has been the subject of fierce debate. One side contends that young carers experience stress and disadvantage as a result of caring and should therefore be given help and support to alleviate the situation. The other side argues that young people would not have to act as carers if their parents – or people they care for – were given the support *they* are entitled to as people with community care needs (see Stalker, 2003 for a smmary of this debate). There is also concern that disabled people's parenting capacity is undermined when their children are allowed to care for them. However, disabled and other parents supported by their children may be keen to avoid social work intervention for various reasons, not least anxiety that their children might be taken into care.

Thus, the circumstances in which children act as carers are likely to be complex and social workers will need to exercise sensitivity and, unless immediate action is required, caution in order to gain trust and acceptance. Young carers are often invisible so social workers working with adults with community care needs should be alert to the presence of young carers. The aims of social work intervention are to minimise the impact of caring on the young person's life – and Scottish Executive (2003b) guidance is very clear that children must not be allowed to take on or continue inappropriate caring roles – and to provide support to families to minimise the need for young people to act as carers.

In terms of support, young carers can be offered information, advice, counselling and the chance to join young carers' projects. Research in Scotland has shown that they get the most out of social and recreational events, often with other young carers (Banks et al., 2002), although there is an argument for more inclusion in mainstream children's activities (Scottish Executive, 2003b). Young people can be encouraged to take up options like homework clubs and buddy systems to facilitate learning and friendships at school, while flexible attendance for older pupils and input from careers and guidance staff will also help young carers to develop and thrive (Banks et al., 2002). At the same time, social workers need to assess the community care needs of the adults whom young people support and ensure services are in place to meet their needs, and/or promote take-up of direct payments whereby help can be purchased for tasks otherwise undertaken by children.

Range of remedies

An essential element within any good service – public, voluntary or private – is a range of accessible, transparent and effective mechanisms through which people can make representations on any aspect of provision they are unhappy about and seek redress. Agencies genuinely committed to participation, empowerment and accountability will see this process as an opportunity to learn and improve the service. Partnership working with people who use services, including those who make complaints, will be improved where social care organisations are open to complaints, take a neutral stance as far as possible, seek common ground, and work towards constructive resolution.

Comments, criticisms and complaints can vary in severity from a social worker failing to return a call or a home carer arriving late, to allegations of serious abuse.[3] Although they may have strong grounds for complaining, people may be resistant to doing so. They may worry about losing a service if they complain. An older person living alone with few external contacts, or an individual with physical or sensory impairments who needs a high level of support with daily living tasks, may rely for 'help' on a paid carer who is mistreating them: they may fear retaliation if they complain. People may not know they have a right to complain and/or may not have received information about how to do so. Those whose first language is not English, or who have communication impairments or learning disabilities, may require support to use remedies effectively. Social workers therefore have an important role in informing people about their right to complain, giving reassurance that no adverse repercussions will ensue, and arranging independent advocacy, communication support and/or interpreting services as necessary.

A continuum of remedies is available to people using services (see also Chapter 2). Regular monitoring and evaluation of client satisfaction, for example through user surveys, residents' meetings and 'suggestion boxes', are low-key and sometimes anonymised avenues for people to raise issues that can be 'caught' and dealt with at an early stage. Dissatisfaction may be related to poor communication, a misunderstanding or simple mistake that can be easily rectified. Most agencies will initially try to resolve issues informally by encouraging the individual or family to talk matters over with their social worker. If necessary, a manager will become involved. This process, described by one complaints officer as a 'golden opportunity' to prevent a dissatisfaction progressing to a complaint, is sometimes referred to as 'conciliation'. However, that is potentially confusing, since conciliation is a distinct activity involving a mediator from an independent organisation who helps disputing parties reach an agreement (for example the Equality and Human Rights Commission offers conciliation in cases of alleged unlawful discrimination).

If informal discussion is unsuccessful, the next step is a formal complaints procedure. Local authorities offer people various ways to lodge complaints, for example by phone, email, letter or a 'freepost' form attached to information leaflets. Social workers can also 'refer' cases to a complaints officer. The authority should acknowledge the complaint within a specified number of days and may contact the complainant to find out more. The latter may be invited to attend a meeting to discuss the issue, accompanied by an advocate or friend if they wish. The authority undertakes to investigate the complaint and respond in full within a set time, typically a month. Local authorities have Review Appeals Panels to consider appeals against decisions made in individual cases.

An example of a recent complaint facing one Scottish local authority[4] concerns an older woman who has been caring for her husband since he became disabled 20 years ago. Two home carers visit three times a day. It is not always possible for two local authority staff, known to the couple, to attend: sometimes an agency carer is teamed with a local authority carer but the authority pledged that it would never deploy together two agency staff who did not know the gentleman. Generally, this works well but on one occasion when the wife was staying with relatives in Wales, two agency staff arrived who did not know how to gain entry to the house, move and handle the client or administer medication. The gentleman was very distressed by this experience and contacted his wife who also became upset and angry. Attempts to resolve the issue informally on her return were unsuccessful, with some escalation of dissatisfaction on the couple's part. The authority, which had admitted fault in the matter, nevertheless undertook a complete investigation that eventually led to an amicable resolution.

If a complainant remains dissatisfied after the normal complaints procedure, including the Review Appeals Panel, has been exhausted, they may take the case to the Scottish public services ombudsman, who can investigate, on an independent basis, complaints of maladministration by public services. Other options include judicial review, whereby the Court of Session reviews and can revoke allegedly illegal or unreasonable actions by public bodies, or the Human Rights Act 1998, if a public body may have acted in a manner incompatible with the European Human Rights Convention. Complainants also have recourse to the Scottish Commission for the Regulation of Care (from

April 2011, Social Care and Social Work Improvement Scotland), if the complaint is against a service regulated by that body, or the Scottish Social Services Council, if it concerns serious 'alleged misconduct' by a social care worker registered with that body. A complaint can be made to either body at any time, thus making it possible to circumvent local authority procedures.

People using non-statutory services have a similar range of remedies. Those using self-directed support should, in the first instance, raise issues with their care manager or direct payments lead officer (Scottish Executive, 2007). If this fails to resolve the matter, they can use local authority complaints procedures and other remedies as described above. If a complaint concerns a personal assistant whom they employ, this should be taken up directly with the employee. Advice about this is available from Independent Living Centres and the Scottish Personal Assistant Employers' Network.

Unfortunately, a small minority of people make vexatious or malicious complaints, while some individuals may be resistant to negotiating or resolving their complaints. This can be stressful for any social worker who is the target of such behaviour: they also need good support and a fair hearing.

It is important that complaints procedures are based on certain key principles. The Crerar Review (Scottish Government, 2007b), which looked at regulation, audit, inspection and complaints procedures for public services in Scotland, recommended that, wherever possible, complaints be resolved simply, consistently, quickly and locally. Other important principles for complaints procedures in adult social care are effectiveness, clarity, confidentiality, impartiality and fairness (see Scottish Commission for the Regulation of Care for more details).[5] Good practice in dealing with complaints includes seeking resolution at the earliest stage, keeping the person informed about progress, communicating the outcome clearly and telling the person about other options if still dissatisfied, and making sure all staff have good knowledge about the range of remedies available. Finally, social workers have an important role in supporting people whose voices are least heard, such as those with dementia, to bring forward complaints as and when appropriate (SCIE, 2009).

Conclusion

Over recent years, social work practice with adults using services and their carers has shifted to a rights-based model promoting mainstream opportunities, self-determination and independence. The best services now focus on supporting better lives, including fostering a sense of belonging for people within local communities. Moreover, anti-discriminatory approaches require social workers to develop inclusive practice and challenge the barriers that prevent people having more control over their lives, for example by meeting individuals' communication needs. Examples of the more personalised support now available include direct payments and individual budgets. Independent advocacy plays a vital role in promoting an individual's interests, but social workers also have a useful part to play in speaking up for people, or supporting them to express their views, where this does not conflict with a worker's role as service representative/employee.

A wide range of people act as informal carers. They have legislative rights to assessment, information and support which, again, should be flexible and well integrated. Social workers should be alert to the presence and needs of young carers and ensure that services are meeting the needs of the adult whom the young carer is supporting.

A range of remedies is available for anyone dissatisfied with social care services. These range from suggestion boxes to formal complaints procedures to human rights legislation. Social workers should inform adults using services and carers about such mechanisms and support people to use them as appropriate.

References

Banks, P., Cogan, N., Riddell, S. et al. (2002) 'Does the covert nature of caring prohibit the development of effective services for young carers'?, *British Journal of Guidance and Counselling*, 30(3): 229–46.

BASW (British Association of Social Workers) (2002) *Code of Ethics*, available online at www.basw.co.uk/about/codeofethics/ [accessed 20 June 2010].

Changing Lives User and Carer Forum (2008) *Principles and Standards of Citizen Leadership*, available online at www.Scotland.gov.uk/Publications/2008/04/17143215/0 [accessed 10 April 2010].

Communication Forum Scotland (n.d.) *Talk for Scotland Toolkit*, available online at www.communicationforumscotland.org.uk/2010/TK_Home.php [accessed 11 April 2010].

Disability Rights Commission (2006) *The Duty To Promote Disability Equality, Statutory Code of Practice Scotland, Making Rights a Reality*, available online at www.dotheduty.org./files/Code_of_practice_scotland.pdf [accessed 9 November 2009].

Duffy, S. (2006) *Keys to Citizenship: A Guide to Getting Good Support for People with Learning Disabilities* (2nd edn), London, Paradigm.

Equality and Human Rights Commission (n.d.) *Independent Living in Scotland*, available online at www.ilis.co.uk/ [accessed 11 April 2010].

Etherington, K., Hatton, C. and Waters, J. (2009) *Way Ahead: Our Early Experience in North Lanarkshire of Demonstrating the Impact of the In Control Approach Glasgow*, North Lanarkshire Council and In Control Scotland.

Higgins, K. (2006) 'Some victims less equal than others', *Scottish Legal Action Group (SCOLAG) Legal Journal*, 346: 162–3.

MacIntyre, G. (2009) *If the Support's Right, She's Right: An Evaluation of Partners for Inclusion*, available online at www.scld.org.uk/library-publications/if-supports-right-shes-right-evaluation-partners-inclusion [accessed 11 April 2010].

NES/IRISS (NHS Education for Scotland/Institute for Research and Innovation in Social Services) (2010) *Sharing Knowledge, Improving Practice and Changing Lives: A Knowledge Management Strategy and Action Plan for Social Services in Scotland 2010–2012*, available online at www.ssks.org.uk/km-strategy.aspx [accessed 11 April 2010].

Nind, M. and Hewett, D. (2001) *A Practical Guide to Intensive Interaction*, Kidderminster, British Institute of Learning Disabilities.

Patrick, H. and Smith, N. (2009) *Adult Protection and the Law in Scotland*, Haywards Heath, Bloomsbury.

SCIE (Social Care Institute for Excellence) (2009) *Guide 15: Dignity in Care*, available online at www.scie.org.uk/publications/guides/guide15/index.asp [Accessed 26 March 2010].

Scottish Executive (2000) *The Same as You? A Review of Services for People with Learning Disabilities*, Edinburgh, TSO.

Scottish Executive (2003a) *Scotland's People: Results from the 2001/2002 Scottish Household Survey*, vol. 7: *Annual Report*, available online at www.scotland.gov.uk/Topics/Statistics/16002/PublicationAnnual [accessed 14 May 2010].

Scottish Executive (2003b) *Community Care and Health (Scotland) Act 2002: New Statutory Rights for Carers: Guidance*, Circular CCD 2/2003, available online at www.sehd.scot.nhs.uk/publications/cc2003_02full.pdf [accessed 7 July 2010].

Scottish Executive (2003c) *One in Eight Care*, available online at www.scotland.gov.uk/Publications/2003/03/16884/20937 [accessed 26 March 2010].

Scottish Executive (2004) *Advocacy for Drug Users: A Guide*, available online at www.scotland.gov.uk/Publications/2004/06/19564/39661 [accessed 30 March 2010].

Scottish Executive (2006) *Changing Lives: Report of the 21st Century Social Work Review Edinburgh, Scottish Executive*, available online at www.socialworkscotland.org.uk/resources/pub/ChangingLivesMainReport.pdf [accessed 11 April 2010].

Scottish Executive (2007) *National Guidance on Self-directed Support*, available online at www.scotland.gov.uk/Publications/2007/07/04093127/0 [Accessed 30 March 2010].

Scottish Executive National Workforce Group (2004) *Scotland's Social Care Labour Market*, available online at www.scotland.gov.uk/Resource/Doc/17002/0025510.pdf [accessed 11 April 2010].

Scottish Government (2007a) *With Inclusion in Mind: The Local Authority's Role in Promoting Wellbeing and Social Inclusion: Mental Health (Care and Treatment) (Scotland) Act 2003 Sections 25–31*, available online at www.scotland.gov.uk/Publications/2007/10/18092957/11 [accessed 11 April 2010].

Scottish Government (2007b) *Report of the Independent Review of Regulation, Audit, Inspection and Complaints Handling of Public Services in Scotland* (Crerar Review), available online at www.scotland.gov.uk/Publications/2007/09/25120506/0 [accessed 26 March 2010].

Scottish Government (2008) *National Minimum Information Standards for all Adults in Scotland*, available online at www.scotland.gov.uk/Topics/Health/care/JointFuture/NMISAnnexB/Q/EditMode/on/ForceUpdate/on   [accessed 26 March 2010].

Scottish Government (2010) *A Working Life for All Disabled People: The Supported Employment Framework for Scotland: Summary Report*, available online at www.scotland.gov.uk/Publications/2010/02/23094107/0 [Accessed 11 April 2010].

Seale, J. and Nind, M. (2010) *Understanding and Promoting Access for People with Learning Difficulties*, Abingdon, Routledge.

Social Services Learning Networks West and Southeast (2009) *Effective Engagement in Social Work Education*, available online at www.serviceusercarer goodpractice.org.uk/intro/purpose [accessed 12 April 2010].

SSSC (Scottish Social Services Council) (2009) *Codes of Practice for Social Services Workers and Employers*, Dundee, Scottish Social Services Council, availableonlineatwww.sssc.uk.com/sssc/all-about-registration-for-social-workers/codes-of-practice.html [accessed 10 April 2010].

Stalker, K., Malloch, M., Barry, M. and Watson, J. (2008) 'Local area co-ordination: strengthening support for people with learning disabilities in Scotland', *British Journal of Learning Disabilities*, 36(4): 215–19.

Tyson, A., Brewis, R., Crosby, N. et al. (2010) *A Report on In Control's Third Phase, Evaluation and Learning 2008–2009*, London, In Control Publications, available online at www.in-control.org.uk/phase3report [accessed 12 April 2010].

Ward, L. and Tarleton, B. (2007) 'Sinking or swimming? Supporting parents with learning disabilities and their children', *Learning Disability Review*, 12(2): 22–32.

Notes

1. See www.bathnes.gov.uk/BathNES/communityandliving/equality/accessible formats/.
2. See www.rnid.org.uk/helpdesk/accessibility/.
3. These are real examples provided by a Scottish local authority complaints officer.
4. Some details have been changed to protect anonymity.
5. www.carecommission.com/indexphp?Itemid=72&id=43&option=com_content &task=view.

Chapter 11

Youth Justice

BILL WHYTE

Introduction

Youth crime policies during much of the twentieth century eroded the distinction between the young person in need and the delinquent youth, only to see these welfare-oriented approaches superseded by punitive law and order ideologies driven by politicians under pressure to be seen to be tough on crime. The combination of two concepts, special responses to the needs of children and young people and equal rights under the law, creates a tension, in social work practice, on how best to reconcile the competing claims of the law, judicial process, punishment and control with the need to consider the best interests, needs and the rights of the child or young person, while effectively reducing offending and its consequences for victims.

Since the Act of Union 1701, Scotland has retained its own distinctive and separate legal system. Nowhere is this better illustrated than in its approach to youth justice and social work. The re-establishment of the Scottish Parliament in 1999 formally devolved law and policy relating to youth justice to the Scottish Government.

Youth justice and children's hearings

The shape of youth justice provision in the early part of the twenty-first century in Scotland is still being moulded and developed and most aspects of policy have been subject to ongoing review. What began as a fundamental review of youth justice (Scottish Executive, 2000) was extended to a full review of the children's hearings system as a whole. The Children's Hearings (Scotland) Bill 2010 is intended to provide an updated framework for the children's hearing system in Scotland (see Chapter 6).

The Social Work (Scotland) Act 1968 (SWA) introduced a distinctive approach to youth justice in Scotland in 1971, which has lasted for nearly 40 years. Scottish youth courts were disbanded and replaced by lay decision-making tribunals – children's hearings – which deal with children at risk and children who offend within a unified welfare system. The centrality of the criminal courts was removed from decision making, so that, for most young people under 16, issues of offence disposal are dealt with by hearings, while matters of adjudication of legal facts (proof when offences are denied and appeals against outcomes) remain matters for the courts. The system was premised on the existence of an integrated social work system in which children's services carried the responsibility for providing meaningful assistance to young people involved in offending and their families, whether subject to voluntary or compulsory measures (for information and discussion of its origins and early workings, see Martin et al., 1981; Cowperthwaite, 1985; Moore and Whyte, 1997).

The Children (Scotland) Act 1995 (CA) provided an updated statutory framework for the system in the context of the United Nations Convention on the Rights of the Child (UNCRC) (OHCRH, 1989) but did not fundamentally change the principles or institutions, with one important departure. Section 16(5) of the Act introduced provision for a hearing (or court) to make a decision not consistent with the 'best interests' principle, if they considered this necessary to protect the public from serious harm; a shift from the best interests of the child as 'the' paramount consideration to the looser UNCRC paramountcy principle – the principle that the best interests and welfare of children must be 'a' primary consideration in any proceedings involving children who offend.

This was one of a series of political 'doctorings' over the years undermining, although not removing, some of the central principles of the hearing system. They highlight shifts from welfare and social work to punitive discourses and the tension facing social workers in providing care within the context of statutory control. The first and most significant for current twenty-first century practice took place as early as 1974 when the Rehabilitation of Offenders Act 1974 (ROA), a piece of UK legislation, included provision in s. 3 that the acceptance of an offence ground at a hearing or later established by a sheriff in a proof hearing 'shall be treated for the purposes of this Act (but not otherwise) as a conviction'. Sections 5(3b) and 5(4A) (as amended) identify the rehabilitation period for the 'conviction'. Few social workers were aware of the significance of this change to a system that explicitly intended to decriminalise children who offend. For most purposes, this was seldom a practical issue until recent years when increasing requirements for enhanced disclosures have resulted in adults who considered they had no 'record' discovering that behaviour as young as eight can be cited in enhanced disclosures.

This issue is subject to ongoing review, particularly in the light of new powers to hold DNA information, and consideration is being given to legislative change to identify specific offences for which a record (rather than a conviction) may be required, ensuring that the remaining children are not subject to criminalisation as originally intended. The powers to amend ROA 1974 as it applies to Scotland, technically, lie with the Scottish Parliament. It is hoped that some remedy will be included in the Children's Hearings (Scotland) Bill 2010.

Scottish law places a statutory duty on local authorities, including social work, to 'promote social welfare', the community's as well as individual's (s. 12(1) of the SWA 1968), and the CA 1995 places a whole authority (corporate) responsible for children 'in need', 'looked after' or 'accommodated' because of their offending. In principle, this should mean that these children and young people have the highest priority for education, housing, leisure and cultural services, drug and mental health services, and are not the sole responsibility of social work. The reality often falls far short of the principle. The overarching assumption underlying the Scottish system is that caring, controlling and assisting positive change to reduce offending will, in the long run, be in the best interests of young people, victims and the community at large. This places complex responsibilities on youth justice social workers to provide meaningful individual and family provision while exercising positive authority and control.

Most children and young people under 16, and many up to 18, who offend are dealt with by the children's hearing system and do not appear in court. Nonetheless, criminal courts do deal with children, subject to safeguards, in that, according to s. 42(1) of the Criminal Procedures (Scotland) Act 1995:

> no child under the age of 16 years shall be prosecuted for any offence except on the instructions of the Lord Advocate, or at his instance [known as the Lord Advocate's Guidelines]; and no court other than the High Court and the Sheriff Court shall have jurisdiction over a child under the age of 16 for an offence.

The Lord Advocate's Guidelines (Angiolini, 2010) provide details on legislative provisions for children in the criminal justice system, legal definitions of a 'child', and instructions on which categories of offences are to be considered for prosecution. Generally, these relate to the gravity of the offence (cases of murder, rape and armed robbery); some offences under road traffic legislation for those over age 14, which can result in disqualification; and offences committed with an adult. In 2009, 80 young people (5 girls and 75 boys) under the age of 16 were found guilty in a Scottish criminal court. Most were over the age of 14 (Scottish Government, 2010, Table 12). These young people present particular challenges to youth justice social workers trying to act in ways that promote their welfare and desistence in a context in which the values of punishment and control dominate.

Scotland's Children: The Children (Scotland) Act 1995 Regulations and Guidance (SWSG, 2004) contains guidance on the broad objectives, direction and intent of the legislation, including the objective of 'reducing or stopping offending' (Annex 1, p. 34). However, it does not provide national objectives or service standards for youth justice social work; the expectation being that local authorities will establish their own service standards as part of children's services planning (s. 19 of the CA 1995). *National Standards for Scotland's Youth Justice Services* (Improving the Effectiveness of the Youth Justice System Group, 2002) were introduced in 2002 but following the concordat of 2007 (Scottish Government/ COSLA) between the Scottish Government and local authorities, these have become 'recommendations' rather than requirements.

A distinct philosophy of youth justice?

While no clear theoretical exposition or any precise definitions of its founding principles were outlined, the Kilbrandon (1964) proposals were based on key assumptions recognisable in current debates. They emphasise non-judicial, child-centred approaches to dealing with offending within the context of meeting the wider social needs of the whole child. Youth justice social work is intended to operate within an integrated children's services system interfacing with criminal justice but not as part of it. This creates practice tensions for social workers' roles in risk/need assessment, intervention planning and outcome evaluation, particularly in relation to serious and persistent criminal behaviour.

In principle, the system is structured around early intervention and diversion from prosecution, where social work is charged with assessing and meeting the needs of the whole child in partnership with parents, where possible, and not simply or exclusively focusing on offending (Whyte, 2008). It is, nonetheless, one of the explicit objectives of the system to help young people to stop offending. The skills set required by youth justice social workers combines good childcare and family practices with criminologically directed skills in tackling offending and 'criminogenic needs'. Consequently, the key principles of the system stress the importance, where possible, of working in partnership with parents and family networks to find community-based solutions directed by social educational principles (Smith and

Whyte, 2008), rather than relying on formal criminalisation and its associated risks highlighted by labelling theories.

Young people who offend are to be viewed not simply as offenders but as young people first, whose upbringing has been unsatisfactory. 'Shared' responsibility for their offending between the young person, the family, the community and the state should allow for possible resolutions without recourse to formal (criminal) proceedings. Theories of victimology and concern for victims, although undeveloped at the time, are nonetheless implicit in the assumptions that young people are often themselves victims of their upbringing and circumstances as well as 'villains' or perpetrators of crime (Whyte, 2008).

Kilbrandon (1964) viewed the criminal process as having two fundamental functions: the adjudication of the legal facts – whether or not an offence had been established beyond reasonable doubt – and decisions concerning disposal once the facts are established. The report contended that the two functions required 'quite different skills and qualities' and that attempting to combine them was a source of 'dissatisfaction' (para. 71). Accordingly, the Scottish system separates adjudication and disposal. Consequently, children's hearings have no power to determine questions of innocence or guilt, which remains the responsibility of the criminal court. Access to representation and legal aid is available to all young people and parents who dispute the facts, deny the offence, are unable to understand the evidence against them, or wish to appeal against the outcome. This is intended to safeguard legal rights and provides a check against overenthusiastic, disproportionate intervention. In practice, the vast majority of young people brought before hearings accept the facts and are therefore dealt with in this welfare setting. Where possible, resolutions, even formal ones, are to be sought in a setting which, by its informality and allocation of time, would ensure, as far as practically possible, effective participation by the young person and adults, assisted by their social worker, in resolving problems and deciding on future action and provision.

Fine principles do not guarantee good practice and critics of the Scottish approach, at the time, pointed to a lack of empirical evidence for the assumptions underpinning the system. Since then, international studies (see Whyte, 2008) have given support to the view that multiple difficulties relating to social adversity, socialisation and social control, particularly parental supervision, are common to many, if not most, young people who offend persistently. Meeting needs, particularly those that sustain and support criminality, as well as addressing deeds should be at the heart of desistence practice for social workers. Contemporary data (McAra and McVie, 2007) supports attempts to synthesise key elements of existing criminological theories, for example that social structure, including the socio-economic status of the family and the ecology of the neighbourhood, can have an influence on the care and social control processes of family and school, on peer groups, and hence, directly or indirectly, on the young person's development. While delinquency in youth can lead to adult offending through the acquisition of criminal habits, skills and associates, formal labelling as an offender can also have the effect of weakening social bonds and increasing the risk of adult offending (Braithwaite, 1989). Commentaries on desistence from crime support approaches in which meeting need and supporting self-control and maturation are key to social work practice aimed at changing lives (Ward and Maruna, 2007).

Scottish youth justice and international standards

Scotland has been under pressure following reports by the UN Committee on the Rights of the Child (1995, 2002, 2008 and see the response of the Scottish Government, 2009a) to raise the age of criminal responsibility, to deal with the relatively high level of detention for young people aged 16 and 17 and the associated anomaly of routinely dealing with young people aged 16 and 17 in adult criminal courts. The Scottish Government's response, *Improving the Lives of Children in Scotland – Are We There Yet?* (2008a, p. 3) stated that 'UNCRC applies to all those aged under 18 in Scotland. It is an international law that recognises that all children and young people have rights'. This is, in effect, a statement of intent to move towards a situation that will address the issues outlined in the *Concluding Observations* (UN Committee on the Rights of the Child, 2008). These include:

- fully implement international standards of juvenile justice (para. 78)
- raise the age of criminal responsibility (para. 78(a))
- establish the principle that detention should be used as a measure of last resort (para. 78(b))
- children in conflict with the law are … never tried as adults in ordinary courts, irrespective of the gravity of the crime they are charged with (para. 78(c))
- ensure that professionals working with children … receive training on their obligation (para. 51(b)).

Scotland is still some way from achieving these international standards. However, growing leverage is present in the publication of Council of

Europe rules, which may be enforceable under the European Convention on Human Rights. The most recent Council of Europe documents with a bearing on youth justice practice include:

- *European Rules for Juvenile Offenders Subject to Sanctions and Measures,* CM/Rec (2008)11[1]
- *Final Draft Guidelines on Child-Friendly Justice,* CJ-S-CH (2010)12[2]
- *Draft Probation Rules R(2010)*[3]
- *Draft European Probation Organisation Statement of Values,* 2010.[4]

While few young people under 16 appear in a criminal court compared to most other UK jurisdictions, Scotland has one of the lowest ages of criminal responsibility in the world, at age eight. No change was proposed by the Kilbrandon Committee on the assumption that most young people would be dealt with by the hearing system and would be decriminalised.

The Criminal Justice and Licencing (Scotland) Act 2010 (CJLA) (s. 38) makes provision to raise the age of immunity from prosecution to 12 from May 2011. This will ensure Scotland will never again face the embarrassment of prosecuting a child under 12 in a criminal court – something that in reality seldom happens. The change is a symbolic gesture to the UN Committee and a statement of intent for the future but does not fundamentally deal with the issue of the criminal records of children aged between 8 and 11. Provisions of ROA 1974 could result in a criminal conviction/record being disclosed many years later, damaging, among other things, future employment opportunities, for behaviour at age 8 to 11.

Changes to the advanced disclosure process included in the CJLA 2010 will mean that this record could stay on the criminal history system well into adulthood. Such records are currently subject to the so-called 40/20 rule; they are routinely kept and disclosed through the organisation Disclosure Scotland, until either the person reaches the age of 40, or 20 years after the 'conviction', whichever is later.

The government has argued that these measures are to ensure that a balance is struck between the rights of children and the rights of communities to be protected. Nonetheless, the extended period of disclosure undermines a key principle of the Kilbrandon philosophy and an essential aspect of social work practice aimed at assisting young people to move on from offending to build a non-criminal identity. It is hoped that the final version of the Childrens' Hearing Bill 2010 will include provisions to limit data retention to the most serious crimes and that future changes to ROA 1974 may see a return to the original Kilbrandon proposals that most children under 16 and even 18 will be fully decriminalised (Whyte, 2008).

Under pressure following the UN Committee's *Concluding Observations* of 2002, the then Scottish Executive re-established youth courts in two pilot areas of Scotland. Despite the name, a youth court is simply an 'adapted' adult summary criminal court with a special focus on young people aged 16 and 17. Evaluations of the two courts published in 2010 (Scottish Government, 2010), while not without methodological limitations, 'found no evidence of lower reconviction rates in either area following the introduction of the youth court but some evidence of possible "net-widening"' (Scottish Government Community Justice Services Division, 2010, Annex A).

These developments reflect political 'doctoring', which often complicates rather than deals with fundamental issues, in this case the transition between hearings and criminal courts and the status of young people aged 16 and 17. They are legally 'children' under CA 1995 but not for the purposes of adult prosecution. Young people of 16 and 17 who are not already within the hearing system cannot be referred there by the procurator fiscal, although, if prosecuted under summary proceedings, they can be referred back to a hearing for disposal or for advice by the criminal court. This inconsistency means that procurators fiscal can prosecute and divert young people, conditionally or unconditionally, but cannot refer 16- or 17-year-olds directly to a hearing for 'compulsory measures', when prosecution is not in the public interest (if it ever is). Research (Waterhouse et al., 2000) highlighted that it is often simpler and more practical for busy procurators fiscal to prosecute than to generate the information required for a decision on how best to deal effectively with a young person under 18 in a non-criminal way. There are no technical reasons in Scottish law why most young people under 18 should not be diverted from the adult criminal justice system and dealt with by the hearing system. It was clearly the intention of the SWA 1968 that they should be dealt with, normally, out of the adult system.

All young people over the age of 16, subject to compulsory measures and reported for offending, are 'jointly reported' to the reporter and the Crown Office and Procurators Fiscal Service. They liaise as to whether or not the young person in question should be prosecuted before the adult criminal courts or referred to a hearing, generally following a social work assessment. An updated agreement between the Crown Office and Procurators Fiscal Service and the Scottish Children's Reporter Administration on jointly reported young people was published in 2010 with the intention of increasing diversion from prosecution (SCRA, 2010).

Section 49 of the Criminal Procedure (Scotland) Act 1995 requires a Sheriff Court and empowers the High Court to refer young people subject to social work supervision, except in respect of offences where the sentence is fixed by law, to the principal reporter to arrange a hearing for advice. A summary criminal court can seek advice from or remit 16- and 17-year-olds to the children's hearings. Despite these provisions, many, if not most, in this age group are routinely prosecuted in adult criminal courts, raising serious questions about prosecution practice in relation to the UNCRC. Social work practice should be UNCRC-rights focused. Social work report writers should be routinely recommending that young people at risk of further offending are maintained in the hearing system beyond 16 and all social work reports to summary courts should recommend remittal back to hearings for this age group.

A key recommendation of the Scottish Prisons Commission's report *Scotland's Choice* (2008), examining Scotland's high custody rate, is the establishment of a specialist youth hearing for young people aged 16 and 17 to remove them from adult criminal proceedings 'to bring Scotland into line with international conventions and to deal more appropriately and effectively' with them (p. 3). At the time of writing, the Scottish Government is still considering this recommendation alongside a decision on whether or not to continue the youth court pilots.

In the light of the new Council of Europe rules, the Scottish Prison Service moved swiftly to establish a dedicated unit, Blair House, in Polmont Young Offenders' Institution for young people aged 16 and 17. It remains to be seen how 'child centred' this regime will be and what special provision will be in place to recognise the status of these young people legally as 'children'.

Further support for recognising the status of young people under 18 as 'children' comes from High Court decisions in England. In 2002, the landmark judgment, *R (Howard League for Penal Reform) v Secretary of State for the Home Department and the Department of Health*, [2003] 1 FLR 484, put beyond doubt the fact that the Children Act 1989 applied to children in prison, and that social service departments are obliged to assess their needs while in custody and plan appropriately for their release. In July 2007, in a Court of Appeal decision in the case of J who was 15 when she committed the offence leading to her detention, three Law Lords confirmed the duty to provide her with the care due under s. 20 of the Children Act 1989. The judgment highlighted that young people aged 16 and 17 in detention should be viewed as children in need and that 'local authorities across the country are failing to provide proper assessments and care plans for vulnerable children (entering and leaving detention) where children are in danger of returning to precisely the same situations that led to their crimes and imprisonment in the first place' (Howard League for Penal Reform, 2007). Although not tested in Scotland, ss. 22 and 25 of the CA 1995 contain almost identical social work duties towards children in need and the provision of accommodation for them as the relevant sections of the 1989 Act. The judgment suggests that any social work assessment for this group should be a comprehensive one and conform to good child-care standards, as directed by *Getting it right for every child.*[5]

Youth justice in practice

Anyone can refer a child to the reporter. In practice, most offence referrals come from the police. In deciding whether or not to act, the reporter must consider that a young person may be in need of 'compulsory measures' to justify referral to a hearing and has powers to require social work reports and assessments to assist in that judgement. The vast majority of offence referrals to reporters are diverted from formal hearings, by doing very little other than communicating with parent/carers or by referring the young people back to social work to receive 'advice, guidance and assistance' under a 'voluntary agreement' as a form of early and preventive intervention under the CA 1995. This is consistent with the UNCRC principle of progressive universal responses. By diverting cases from hearings, the reporter and social worker have a crucial role in minimising the risk of 'net-widening', which can be associated with welfare-oriented systems.

Arrangements can be made with the agreement of parents and the young person to confiscate weapons, provide a letter of apology to victims, or agree to make restitution with the assistance of a voluntary agency. Other restorative practices including conferencing, while victim awareness programmes are available to reporters in many local authority areas, and legislation makes provision for reporters to give victims information on decision making and outcomes.

A hearing does not have the power to imprison, fine, order compensation or impose a community sentence. However, the disposals that are available to it include powers of compulsory supervision, with the power to attach a wide range of conditions and controls, including reparation and mediation, or attendance at offence-focused or educational programmes and out of home placement. Movement restriction conditions (MRC) – electronic tagging – can be ordered as part of supervision or as an alternative to secure accommodation, providing the criteria for secure accommodation are met (see below). An MRC cannot be imposed without a written social work plan covering the range of elements in the programme and how it will be delivered. Intensive support and monitoring (ISM) programmes, including tagging, can be ordered from social workers. MRCs and ISMs were introduced by s. 135 of the Antisocial Behaviour etc. (Scotland) Act 2004 (ASBA). There are major 'standards' inconsistencies between the hearing system and the criminal justice system, in that a 16/17-year-old can be released from a young offenders institution under home detention curfew (tagging) with no requirement for a social work support plan and package.

Residential conditions can also be required and may include confinement in secure (locked) accommodation. The criminal court can also order secure accommodation. A secure accommodation authorisation enables a young person to be placed and kept in secure accommodation within a specified residential establishment. The authorisation made by a hearing (or sheriff on appeal) may only be made in conjunction with compulsory measures. Two key conditions must be met before any authorisation can be granted – the risk of absconding and the risk to the child's welfare (that the child is likely to self-harm, or is likely to cause injury to another person). The hearing must be satisfied that the other options available, including an MRC, have been considered (see Secure Accommodation (Scotland) Regulations 1996, SI 1996/3255). Changes to practice in secure care are proposed following the review *Securing our Future Initiative: A Way Forward for Secure Care* (Scottish Government/COSLA, 2009a). Providing intensive individual and family services and minimising the use of secure accommodation or tagging require social workers to manage a difficult balance of care and control within the community.

Local authorities are legally required to give effect to hearing disposals. All children subject to compulsory measures will, in principle, have an allocated social worker responsible for supervision and, for example, individual and family work, crime-focused programmes and school-related work aimed at, among other things, reducing reoffending. Given its extensive powers to continue compulsory measures, the hearing must review all supervision requirements within a year or they automatically lapse. They cease 'to have effect ... on his attaining the age of 18 years' (s. 73(3) of the CA 1995). Young people and their parents can ask for a review, subject to conditions contained in s. 73(6) and the 'child, parents or relevant persons' have the right of appeal to the court against the decision of a hearing. The social worker can request a review at any time, particularly where 'breaches' of agreements have occurred, and this is crucial in modelling positive authority.

The hearings' powers of disposal, including secure care, are being updated by the Children's Hearings (Scotland) Bill 2010, with supervision requirements becoming compulsory supervision orders. Interim compulsory supervision orders are proposed for the first time. Despite the extensive powers given to social workers, the stated aim of the hearing and practice remains that of involving parents in a non-coercive way in order to 'strengthen, support and supplement ... the natural beneficial influences of the home and family' (Kilbrandon, 1964, para. 35).

Children's hearings cannot impose orders on parents. Parenting orders under the ASBA 2004 have never been used and social workers are expected to try and engage even the most difficult parents in the care and control of their young people. Models of social work practice supported by this approach include family conferencing and structured family work aimed at building human and social capital to assist young people to mature and desist from offending (see Whyte, 2008).

Local authorities have specific duties of 'after care' for anyone under 19 years who was looked after at any time after they ceased to be of school age (s. 29(1)) of the CA 1995). Local authorities are empowered to provide advice, guidance and assistance (s29(2)) for this same group when they are over 19 but less than 21 if they apply for it (see The Arrangements to Look After Children (Scotland) Regulations, 1996, as amended). Local authorities are also empowered to provide this same group with financial assistance, until they are 21, towards the expense of education and training and to make contributions towards accommodation and maintenance (s. 30 of the CA 1995). Good models of social work throughcare, maintaining change over time, are assumed in the structures of the system (see Whyte, 2008, Ch. 8).

Youth justice: future developments

Youth justice practice in Scotland is founded on developments identified in the review *It's a Criminal Waste: Stop Youth Crime Now* (Scottish Executive, 2000). The report concluded that the hearing system was, in principle, appropriate for dealing with young people right up to 18 involved in serious and persistent offences. However, social work practice still had to demonstrate its ability to deal with the most serious and persistent young offenders. Social work practice was considered not sufficiently crime focused or influenced by research evidence on effective practice. Public confidence in social workers' ability to care for and control the most difficult young people was said to be poor.

Dealing with Offending by Young People (Audit Scotland, 2002, 2007) identified that a disproportionate amount of resources were spent on running the system rather than on direct services for young people involved in persistent and serious offending. By 2007, following *Scotland's Action Programme to Reduce Youth Crime* (Scottish Executive, 2002), Audit Scotland found that funding had increased from £235m in 2000/01 to over £330m in 2005/06. However, the impact of the investment had not yet been demonstrated and local authorities had made limited progress on several key recommendations of the 2000 report, particularly in relation to integrated multidisciplinary approaches and performance/management information. On the positive side, all local authorities had appointed youth justice coordinators to contribute to strategic planning and service development, and specialist youth justice social workers.

Resulting developments mean that local authorities should have a multidisciplinary strategic group responsible for planning for young people who offend, within an integrated framework of children's services outlined within the *Getting it right for every child* programme. Youth justice coordinators and specialist youth justice teams or specialist social workers, generally located within children and family services, are responsible for day-to-day provision. In addition to the emphasis on diverting young people from the criminal justice system, prevention and early intervention have been improved by the development of pre-screening groups in most local authorities to divert children from hearings.

The report identified the need to establish a national resource to support research in practice, to assist improved models of practice and to expand the range of provision. The Criminal Justice Social Work Development Centre for Scotland,[6] a government-funded centre based in the University of Edinburgh, was remitted to support youth justice practice across Scotland. In 2010, a national youth justice practice team was established within the Criminal Justice Social Work Development Centre for Scotland to provide direct support to youth justice coordinators, specialist youth justice social workers and managers and to develop good practice guidance.

The Scottish Government's *Reducing Reoffending* strategy (2006) provides an overarching framework for criminal and youth justice across children's hearings and criminal justice. The Youth Justice Programme Implementation Board is responsible for establishing and implementing a joint multidisciplinary framework for reducing offending and reoffending by young people involved in serious offending. The intention is that this and the work of the National Youth Justice Strategy Group, which focuses on younger children involved in offending, will set out a joint vision of what national and local agencies should do to prevent, divert, manage risk and support behaviour change with children and young people who offend, or who are at risk of offending.

These developments are intended to encourage better ways of working that aim to ensure agencies can provide children and young people who offend with the help they need to turn their lives around, achieving long-term benefits for them and the communities in which they live. There is a growing focus on improving practice with young people involved in violence and sexually harmful behaviour. New protocols are being developed between Multi-agency Public Protection Arrangements and child protection procedures for young people involved in sexual or violent offending dealt with through the hearing system. (For a detailed discussion on risk and need assessment and the use of standardised tools in practice, see Whyte, 2008, Ch. 4.)

These young people present major control issues for social work. However, the use of secure accommodation and custody has shown no good outcomes in worldwide research and almost all young people struggle and present major risks on their return to the community. The role of intensive support, electronic monitoring and 'wrap around' using people rather than buildings to provide 'security' for young people remains a significant social work practice challenge for the future.

A series of policy documents are intended to be harmonised with the expectations of the childcare framework outlined under the *Getting it right for every child* programme. These include *Preventing Offending by Young People: A Framework for Action* (Scottish Government, 2008b), which focuses on:

- prevention
- early and effective intervention
- managing high risk
- victims and community confidence
- planning and performance improvement.

Meeting Need, Managing Risk and Achieving Outcomes (Scottish Government, 2009b) focuses on responding effectively to the needs of a small but significant number of children and young people who present a risk of serious harm to themselves and others, and who have complex needs, including children and young people involved in sexually harmful behaviour, sexual offences and violence. *Promoting Positive Outcomes: Working Together to Prevent Antisocial Behaviour in Scotland* (Scottish Government/COSLA, 2009b) provides an updated framework for preventing antisocial behaviour, playing down some of the more punitive and enforcement-focused policies of the previous government.

Scotland's distinctive approach to youth justice continues to change and develop. There has never been a more challenging time to be a youth justice social worker. The politicised nature of practice, ambivalence towards young people in general, the demonisation of those who break the law, and a lack of public confidence sit alongside increased international demands for child-centred and rights-based approaches as effective responses to reducing and preventing offending by young people.

References

Angiolini, E. (2010) *Lord Advocate's Guidelines to Chief Constables Reporting to Procurators Fiscal of Offences Alleged to Have Been Committed by Children: Revised Categories of Offences*, available online at www.copfs.gov.uk/Resource/Doc/7/0000608.pdf [accessed 9 July 2010].

Audit Scotland (2002) *Dealing with Offending by Young People: Main Report*, available online at www.audit-scotland.gov.uk/docs/central/2002/nr_021204_youth_justice.pdf [accessed 9 July 2010].

Audit Scotland (2007) *Dealing with Offending by Young People*, available online at www.audit-scotland.gov.uk/docs/central/2007/nr_070823_youth_justice_update.pdf [accessed 9 July 2010].

Braithwaite, J. (1989) *Crime, Shame and Reintegration*, Cambridge, Cambridge University Press.

Cowperthwaite, D. (1985) *The Emergence of the Scottish Children's Hearings system: An Administrative/Political Study of the Establishment of Novel Arrangements in Scotland for Dealing with Juvenile Offenders 1960–1982*, Southampton, University of Southampton.

Howard League for Penal Reform (2007) Howard League Hails Court of Appeal Victory, Press Release, available online at www.howardleague.org/fileadmin/howard_league/user/pdf/Press_2007/Howarrd_League_hails_Court_of_Appeal_Victory_26_July_2007.pdf [accessed 9 July 2010].

Improving the Effectiveness of the Youth Justice System Group (2002) *National Standard for Scotland's Youth Justice Services*, available online at www.scottishthroughcare.org.uk/docs/policy/National_Standards_for_Youth_Justice_Services. pdf [accessed 30 June 2010].

Kilbrandon, C.S. (1964) *Report of the Committee on Children and Young Persons, Scotland*, (Kilbrandon Report), Cmnd 2306, available online at www.scotland.gov.uk/Resource/Doc/47049/0023863.pdf [accessed 12 July 2010].

McAra, L. and McVie, S. (2007) 'Youth justice? The impact of system contact on patterns of desistance from offending', *European Journal of Criminology*, 4(3): 315–45.

Martin, F., Fox, S.J. and Murray, K. (1981) *Children out of Court*, Edinburgh, Scottish Academic Press.

Moore, G. and Whyte, B. (1997) *Social Work and Criminal Law*, Edinburgh, Mercat Press.

OHCHR (Office of the United Nations Commissioner for Human Rights) (1989) *Convention on the Rights of the Child*, available online at www2.ohchr.org/english/law/crc.htm. [accessed 12 July 2010].

R (Howard League for Penal Reform) v Secretary of State for the Home Department and the Department of Health (interested party) [2002] EWHC 2497 (Admin), 29 November 2002; [2003] 1 FLR 484, paras 10 and 11.

Scottish Executive (2000) *Its a Criminal Waste: Stop Youth Crime Now: Report of Advisory Group on Youth Crime*, available online at www.scotland.gov.uk/youth/crimereview/docs/agyc-00.asp [accessed 9 July 2010].

Scottish Executive (2002) *Scotland's Action Programme to Reduce Youth Crime 2002*, available online at www.scotland.gov.uk/Resource/Doc/158894/0043162.pdf [accessed 30 June 2010].

Scottish Government (2006) *Reducing Reoffending: National Strategy for the Management of Offenders*, available online at www.scotland.gov.uk/Publications/ 2006/05/19094327/0 [accessed 9 July 2010].

Scottish Government (2008a) *Improving the Lives of Children in Scotland – Are We There Yet?: Consultation on the Scottish Government's Response to the 2008 Concluding Observations from the UN Committee on the Rights of the Child*, available online at www.scotland.gov.uk/Publications/2008/12/ 18090842/0 [accessed 9 July 2010].

Scottish Government (2008b) *Preventing Offending by Young People: A Framework for Action*, available online at www.scotland.gov.uk/Publications/ 2008/06/ 17093513/0 [accessed 9 July 2010].

Scottish Government (2009a) *UN Convention on the Rights of the Child: Scottish Government's Detailed Response to the UN Committee's 2008 Concluding Observations*, available online at www.scotland.gov.uk/Publications/2009/10/ 28095627/3 [accessed 30 June 2010].

Scottish Government (2009b) *Getting it right for children and young people who present a risk of serious harm: Meeting Need, Managing Risk and Achieving Outcomes*, available online at www.scotland.gov.uk/Publications/ 2008/05/16160941/0 [accessed 9 July 2010].

Scottish Government (2010) *Statistical Bulletin: Crime and Justice Series: Criminal Proceedings in Scottish Courts, 2008–9*, available online at www. scotland.gov.uk/Publications/2010/03/03114034/0 [accessed 9 July 2010].

Scottish Government Community Justice Services Division (2010) *Review of the Hamilton and Airdrie Youth Courts: Report*, available online at www. scotland.gov.uk/Publications/2009/12/09093018/0 [accessed 9 July 2010].

Scottish Government/COSLA (Convention of Scottish Local Authorities) (2007) *Concordat between the Scottish Government and Local Government*, available online at www.scotland.gov.uk/Publications/2007/11/13092240/ concordat [accessed 20 June 2010].

Scottish Government/COSLA (Convention of Scottish Local Authorities) (2009a) *Securing our Future Initiative: A Way Forward for Scotland's Secure Care Estate: A Response from the Scottish Government and COSLA*, available online at www.scotland.gov.uk/Publications/2009/04/23163903/0 [accessed 9 July 2010].

Scottish Government/COSLA (Convention of Scottish Local Authorities) (2009b) *Promoting Positive Outcomes: Working Together to Prevent Antisocial Behaviour in Scotland*, vol. 1, available online at www.scotland.gov. uk/Publications/2009/03/18112243/0 [accessed 9 July 2010].

Scottish Prisons Commission (2008) *Scotland's Choice: Report of the Scottish Prisons Commission*, available online at www.scotland.gov.uk/Publications/ 2008/06/30162955/0 [accessed 9 July 2010].

SCRA (Scottish Children's Reporter Administration) (2010) *Joint Agreement in Relation to the Cases of Children Jointly Reported to the Procurator Fiscal*

and Children's Reporter, available online at www.copfs.gov.uk/Resource/
Doc/13547/0000614.pdf [accessed 9 July 2010].

Smith, M. and Whyte, B. (2008) 'Social education and social pedagogy:
reclaiming a Scottish tradition in social work', *European Journal of Social
Work*, **11**(1): 15–28.

SWSG (Social Work Services Group) (2004) *Scotland's Children: The Children (Scotland) Act 1995 Regulations and Guidance*, vol. 2, *Children
Looked After by Local Authorities*, available online at www.scotland.gov.
uk/Publications/2004/10/20067/44747 [accessed 9 July 2010].

UN Committee on the Rights of the Child (1995) *Concluding Observations:
United Kingdom of Great Britain and Northern Ireland*.

UN Committee on the Rights of the Child (2002) *Concluding Observations:
United Kingdom of Great Britain and Northern Ireland*.

UN Committee on the Rights of the Child (2008) *Concluding Observations:
United Kingdom of Great Britain and Northern Ireland*, available online at
www.unhcr.org/refworld/publisher,CRC,CONCOBSERVATIONS,GBR,0.
html [accessed 12 July 2010].

Ward, T. and Maruna, S. (2007) *Rehabilitation: Key Ideas in Criminology*,
Oxford, Routledge.

Waterhouse, L., McGhee, J., Whyte, B. et al. (2000) *The Evaluation of Children's Hearings in Scotland*, vol. 3, *Children in Focus*, Edinburgh, Scottish
Executive Central Research Unit.

Whyte, B. (2008) *Youth Justice in Practice*, Bristol, Policy Press.

Notes

1. http://book.coe.int/EN/ficheouvrage.php?PAGEID=36&lang=EN&produit_
   aliasid=2447.
2. http://www.coe.int/t/dghl/standardsetting/childjustice/default_en.asp.
3. https://wcd.coe.int/ViewDoc.jsp?id=1575813&Site=CM&BackColorInternet=
   C3C3C3&BackColorIntranet=EDB021&BackColorLogged=F5D383.
4. http://www.cep-probation.org/default.asp?page_id=65&news_item=256.
5. See information about the *Getting it right for every child* programme at http://
   www.scotland.gov.uk/Topics/People/Young-People/childrensservices/girfec.
6. See information about the Criminal Justice Social Work Development Centre
   for Scotland at http://www.cjsw.ac.uk/.

Chapter 12

Adult Criminal Justice

TRISH McCULLOCH AND FERGUS McNEILL

Introduction

Crime and justice in Scotland continue to occupy a prominent and often contentious position in public and political spheres. On one level, and in common with developments in other jurisdictions, recent penal developments in Scotland can be seen to reflect late modern preoccupations with risk, punishment and control. Yet, at the same time, Scotland maintains an explicit and well-defended commitment to the welfare, social inclusion and integration of all citizens, including those who offend; a commitment which, even in the recent past, it has had to defend on a national and global level.

Upon this embattled landscape stand Scotland's exceptionally high prison rates (and associated costs) and its persistently troubling reoffending figures. Once again, these problems have converged to place due and mounting pressure on government to develop and promote new and improved ways of meeting the challenges that are crime and its control. Criminal justice social workers practising in this context face a challenging and engaging task. In this chapter, we seek to examine that task with a view to illuminating both the 'what' and the 'how' of contemporary professional practice. We begin by mapping out the distinctive and changing terrain of contemporary criminal justice social work, giving attention to its position within broader judicial, political and societal contexts. We then consider the social work tasks that arise in three key areas, the provision of services to the court, the supervision of community sentences, and the delivery of prisoner throughcare and resettlement. Finally, attention is given to the emerging research evidence relating to each of the above areas and to the implications of that for effective practice.

Criminal justice social work in context

Scotland's criminal justice system has long been recognised for its distinctive nature, traditions and practice (Young, 1997). Typically, commentators draw attention to the 'common law' nature of Scottish criminal law and the pivotal and discretionary role played by prosecutors and sentencers in the criminal justice process. While opinions vary as to the virtues or otherwise of these traditions, most agree that each brings a level of flexibility and discretion to Scottish justice, which sets it apart from the judicial practices of many other jurisdictions.

As McNeill and Whyte (2007) noted, Scotland's arrangements for the supervision of offenders in the community are equally distinctive. In contrast to the rest of the UK, responsibility for providing offender services to the criminal justice system, in the form of assessment, supervision and throughcare of offenders, continues to rest with local authority social work departments. For the past two decades, this has typically been delivered via specialist criminal justice social work teams who, under the directives of *National Objectives and Standards for Social Work Services in the Criminal Justice System* (SWSG, 1991), are tasked to deliver a range of services and schemes. For those less familiar with recent penal developments in this country and beyond, this configuration of criminal justice services is significant and attests to Scotland's long-standing commitment to the promotion of social welfare within Scottish justice.

It is conventional to date both the local authority-based organisation of criminal justice social work and its social welfare ideology to the Kilbrandon reforms enshrined in the Social Work (Scotland) Act 1968. However, the Scottish probation services that were formally established by the Probation (Scotland) Act 1931 were always coterminous with council boundaries rather than sheriffdoms (see Morison, 1962; McNeill, 2005). Equally importantly, the development of penal welfarism has deeper roots and a longer history (Garland, 1985).

Shortly after the Kilbrandon reforms, by the late 1970s, academic and professional commentators were bemoaning the demise of Scottish probation within the generic departments (Marsland, 1977; Moore, 1978). That said, the late 1970s did augur in community service, perhaps the most significant innovation in criminal justice social work since the probation order itself. The Community Service by Offenders (Scotland) Act 1978 introduced the community service order and by 1986 it was available in 50 courts. Because its further expansion was hampered by the vagaries of diverse local authority-based funding arrangements throughout the country, central Scottish Office funding followed in 1989, linked to national objectives and standards. This became a model for all social work services in the criminal justice system two years later (SWSG, 1991).

The incentives that prompted the then Scottish Office to pursue these reforms are remarkably similar to those that concern today's Scottish

Government, but in the 1980s, prison overcrowding was associated not just with high fiscal costs but also with adverse media coverage related to prison riots and prison suicides. The first objective in the new national standards was 'to enable a reduction in the use of custody ... where it is used for lack of a suitable, available community based social work disposal' (SWSG, 1991, s. 12.1). However, the standards were also premised on the view that reducing the use of custody required improvement in the credibility of community-based disposals, and that signalled the importance of enhancing the effectiveness of practice in reducing reoffending (see below). In this respect, the standards also signified and enshrined a recalibration of the underlying ideology of criminal justice social work. As Paterson and Tombs (1998) noted, they implied a 'responsibility model' – a sort of hybrid of welfare and justice – where offenders were to be held to account for their offending choices, but those choices were to be understood as being situated in particular personal and social contexts.

However, by the late 1990s, in Scotland as in several other jurisdictions, public protection was emerging as the dominant purpose of or metanarrative for probation work (see Robinson and McNeill, 2004). By the time of the publication of *Community Penalties: The Tough Option* (Scottish Office, 1998), the minister responsible declared that 'Our paramount aim is public safety' (s. 1.2). A plethora of reports, guidance documents and revision to the national standards reflected these important changes in emphasis (for a full discussion, see McIvor and McNeill, 2007; Weaver and McNeill, 2010).

Following the devolution settlement and the establishment of the Scottish Parliament in 1999, the pace of change in Scottish criminal justice and youth justice has been unrelenting. Under the Labour–Liberal Democrat coalitions that were in government between 1999 and 2007, the ironic effect of devolution was a 'detartanisation' of Scottish criminal justice (McAra, 2008), as many of the ideas and programmes of the UK's New Labour government filtered north from Westminster to Holyrood. Perhaps most significantly for criminal justice social work, the Labour Party manifesto in the 2003 election proposed the establishment of a single correctional service, removing criminal justice social work from local authorities and combining it with the Scottish Prison Service in a single agency. In the face of strong opposition to these plans, the Labour–Liberal Democrat coalition introduced instead the Management of Offenders (Scotland) Act 2005, which established eight Community Justice Authorities, charging them with the task of developing strategic plans with their key partners (the police, courts, prosecution, prison, victims' organisations, health boards and others) to reduce reoffending (see McNeill and Whyte, 2007).

If the focus on protecting the public by reducing reoffending through offender management had signalled a detartanisation of Scottish criminal justice social work, then the election of a minority Scottish National Party administration in 2007 perhaps has allowed (predictably) for its potential retartanisation. From the outset, the SNP Government had a different approach (required by its minority position). The key documents produced since 2007 are *Reforming and Revitalising: Report of the Review of Community Penalties* (Scottish Government, 2007), *Scotland's Choice* (Scottish Prisons Commission, 2008), the government response *Protecting Scotland's Communities: Fair, Fast and Flexible Justice* (Scottish Government, 2008) and the Criminal Justice and Licensing (Scotland) Act 2010. Although none of these dispenses with protecting the public through reducing reoffending as part of the purpose of punishment, collectively they attest to the emergence of an increasing emphasis on reparation – offenders paying back for their crimes.

For example, the central message of the Scottish Prisons Commission's (2008, p. 3) report can be found in its first two recommendations:

1. To better target imprisonment and make it more effective, the Commission recommends that imprisonment should be reserved for people whose offences are so serious that no other form of punishment will do and for those who pose a significant threat of serious harm to the public.
2. To move beyond our reliance on imprisonment as a means of punishing offenders, the Commission recommends that paying back in the community should become the default position in dealing with less serious offenders.

The commission's remedy for Scotland's overconsumption of imprisonment centres on a range of measures that it considers necessary to enact its second recommendation. The concept of 'payback' is defined as follows:

In essence, payback means finding constructive ways to compensate or repair harms caused by crime. It involves making good to the victim and/or the community. This might be through financial payment, unpaid work, engaging in rehabilitative work or some combination of these and other approaches. Ultimately, one of the best ways for offenders to pay back is by turning their lives around. (Scottish Prisons Commission, 2008, para. 3.28)

Several ways of paying back are identified – through restorative justice practices, financial penalties, unpaid work, restriction of liberty and, perhaps most interestingly in this context, through 'paying back by working at change'. Working at change, in turn, is linked to engagement in a wide range of activities that might seem likely to address the issues underlying offending behaviour. Notably, the notion of paying back by turning one's life around represents a neat, if underdeveloped, reframing of engagement in rehabilitation as an act of reparation.

The government's response to the commission's proposals is contained in the Criminal Justice and Licensing (Scotland) Act 2010. Among the measures is the introduction of a single 'community payback order', which is intended to replace or subsume most current community disposals, allowing sentencers to determine which particular conditions (or forms of payback) are appropriate in individual cases. As has been suggested elsewhere (McNeill, 2009), the concept of 'payback' is one with which criminal justice social work must now engage. Under the new Act, it will lie as much with social work practitioners as with policy makers to give real meaning to the concept, and in order to avoid the development of the concept and the order in ways that are inimical to the best of criminal justice social work's traditions and values, it is vital to populate the notion of payback positively.

In summary, for decades, criminal justice social work has pursued three purposes: reduction in the use of custody; public protection through reduced reoffending; and the rehabilitation and social inclusion of offenders (McNeill et al., 2005). Although one or other of these purposes has tended to be given priority, most policy documents tend to recognise their interdependence. But now, there is a 'new kid on the block' – reparation (or payback) – and it falls to criminal justice social work to determine where and how it fits with these existing and enduring priorities.

Criminal justice social work in practice

The above discussion sets out the shifting purposes and contexts of contemporary criminal justice social work. The attending question then is 'what does this mean in practice?' or, put more precisely, 'what is it that criminal justice social workers do?' In this section, we provide an overview of the criminal justice social work task as it occurs in three key areas.

Services to the court

Social workers are routinely involved in the provision of advice, information and services that can assist the criminal court in sentencing. Social workers also have a duty to provide services for offenders and their families, victims and witnesses while attending court. The range of duties associated with these tasks are detailed within the *National Objectives for Social Work Services within the Criminal Justice System* (Scottish Executive, 2004, para. 8) and include, for example, dealing with requests for reports, interviewing offenders pre and post sentence and liaising with other professional groups.

Among the many duties in this area, the provision of 'reports' (known as social enquiry reports in Scotland) occupies a critical part of the sentencing process and, as such, the social work task. National standards identify the purpose of social enquiry reports as being:

> to assist sentencing. They provide information about offenders and their circumstances of general relevance to the courts. On the basis of a risk and needs assessment, they also advise the courts on the suitability of offenders for those community based disposals. (Scottish Executive, 2004, para. 1.2)

The above standard usefully highlights the core functions of social enquiry reports. It also, importantly, identifies the process at the heart of that activity, that is, assessment. In a professional climate where the practice of 'report writing' (as it is most commonly referred to) has become increasingly standardised and fragmented (Robinson, 2003; Gorman, 2006), the relationship between social enquiry practice and professional assessment is easily eroded. In part, this reflects broader global trends affecting public service provision – including, for example, the rise of managerialism – however, it also reflects the particular content and context of criminal justice social work practice, features of which present particular challenges to the practice of social enquiry.

For example, McNeill and Whyte (2007) highlight the long-standing tension of defining the social work 'client' in the social enquiry process, the often conflicting expectations of sentencers, offenders, victims and other stakeholders, and the inevitable tensions that arise in operating at the intersection of two systems with intrinsically different ideological bases. Others draw attention to the impact of wider penal trends on the development of social enquiry and pre-sentence reports (as they are known in England and Wales). For example, Nash (2003) and Gelsthorpe et al. (2010) highlight significant changes in the purpose, focus and content of pre-sentence report writing in recent years, changes that both observe are best understood in the context of 'changing representations of offenders against a backdrop of late modern moves towards risk thinking, managerialism and populist punitiveness' (Gelsthorpe et al., 2010, p. 1). Reviewing similar trends, Gorman (2006) charted what he considers to be the progressive sacrifice of individualised assessment, narrative skill and professional autonomy to an increasingly depersonalised, automated and hyper-regulated report-writing practice. Robinson's (2005) analysis raises similar concerns and presents a vision of offender management in which the process of assessment increasingly resembles an assembly-line process, where the principal task becomes one of 'sifting' and 'sorting' the typically messy narrative that emerges from the offending subject. While this process may make for a more efficient progression to the next stage of 'correction', it is a process that appears much less conducive to meaningful progression for offenders.

Assuming, then, that social enquiry practice, and the process of assessment within that, is, at least in part, seeking to inform effective and meaningful progression for offenders (via appropriate and effective judicial decision making), it is imperative that those engaged in this task do so with a clear sense of purpose. Moreover, in the current trend towards standardised and technicist approaches to professional assessment, there is a need, perhaps now more than ever, for workers to engage in that purpose with a critical appreciation of the research evidence that underpins effective assessment (see below).

Community sentences

At the time of writing, social work's role in the supervision of community sentences and disposals occurs in various forms. For example, social workers may have a role in supporting diversion from prosecution by supporting access to relevant support services. Social workers are directly responsible for the supervision of probation orders, in the form of standard probation, probation with requirements, and intensive probation. Social workers are also involved in supporting community-based reparation and mediation measures, whether in the form of unpaid work, restorative justice or community reparation orders.

While it looks likely that the nomenclature surrounding the social work role and task in this area is set to change, it remains to be seen to what extent this most recent reconfiguration of services, if enacted, will alter and impact on the day-to-day practice of community sentences. For the time being, it is reasonable to assume that the three enduring purposes long associated with criminal justice social work – currently headlining with the goal of public protection through reduced reoffending – will continue to dictate both the what and the how of practice in this area, albeit with an enhanced attention to reparation. In day-to-day practice, then, and in various guises, this can helpfully be translated into three core and interactive tasks:

1. The nurturing and development of worker–offender relationships capable of supporting offenders to engage and comply with imposed orders.

2. The development and enactment, in partnership with the offender, of an individualised action plan capable of supporting and sustaining change, for example via the targeting of assessed needs, risks and strengths.
3. The regular review of activities towards an improved targeting of resources, service delivery and approach.

Of course, how workers and offenders go about the above tasks is appropriately varied, influenced as it is by a myriad of factors, including, for example, the individual offender, the worker's experience, values and beliefs, professional and organisational directives, and research evidence. However, as a baseline, it is reasonable to suggest that if workers are morally and practically engaged in these processes, there is scope for optimism regarding what can be achieved.

Prisoner throughcare and resettlement

Prisoner throughcare and resettlement refers to the provision of a range of social work and associated services to prisoners and their families from the point of sentence or remand, during the period of imprisonment, and following release into the community (Scottish Executive, 2004). In practice, this typically consists of two elements: pre-release work in prison and post-release supervision in the community.

When one considers this task in the current context, that is, a context of escalating prison numbers, unacceptable reoffending rates and frequently asserted commitments to curtail the 'revolving door' of custody, it would be reasonable to expect the area of throughcare and resettlement to occupy pole position in the line-up of criminal justice social work provision. Indeed, in 2005/06, nearly three-quarters of prisoners released from a short sentence (6 months or less) were reconvicted and over half (54%) returned to prison on a custodial sentence (Scottish Government, 2009). If these statistics were not disturbing enough, research studies consistently highlight the high level of (unmet) personal, social and psychological needs presented by prisoners upon release (Haines, 1990; Vanstone, 2007).

Notwithstanding this, until recently, throughcare provision has found itself on the margins of criminal justice social work services, with policy and practice efforts variously described as patchy, poorly developed, and failing to meet basic resettlement needs (McIvor and Barry, 1998; McIvor and McNeill, 2007; Munro and McNeill, 2010). Partly in response to this troubling picture, recent penal developments in Scotland have placed increasing emphasis on the role of throughcare and resettlement in achieving broader governmental objectives of public protection and reduced reoffending. In turn, a range of new provisions has been proposed and established, including, for example, new arrangements and priorities for partnership working in throughcare, new measures to secure 'end-to-end' sentence management of offenders, and enhanced provisions for the supervision and surveillance of prisoners on release, with particular attention to arrangements for sexual and violent offenders.

Professional and academic responses to recent developments have been mixed. On the one hand, there has been broad support for what has been seen as the long overdue revival of throughcare as a now fundamental feature of government efforts to promote public protection. On the other hand, legitimate concerns have been raised regarding the associated costs of new initiatives (Tata, 2007), the perceived ratcheting up of surveillance practices over an ever-expanding post-release population (Munro and McNeill, 2010), and the inevitable tensions that arise in seeking to balance public protection and risk management priorities with questions of justice and rights (Tata, 2007).

Whatever one's view – and to some extent we are, again, in a 'wait and see' position as many of the new provisions remain in a formative phase – social work's role in this fast-changing landscape remains pivotal and will almost certainly expand. For example, we can expect to see a much enhanced role for social work in the assessment of prisoners – as an ongoing feature of sentence management. There are already more explicit expectations in respect of joint planning and partnership working. And the increasingly varied demands made of social work in terms of post-release supervision look set to increase considerably. Yet, amid this state of flux, there is much that remains the same. The overall aim of the service remains intact, that is, to assist prisoners to reduce their risk of reoffending and to help them resettle and reintegrate within the community. Moreover, the recognised 'processes' by which that can be achieved remain consistent with the core activities identified above in relation to community sentences (Vanstone, 2007). Further, the shifting, complex and morally challenging environment in which social workers are required to undertake this task is one that workers are more than accustomed to. As we face the challenge of delivering effective throughcare in an unfolding and uncertain terrain, we can perhaps take comfort from the fact that success will most likely be achieved through practices marked by both continuity and change.

Research evidence

As we turn to consider the research evidence currently informing criminal justice social work practice, it goes without saying that a comprehensive review of the research in this area is beyond the scope of this chapter. For a fuller discussion, readers are directed to McNeill (2009) and Ward and Maruna's (2007) work in this area. For our purposes here, we seek simply to provide a brief overview of promising approaches in offender assessment and supervision.

Assessing risk, needs and strengths

Over the past two decades, effective assessment in criminal justice social work, and offender management more broadly, has become firmly associated with a 'risk/needs' approach to assessment and intervention. Informed by the work of Andrews and Bonta (1994, 1995), this approach involves the use of standardised assessment tools – used in conjunction with professional judgement – to enable practitioners to arrive at a prediction of an offender's future 'risk of reoffending' and 'risk of harm' (Kemshall, 1996). The process also involves the identification of offence-related ('criminogenic') needs and, ideally, attention to how motivated offenders are to address identified needs and risks. Much has since been written about the use, merits and limitations of this approach to assessment and space does not permit detailed coverage here. To summarise, it is now widely acknowledged that standardised risk/need assessment tools, when used alongside professional judgement, can greatly enhance the process and quality of assessment and decision making in criminal justice practice. Not surprisingly, however, research also documents a number of associated problems and pitfalls. Specifically, existing studies highlight the considerable demands of such an approach on practitioners' time (Robinson, 2003), the potential for discrimination of minority groups (Hannah-Moffat, 2005), an overpresentation of negatives and deficits (Ward and Maruna, 2007), and an approach to assessment that is potentially mechanical, stereotyped and distancing.

As we look to research then, arguably the challenge of effective assessment practice only broadens. Perhaps this is to be welcomed. Our discussion of assessment began by tracing a trend in social enquiry towards an increasingly technicised task. Attention to the related research evidence indicates that this is one potential outcome of practice developments in this area. However, the above discussion also highlights that the development of structured approaches to assessment can offer benefits when used appropriately. As we continue to grapple with the many and varied demands of effective assessment in criminal justice social work, it is perhaps prudent to appraise and apply recent research evidence in the context of the broader knowledge and research base informing effective assessment practice. It is a research base that routinely highlights that assessment is a process not a task, the importance of relationship and partnership in that process (Burnett and McNeill, 2005; McCulloch, 2005), and the importance of engaging in thoroughly individualised and contextualised assessments of risk, needs and strengths (Milner and O'Byrne, 2009).

Offender supervision: what's promising in reducing reoffending?

The rise of public protection and reduced reoffending as the bold new headline for criminal justice social work has done much to focus research attention on the means by which that goal can be achieved. However, despite the substantial progress that has been made in this area, research, policy and practice continue to highlight that our understanding of, and efforts towards, effective practice remains a work in progress. In part, this reflects the multifactorial nature of crime and its causes, a feature which should remind us that the challenge of reducing reoffending in practice is considerable. Yet, acknowledging this challenge, we also know that most offenders, including many persistent offenders, do give up crime, despite the many needs they have and the many obstacles they face. With this in mind, we turn now to consider current evidence about the means of effective offender supervision, that is, the practices and processes shown to be most promising in assisting individuals to achieve reduced reoffending, desistance and, ultimately, a good life. Our discussion focuses on three promising approaches, that of the risk-need-responsivity model, desistance-focused practice, and the good lives model.

The risk-need-responsivity (RNR) model is associated principally with the work of Canadian correctional psychologists Don Andrews, Jim Bonta, Paul Gendreau and Robert Ross. The most prominent of the models considered here, RNR has underpinned most policy and practice developments that have come to be associated with the 'what works' movement of the past two decades. By way of summary, McNeill (2009, p. 24) provides a basic outline:

> The RNR principles are that levels of service should be proportionate to the level of assessed risk (high risk individuals require the most intensive intervention); that treatment should be focussed on changing criminogenic needs (these being dynamic factors which, when changed, are associated with reduced recidivism); and that the style and mode of the intervention should engage the offender and suit his or her learning style and cognitive abilities. These three principles require the development of comprehensive and validated assessment instruments to guide assessment and intervention and the development of treatment programmes that are highly structured, cognitive behavioural in orientation, implemented by well trained and supported

staff, delivered with integrity, based on manuals, and located in organisations committed to rehabilitation in general and programmes in particular.

As the above approach has been 'tried and tested' over the past two decades, there is evidence to suggest that offenders supervised in accordance with RNR principles are more likely to desist. However, there is also considerable evidence – much of which emerges from implementation studies – pointing to its limitations. Reviewing this evidence, Ward and Maruna (2007) conclude that it may not be that RNR is at fault in targeting risk, need and responsivity, but rather that the targeting of risk may be a necessary but not a sufficient condition for reducing reoffending. The authors go on to suggest that to accommodate differences among offenders, a 'specific case formulation' is required, rather than too generalised an application of the principles. Part of the task, then, is not just to identify risk and needs, but to work out, case by case, how risk and needs interact to influence offending in specific contexts and, from such an understanding, how risk and needs can be best addressed. This conclusion resonates with the findings of other studies, which point to a need to also attend to the broader processes and outcomes of change interventions, including, for example, the construction of helping relationships, the dynamics of motivation and compliance, and the importance of recognising broader rewards and reasons for change (McCulloch and McNeill, 2008). Of course, there is an unavoidable tension here, insofar as RNR centres on a belief in 'targeted', 'structured' and often 'standardised' approaches to intervention, while its critics point to the need for a broader, more subjective and more contextualised approach to change.

The desistance literature exists less as a model of intervention and more as a paradigm for understanding and supporting the change processes involved in desisting from crime, that is, ending offending. By way of summary, Maruna (2001) identifies three broad theoretical perspectives in the desistance literature: maturational reform, social bonds theory, and narrative theory. Respectively, these perspectives address how desistance relates to age and maturity, to social ties and social bonds, and to changing personal identities. Bringing these perspectives together, Farrall (2002, p. 11) stressed the significance of the relationships between 'objective' changes in the offender's life and their 'subjective' assessment of the value or significance of these changes:

> the desistance literature has pointed to a range of factors associated with the ending of active involvement in offending. Most of these factors are related to acquiring 'something' (most commonly employment, a life partner or a family) which the desister values in some way and which initiates a re-valuation of his or her own life.

Rather than the three perspectives competing, desistance is seen to reside somewhere in the interfaces between developing personal maturity, changing social bonds associated with certain life transitions, and the individual subjective narrative constructions (or personal stories) that offenders build around these key events and changes. Put simply, it is not just the events and changes that matter, it is what these events and changes mean to the people involved.

The implications for practice of this developing evidence base have begun to be explored in a small number of studies that have focused on the role that probation or social work may play in supporting desistance. For example, Rex (1999) and others underline the importance of strong relationships between offenders and their supervisors, characterised by mutual respect, loyalty and commitment. Other studies point to the importance of offenders' own resources and networks in resolving problems and supporting change (Farrall, 2002; McCulloch, 2005). Reflecting something of a renaissance in attention to the social contexts of persistence and desistance, each of these studies suggest that, in addition to addressing individual decision making, motivation and reasoning skills (also known as 'human capital'), interventions must pay greater heed to the community, social and personal contexts (or social capital) in which they take place. Necessarily, this requires a decentring of the offending subject – or, more precisely, their perceived deficits – in favour of an attention to the broader social contexts and conditions required to support and sustain change. Farrall (2002, p. 214) puts this point more directly and identifies the need to now 'conceptualise probation intervention as being aimed at altering some aspect of an individual's social and personal circumstances'. While this point may seem obvious to those practising within a Scottish context, recent practice developments suggest it is a point worth restating.

The good lives model (GLM) represents a relatively recent development in offender supervision (Ward and Brown, 2004; Ward and Marshall, 2004) and is an approach to practice that focuses less on offender deficits and more on a holistic and strengths-based approach to individuals and their change process. The basic principle underpinning GLM is that each of us, including those who offend, are predisposed to seek certain goals or 'primary human goods' (including life, knowledge, excellence in play and work, agency or autonomy, friendship, community) and typically do so via the means available to us. The means by which we achieve these goals are known as 'secondary goods' and might include certain types of work, networks or relationships. In light of our preceding discussion around desistance (in particular the necessity of attending to the interplay between human and social capital), this conception of human behaviour and human agency is particularly resonant and raises a number of implications for offender supervision. The principal implication is that interventions seeking to promote desistance or a 'good life' should aim to promote an individual's good as well as to manage and reduce risk. There is, of course, a necessary balance here. As McNeill (2009, p. 27) noted, too strong a focus on personal goods may produce a happy but dangerous offender, while too strong a focus on risk may produce a dangerously defiant or disengaged offender. The task for the worker is to create a change relationship in which the individual offender is recognised, valued and respected and through which individual (change) priorities can be jointly established and pursued in line with their life plans, associated risk factors and life capacities.

Ward and Maruna's (2007) evaluation of the GLM cited a wealth of empirical evidence to support this approach to practice. However, the authors are also quick to acknowledge that, thus far, 'there is a paucity of specific correctional programs that have been explicitly developed with GLM in mind' (Ward and Maruna, 2007, p. 171). Certainly, there are a number of questions that might be asked about the GLM in the Scottish context. For example, are the primary human goods cited as universal, as the model suggests? Further, are today's workers in a position to negotiate and support the 'person-centred' priorities associated with the pursuit of a 'good life'? These questions and others now need to come to the fore as the GLM is more fully tested in the contexts in which change efforts take place. Certainly, there is much within the GLM that offers an antidote to some of the limitations associated with RNR and the correctional climate currently dominating practice. However, there is also much within its core values and principles that will inevitably make its implementation in that same climate challenging.

If the above discussion of promising approaches in the field of offender supervision feels like a challenging task, then we have perhaps scratched the surface of the challenge of the task. As those engaged in the process of desistance will attest, sustained change is rarely easy, it rarely goes entirely according to plan and it is rarely unidirectional. It is, more often than not, associated with effort, vacillation, persistence, partnership and hope. The task of the worker in this process is, at its simplest, to contribute to and impact on that process for good.

Conclusion

In this chapter, we have sought to illuminate both the 'what' and the 'how' of the criminal justice social work task. In doing so, we have given attention to the embattled landscape in which that task is unfolding, to the nature of the task itself and to the developing research evidence that seeks to inform it. The story that emerges is one of change, continuity, challenge and opportunity. More significantly, it is a story that requires each of its actors, from our many and diverse vantage points, to populate and direct that story towards a positive and sustainable future.

References

Andrews, D. and Bonta, J. (1994) *The Psychology of Criminal Conduct*, Cincinnati, OH, Anderson.

Andrews, D. and Bonta, J. (1995) *The Level of Service Inventory – Revised: Manual*, New York, Multi-Health Systems Inc.

Burnett, R. and McNeill, F. (2005) 'The place of the officer-offender relationship in assisting offenders to desist from crime', *Probation Journal*, 52(3): 247–68.

Farrall, S. (2002) *Rethinking What Works with Offenders: Probation, Social Context and Desistance from Crime*, Collumpton, Willan.

Garland, D. (1985) *Punishment and Welfare: A History of Penal Strategies*, Aldershot, Gower.

Gelsthorpe, L., Raynor, P. and Robinson, G. (2010) 'Pre-sentence reports in England and Wales: Changing discourses of need, risk and quality', in F. McNeill, P. Raynor and C. Trotter (eds) *Offender Supervision: New Directions in Theory, Research and Practice*, Cullompton, Willan.

Gorman, K. (2006) 'Constructing a convincing narrative: the art of persuasive storytelling within the tight constraints of formal pre-sentence assessments for the criminal courts', in K. Gorman, M. Gregory, M. Hayles and N. Parton (eds) *Constructive Work with Offenders*, London, Jessica Kingsley.

Haines, K. (1990) *Aftercare Services for Released Prisoners: A Review of the Literature*, Cambridge, Institute of Criminology.

Hannah-Moffat, K. (2005) 'Criminogenic needs and the transformative risk subject: hybridizations of risk/need in penality', *Punishment and Society*, 7(1): 29–51.

Kemshall, H. (1996) *Reviewing Risk*, London, Home Office.

McAra, T. (2008) 'Crime, criminology and criminal justice in Scotland', *European Journal of Criminology*, 5(4): 481–504.

McCulloch, T. (2005) 'Probation, social context and desistance: retracing the relationship', *Probation Journal*, 52(1): 8–22.

McCulloch, T. and McNeill, F. (2008) 'Desistance focussed approaches', in S. Green, E. Lancaster and S. Feasey (eds) *Addressing Offending Behaviour*, Collumpton, Willan.

McIvor, G. and Barry, M. (1998) *Social Work and Criminal Justice*, vol. 7, *Community Based Thoughcare*, Edinburgh, TSO.

McIvor, G. and McNeill, F. (2007) 'Probation in Scotland: past, present and future', in L. Gelsthorpe and R. Morgan (eds) *The Probation Handbook: A Policy, Practice and Research Handbook*, Cullompton, Willan.

McNeill, F. (2005) 'Remembering probation in Scotland', *Probation Journal*, 52(1): 25–40.

McNeill, F. (2009) *Towards Effective Practice in Offender Supervision*, Edinburgh, Scottish Centre for Crime and Justice Research.

McNeill, F. and Whyte, B. (2007) *Reducing Reoffending: Social Work and Community Justice in Scotland*, Cullompton, Willan.

McNeill, F., Batchelor, S., Burnett, R. and Knox, J. (2005) *21st Century Social Work: Reducing Reoffending: Key Pracice Skills*, Edinburgh, Scottish Executive.

Marsland, M. (1977) 'The decline of probation in Scotland', *Social Work Today*, 8(23): 17–18.

Maruna, S. (2001) *Making Good: How Ex-convicts Reform and Rebuild their Lives*, Washington, DC, American Psychological Association.

Milner, J. and O'Byrne, P. (2009) *Assessment in Social Work*, Basingstoke, Palgrave Macmillan.

Moore, G. (1978) 'Crisis in Scotland', *Howard Journal of Criminal Justice*, 17(1): 32–40.

Morison, R.P. (1962) *Report of the Departmental Committee on the Probation Service* (Morison Report), Cmnd 1650, London, HMSO.

Munro, M. and McNeill, F. (2010) 'Fines, community sanctions and measures', in H. Croall and G. Mooney (eds) *Criminal Justice in Scotland*, Cullompton, Willan.

Nash, M. (2003) 'Pre-trial investigation', in W.H. Chui and M. Nellis (eds) *Moving Probation Forward: Evidence, Arguments and Practice*, Harlow, Pearson.

Paterson, F. and Tombs, J. (1998) *Social Work and Criminal Justice*, vol. 1, *The Impact of Policy*, Edinburgh, Scottish Office Central Research Unit.

Rex, S. (1999) 'Desistance from offending: experiences of probation', *Howard Journal of Criminal Justice*, 36(4): 366–83.

Robinson, G. (2005) 'What works in offender management?', *Howard Journal of Criminal Justice*, 44(3): 307–18.

Robinson, G. and McNeill, F. (2004) 'Purposes matters: the ends of probation', in G. Mair (ed.) *What Matters in Probation Work*, Cullompton, Willan.

Scottish Executive (2004) *National Objectives for Social Work Services in the Criminal Justice System: Standards – Social Enquiry Reports and Associated Court Services*, available online at www.scotland.gov.uk/Publications/2004/12/20474/49335 [accessed 7 July 2010].

Scottish Government (2007) *Reforming and Revitalising: Report of the Review of Community Penalties*, Edinburgh, Scottish Government.

Scottish Government (2008) *Protecting Scotland's Communities: Fair, Fast and Flexible Justice*, Edinburgh, Scottish Government.

Scottish Government (2009) *Reconviction Rates in Scotland: 2005–06 and 2006–07 Offender Cohorts*, available online at www.scotland.gov.uk/Publications/2009/08/28132734/Crime-Justice [accessed 7 July 2010].

Scottish Office (1998) *Community Sentencing: The Tough Option – Review of Criminal Justice Social Work Services*, Edinburgh, Scottish Office.

Scottish Prisons Commission (2008) *Scotland's Choice: Report of the Scottish Prisons Commission*, Edinburgh, Scottish Prisons Commission.

SWSG (Social Work Services Group) (1991) *National Objectives and Standards for Social Work Services in the Criminal Justice System*, Edinburgh, SWSG.

Tata, C. (2007) *The End to 'Dishonesty' in Sentencing? The Custodial Sentences Act will be Fogged by Confusion*, available online at www.cjscotland.org.uk/index.php/cjscotland/dynamic_page/cjscotland/dynamic_page/?title=custodial_sentences [accessed 7 July 2010].

Vanstone, M. (2007) 'The resettlement of prisoners in England and Wales: learning from history and research', in G. McIvor and P. Raynor (eds) *Developments in Social Work with Offenders*, London, Jessica Kingsley.

Ward, T. and Brown, M. (2004) 'The good lives model and conceptual issues in offender rehabilitation', *Psychology, Crime and Law*, 10(3): 243–57.

Ward, T. and Marshall, W. (2004) 'Good lives, aetiology and the rehabilitation of sex offenders: a bridging theory', *Journal of Sexual Aggression*, 10(2): 153–69.

Ward, T. and Maruna, S. (2007) *Rehabilitation: Beyond the Risk Paradigm*, London, Routledge.

Weaver, B. and McNeill, F. (2010) 'Public protection in Scotland', in A. Williams and M. Nash (eds) *The Handbook of Public Protection*, Cullompton, Willan.

Young, P. (1997) *Crime and Criminal Justice in Scotland*, Edinburgh, TSO.

Partnership with Service Users

ANDREW KENDRICK

Introduction

In February 2010, the Scottish Government published a national strategy for self-directed support. This represents one aspect of the recent developments in the reconfiguration of the relationship between the state and the users of social work and social care services:

> This strategy responds to increasing interest in reshaping care and support in Scotland. It aims to set out and drive a cultural shift around the delivery of care and support that views people as equal citizens with rights and responsibilities. (Scottish Government, 2010a, p. 1)

The strategy is seen as supporting the empowerment of individuals to gain equality of opportunity, and self-directed support 'should involve partnership between those who require support and those who commission and provide it' (Scottish Government, 2010a, p. 14). This strategy embraces a number of concepts and terms, which, at face value, it would be hard to disagree with. In his discussion of personalisation, Ferguson (2007) drew on Raymond William's idea of keywords, such as the 'warmly persuasive word ... community':

> Such keywords ... tend to share two main characteristics. First they are capable of incorporating multiple meanings, which often bear little relationship to each other and are sometimes contradictory ... Second, the connotations of keywords are often overwhelmingly positive and they are therefore very hard to be 'against', without sounding mean or curmudgeonly. Who, for example, could be *against* empowerment or *against* 'choice' in health and social care services? (Ferguson, 2007, p. 388)

Partnership is such a word and, in this chapter, I will discuss the contested nature of partnership with service users, and the way in which it has become central to the development of social work and social care services, fundamentally changing the nature of the relationship between social work and social care professionals and service users. Braye and Preston-Shoot (1995, pp. 35–6) contrast a range of new 'radical values' such as advocacy, empowerment, participation, partnership and user control, which challenge oppression and structural inequality, with 'traditional values', which focus on the individualised relationship between the social worker and the service user, and the adjustment of service users to existing conditions in society. Turner and Balloch (2001) argue that taking user involvement and empowerment seriously requires agencies to work in partnership with service users.

However, it must also be acknowledged that the development of partnership varies across different service user groups, and the way that partnership is discussed and conceptualised can also be very different. There is a marked contrast, for example, in the language of partnership and the nature of the relationship between service users and professionals when considering looked after children and young people, offenders or disabled service users. This is partly explained by the articulation of these concepts with issues of risk (Kemshall, 2010).

The meaning of working in partnership

Over recent years, there has been a constant exhortation for the development of partnership working and for interagency and interprofessional collaboration. Partnership working has become a core aspect of policy and practice over many years (Balloch and Taylor, 2001). According to Dowling et al. (2004, p. 309):

> The message is clear – the pressure to collaborate and join together in partnership is overwhelming. Partnership is no longer simply an option, it is a requirement.

This long-standing focus on cooperation, collaboration, partnership and 'joined-up working' has not necessarily led to a clear understanding of the nature and effectiveness of such relationships. In 1994, Leathard (1994, p. 5) described this area as a 'terminological quagmire', and the continued lack of clear definitions and conceptualisation bedevils the development of a clear evidence base for demonstrating the success (or otherwise) of partnerships. Research has focused more on process issues than on outcomes (Dowling et al., 2004). Rummery stated (2009, p. 1798): 'A lack of clarity around definitions of "partnership" and associated terms has diverted attention away from a focus on outcomes (if we do not know what a "partnership" is, how can we measure it?).'

For a long period, partnership has referred primarily to the relationship between government departments, local authorities and other agencies.

Increasingly, however, partnership is being used to discuss the relationship between agencies and professionals who deliver services, and those who use them. While this is an important shift in the concept of partnership, a distinction needs to be made between the focus on partnership in terms of services for individual service users or partnership in the strategic development and planning of service provision (Braye, 2000). According to Hunter and Ritchie (2007, p. 11):

> While partnership in strategy and governance and partnership at an individual and family level are informed by the same values, they typically happen in different settings through different intonations and require complementary rather than identical skills and methods.

Service users are increasingly being seen as partners in the planning and delivery of services in health and social care services, but there is still a steep hill to climb and concern that there is a continuing risk that they are excluded (Beresford and Branfield, 2006). Turner and Balloch (2001) commented that a decade after the passing of the NHS and Community Care Act 1990, there has been slow progress in the involvement of service users in the planning and delivery of services. More recently, Rummery (2009) stated that the involvement of users as partners has been underexplored, and only 7 of the 76 studies in her international review of partnerships in health and social care involved service users as partners. So despite evidence of the importance of service user involvement in partnerships for more effective service provision, better communication and improved service outcomes, there is continuing need to further develop this aspect of partnership (Beresford and Branfield, 2006; Rummery, 2009).

A seminal model that has been applied widely in the debates on service user involvement is Arnstein's (1969) ladder of participation. Arnstein describes eight steps in her ladder and breaks these into three broad categories: manipulation and therapy (non-participation); informing, consultation and placation (tokenism); and partnership, delegated power and citizen control (citizen power):

> Further up the ladder are levels of citizen power with increasing degrees of decision-making clout. Citizens can enter into a (6) Partnership that enables them to negotiate and engage in trade-offs with traditional power holders. At the topmost rungs, (7) Delegated Power and (8) Citizen Control, have-not citizens obtain the majority of decision-making seats, or full managerial power. (Arnstein, 1969, p. 217)

Arnstein, then, sees partnership as a form of participation where there is real power in decision making. Braye (2000, p. 20) suggests that:

full participation is a process where power to determine the outcome of decisions is shared equally between the parties ... The word partnership is sometimes used to describe forms of participation that involve power sharing as distinct from those that do not.

More recently, Tritter and McCallum (2006) have critiqued Arnstein's ladder of participation on a number of levels. They argue that Arnstein's ladder has missing rungs because it implies that user empowerment is the sole aim, whereas user involvement is more complex, for example the role of users in framing problems by involvement in needs assessment. Tritter and McCallum also suggest that the nature of user involvement necessitates multiple ladders, specifically because of the varying roles of users in relation to individual treatment or care, service development, research or teaching. Tritter and McCallum (2006, p. 165) suggest a more complex mosaic, which:

> captures interactions between individual users, their communities, voluntary organisations and the health care system on which successful user involvement depends. The importance of user involvement is the engagement of diverse users and health professionals as co-producers.

Empowerment

Arnstein's ladder of participation was based on the degree of power that citizen representatives held, and empowerment of service users is central to debates about partnership. Empowerment is a contested term, with a range of meanings (Adams, 2008). Braye and Preston-Shoot (1995, p. 48) define empowerment as:

1. Extending one's ability to take effective decisions.
2. Individuals, groups and/or communities taking control of their circumstances and achieving their own goals, thereby being able to work towards maximising the quality of their lives.
3. Enabling people who are disempowered to have more control over their lives, to have a greater voice in institutions, service and situations which affect them, and to exercise power over someone else rather than simply being the recipients of exercised power.
4. Helping people to regain their own power.

It can be seen that these definitions could cover a range of relationships between service users and social work and social service professionals, with service users being more or less active in the process. It also raises issues, as we have seen, about the service user as an individual or as part of a collective community. Turner and Evans (2004), for example, highlight the major influence that the vision and leadership of service users working at local and national levels has had on empowerment practice.

In contrast, Langan (1998, p. 214) considers that empowerment implies an individualistic conception of power that 'by reducing social relationships to the interpersonal level, obscures the real power relations in society ... Too often, empowerment means reconciling people to being powerless'.

Batchelor and Burman (2004, p. 277), in highlighting the importance of self-efficacy and empowerment for work with female offenders to be effective, pointed out that 'empowering women' has been appropriated as a means of 'responsiblising women', and making them responsible for their own risk assessment and engaging with programmes of change. However, they are constrained by structural conditions of oppression, inequality and social exclusion (Batchelor and Burman, 2004; see also Kemshall, 2010). Twigg (2000, p. 112) stated that:

> At the heart of user empowerment lies the attempt to redress the unequal power relations of social care ... User empowerment is a conscious attempt to redress this situation of disadvantage and put the wishes of users at the heart of service.

Twigg goes on to say, however, that this structural weakness means that user empowerment 'relies on goodwill and the reorientation of service providers to make greater space in their practice for the expressed wishes of users' (Twigg, 2000, p. 112). This can be considered to be central to social work and Braye (2000, p. 16) considers that:

> at the heart of the professional mandate is a will to understand oppression and a commitment to counter it through practice which is participative and empowering, whether the focus is upon the professional/agency/user relationship or their joint efforts to address barriers elsewhere.

On the other hand, the service user mandate for participation is not simply about greater involvement in the individual service user relationship, service users 'also fundamentally challenge the dominant paradigms upon which provision is based and the models used for understanding needs and entitlement' (Braye, 2000, p. 17).

As we have seen, the relationship between service users and service providers varies radically across different service user groups, and the nature of empowerment practice is affected by contrasting issues of care and control (Thomson, 2007; Adams, 2008). The ability to challenge dominant paradigms is similarly constrained by the different contexts and discourses of empowerment, and the different balance between rights to autonomy and protection, risk management and empowerment (Braye, 2000). So, while empowerment may be another 'warmly persuasive word', it is a complex and contradictory concept.

Personalisation and co-production

Ferguson (2007) noted the remarkably short space of time in which personalisation has moved to occupy a central place in social work policy, philosophy and legislation in the UK. Carr (2010, p. 2) describes personalisation as:

> thinking about care and support services in an entirely different way. This means starting with the person as an individual with strengths, preferences and aspirations and putting them at the centre of the process of identifying their needs and making choices about how and when they are supported to live their lives.

Personalised services were central to the agenda of *Changing Lives: Report of the 21st Century Social Work Review* and 'personalisation is driving the shape of all public services, with a growing public expectation that services will meet their need, helping them achieve personal goals and aspirations' (Scottish Executive, 2006, p. 9). *Changing Lives* drew heavily on the work of Charles Leadbetter and commissioned a report on personalisation (Leadbetter and Lownsbrough, 2005).

Linked to debates about personalisation has been the development of models of co-production. Hunter and Ritchie (2007, p. 15) define co-production as a particular form of partnership between service users and the people and agencies who provide services:

> In the co-production model, the state has an important role in creating the conditions for productive partnership between professionals and 'problem-owners'. People who own the problem and professionals have a greater role overlap in defining the problem and developing solutions.

There is a similarity between this conception of co-production and Leadbetter's (2004) concept of deep personalisation, which gives users a far greater role for designing solutions.

Ferguson (2007) questions the personalisation agenda, and the writings of Leadbetter, on a number of fronts. He highlights the critiques of consumerism and customer choice and neoliberal globalization from the stance of the anti-capitalist movement. He highlights Leadbetter's failure to address the issue of structural inequality, and while 'this is not to deny the importance of service users' exercising control over services ... it does mean ... that the choices that are available to them will often be very limited, especially for those designated as "involuntary clients"' (Ferguson, 2007, p. 396). The extent to which consumerism and the market for services has empowered users has been seriously questioned (Scourfield, 2007), as has the description of the service user as a rational consumer or 'homo economicus' (Houston, 2010).

Development of partnership with service users in Scotland

Social work and social care services interact and intervene in people's lives in a variety of ways. Some of these will be viewed primarily as supportive and caring interventions, others as restricting and controlling. While there may be an argument that even the most restrictive and controlling interventions, where individuals are deprived of their liberty, will also encompass care and support, the balance of the relationship between social workers and service users will vary widely (Forbes and Sashidharan, 1997). The development and nature of partnership will also vary widely. Croft et al. (2004, p. 32) do point out though, that social models place service users' knowledge and experiences at the centre, irrespective of whether the focus is on social support or social control:

> Social model approaches are now being developed to provide a broad framework which addresses the (similar and different) issues faced by mental health service users, older people, people with learning difficulties and people from black and minority ethnic groups.

In the remainder of this section, I will focus on five service user groups: disabled people, users of mental health services, offenders, children and young people, and older people.

Disabled people

Disabled people have been at the vanguard in driving forward developments in partnership working with social work and social care professionals. The social model of disability has been the philosophy underpinning the independent living movement established by disabled people (Croft et al., 2004). In calling for the empowerment of disabled people, Morris (1997) described the timeline from the 1960s and the development of civil rights campaigns against institutionalisation, the foundation of the Union of the Physically Impaired Against Segregation in 1974, and the development of the independent living movement, through to the implementation of direct payments. Similarly, in Scotland, Pearson and Riddell (2006) detailed the role of campaigning organisations of disabled people in the establishment of indirect payment schemes such as the Independent Living Fund, prior to the implementation of direct payments through the Community Care (Direct Payments) Act 1996.

There is a wide range of local and national disability organisations in Scotland; a recent mapping exercise identified over 1,400 organisations – 85% of these operating at a local level and 15% at a national level (Johnston et al., 2009). While this survey identified a large number of organisations, there was unequal distribution across the country, with a gap in available representation and services in the west and northwest of Scotland. Three-quarters of the local organisations and two-thirds of the national organisations are user led. There was also clear evidence of networking and forums of disability organisations (Johnston et al., 2009). Examples include the Scottish Consortium of Learning Disability (www.scld.org.uk) – a partnership of 12 organisations – whose aim is to work in partnership with people with learning disabilities of all ages and family carers to challenge discrimination and develop and share good practice, and Disability Agenda Scotland (www.disabilityagendascotland.org.uk) – an alliance of six of Scotland's major disability organisations – which aims to promote the interests of disabled people whose views are hard to reach because people are not involved in consultation processes, are not included in or have no influence on lobby groups, have communication support needs that are not met or are poorly understood, or they may simply not be asked.

The range of disabled people's organisations evidences the strength of a collective voice and responsibility in the disability rights movement, and this links directly to the developments of partnership between individual service users and service providers and the protection of individuals' rights (Morris, 1997).

Users of mental health services

Kemp (2010, p. 25) considers that service user involvement has now been established as a significant feature of mental health service provision, and 'a different value base is emerging based on partnership and collaboration with service users'. There has been a considerable development in mental health service user organizations since the late 1980s, building on the influence of the anti-psychiatry movement in the 1960s and 70s.

Quinn and Knifton (2005) describe a mental health awareness and anti-stigma programme in east Glasgow – Positive Mental Attitudes, a partnership of public and voluntary sector agencies, community groups and service users. There has been a high degree of service user participation in the design, planning and delivery of each part of the programme, which involved lessons in local secondary schools, information seminars and policy development for local employers, anti-stigma training workshops for public service workers, and a range of social marketing and arts work in the local community. Quinn and Knifton (2005, p. 43) state that:

> Positive Mental Attitudes has been developed in one low-income locality and has evaluated well in terms of achieving attitudinal and behavioural change and promoting the involvement of a wide range of partners and service users in its development.

User involvement in treatment and care, service user groups, and service and policy development is also central to recovery approaches (Brown and Kandirikirira, 2007) and the work of the Scottish Recovery Network. In Scotland, a range of local initiatives such as the Highland User Group and Edinburgh Users Forum, and national organisations such as the Scottish Association for Mental Health are developing strong user partnerships. Voices Of eXperience (VOX) is a national mental health service user-led organisation that works 'in partnership with mental health and related services to ensure that service users get every opportunity to contribute positively to changes in the services that serve them and wider society' (www.voxscotland.org.uk/about).

However, the policy developments in mental health that call for user participation and involvement must be set alongside the more coercive policy drivers of risk and dangerousness (Forbes and Sashidharan, 1997; Hothersall et al., 2008; Kemp, 2010). Wilson and Daly (2007) suggested that mental health social work, with its recourse to coercive legislation, sits uneasily alongside the rights-based agenda of the service user movement, and called for a refocusing debate to consider social workers' responses to these challenges.

Children and families

Partnership working with children and young people is primarily located within the discourse of children's rights, underpinned by the focus on participation in the 1989 United Nations Convention on the Rights of the Child (UNCRC). Milligan and Stevens (2006, p. 134), for example, focus on rights to participation in relation to collaborating with children and young people, and conclude that 'the child should be listened to and respected as a partner in their own care and collaboration with the child should form the basis of all work'. However, rights to participation may be in tension with rights to protection (Kendrick, 2000; Emond, 2008).

Partnership with parents has also been a central principle of child welfare in the UK, particularly in relation to the maximum involvement of parents in decision-making processes (Hill, 2000; Cox, 2007). However, Hill (2000, p. 65) also stresses that there are tensions in this process when taking account of the best interests of the child:

> Unless carefully integrated in practice, the language of partnership may disguise rather than resolve tensions between agencies, carers and parents, distract from real differences of opinion about what is best for children and gloss over differences in power and resources.

While this discussion of partnership with children, young people and parents has tended to focus on their involvement and participation in individual planning and decision making, the rights agenda stimulated by the UNCRC has also led to a discussion of partnership in relation to service development and planning, and early in its life, the Scottish Parliament commissioned research which found that children and young people have a strong wish to be consulted, particularly on issues directly affecting their daily lives (Stafford et al., 2003).

The Scottish Children's Commissioner for Children and Young People (SCCYP) places participation of children and young people at the centre of their work. Recent activity has involved looked after children and young people, for example guidance on encouraging outdoor activities in residential childcare (SCCYP, 2010), and the age of leaving care in Scotland (SCCYP, 2008). Who Cares? Scotland has also been influential in campaigning and promoting the views and experiences of young people at a local and national level. For example, Who Cares? Scotland consulted over 100 children and young people in care for the National Residential Child Care Initiative, which focused on the development of residential services in Scotland (Bayes, 2009). Working in partnership with children and young people in care, it also launched the Give Me a Chance anti-stigma campaign (Who Cares? Scotland, 2010).

Offenders

Partnership with service users takes on a particular resonance when looking at the relationship of social work and social workers with offenders. In commenting on a probation circular in England and Wales that called for the identification and promotion of best practice in the engagement of offenders in the development of services, Pycroft (2006, p. 36) suggests that the idea of 'the offender as service user is seen to have no place in contemporary probation practice'. In similar fashion, Needham (2009, p. 111) analysed New Labour's criminal justice policy in terms of narratives of consumerism, but the 'terms empower, engage, participate and involve are used relatively seldom', and there was little evidence of choice and personalisation.

While Whyte (2007, p. 119) agrees that adversarial criminal justice provides 'limited opportunity for "user" or "stakeholder" involvement in decision making', he goes on to suggest that developments in community justice aim to 'empower citizens, voluntary groups and neighbourhood associations as partners in the justice process'. A recent example of such developments is Circles of Support and Accountability, a community contribution to reducing sex offending, working in close partnership with criminal justice agencies. The Scottish Government commissioned research to explore the feasibility of establishing pilot circles in Scotland, taking account of the experience in Canada and England and the distinctive features of the Scottish criminal justice system. Circles use volunteers to provide support to a high-risk, high-needs sex offender's reintegration into the community. They hold the volunteer accountable by challenging attempts to minimise offending behaviours and thought processes, and by reporting concerns to the authorities (Armstrong et al., 2008, p. 5). Several circles are currently running in Scotland, operating informally out of churches, and proposals have been made to the Scottish Government to fund a circles pilot.

Further, developments in restorative justice involve offenders directly with victims, community members, parents and families (Marshall, 1999). SACRO, a national community justice voluntary organisation working across Scotland, maintains a website (www.restorativejustices-cotland.org.uk) that provides up-to-date information on the use of restorative justice in Scotland across a range of settings and contexts. It highlights the values of restorative justice, and a range of resources on the variety of approaches used in Scotland. These include restorative justice conferences, circles, family group conferences, conversations, face-to-face meetings, shuttle dialogue, police warnings, and victim awareness programmes (Scottish Restorative Justice Consultancy and Training Service, 2008). According to Whyte (2007, p. 131):

> Restorative practices have the potential to provide a form of partnership between the state and individuals, families and communities as co-producers, whereby people can participate as citizens and stakeholders with expert knowledge and not simply as passive recipients of justice.

Older people

The changing demography of Scotland will have significant implications for social work and social care services for older people. Dewar et al. (2004) investigated the involvement and participation of older people in the development and delivery of services and identified a range of mechanisms to involve or consult older people as a specific community of interest, as well as 'generic' involvement mechanisms. The former included older people's forums, an older people's assembly, older people's networks and user panels, and older people's services user groups or planning groups. Dewar et al. (2004, p. 16) stated that:

> The majority of examples of involvement activities given by professionals were information giving and consultation. There was awareness among professionals that involvement could be developed further.

The importance of older people having real power and influence was also stressed and 'professionals were keen to see more partnership working between public agencies and older people' (Dewar et al., 2004, p. 19). *All Our Futures* (Scottish Executive, 2007) also identified models of good practice where local authorities work in partnership with older people to involve them in planning and decision making in service delivery, and recommended the establishment of a National Forum on Ageing. According to Jeffery (2010, p. 24):

> One of the clear features of *All Our Futures* is this focus on the older person as individual citizen. And the Scottish Government has added action to aspiration, for example: in securing opportunities for involvement of older people in the implementation of *All Our Futures*; [and] in researching and delivering a prominent anti-ageism campaign ('See the Person, Not the Age') that has run from the summer of 2008.

In order to develop this agenda, the Scottish Government has funded the National Forum on Ageing Futures Group – an independent think tank consisting of a range of individuals and organisations – to take forward the debate about the contribution of older people in focusing government and public services on creating opportunities for all Scotland to flourish (National Forum on Ageing Futures Group, 2009).

The clear demographic trends and profile of the ageing population, along with its cost implications in the context of severe financial constraint, have led the Scottish Government, in partnership with COSLA and the NHS, to launch *Reshaping Care for Older People*:

It is clear that our current set-up will not be able to cope with such an increase in numbers. So Scotland needs to put in place a plan to remedy this – not just for today's older people but for the benefit of us. We must build a care system that ensures we all get the level of care and support that we need to enjoy our later years. (Scottish Government, 2010b, p. 2)

Reshaping Care for Older People is being taken forward through an extensive programme of engagement events at local and national level. But the agenda has clearly been laid in terms of devising and implementing 'new ways of delivering services which redistribute pressure from systems to individuals and enable Scots to take charge of their own destinies' (Scottish Government, 2010b, p. 7).

Conclusion

Working in partnership is high on the agenda of service users, social workers and central and local government, yet it remains elusive. The organisational and resource barriers that can be placed in the way of partnership working with service users, both individually and collectively, need to be challenged by social workers in order to ensure that participation is not tokenistic or manipulative. In work with individuals and families, the values that underpin social work practice are those which are valued by service users and are at the centre of partnership working: active listening, empathy, respect, reliability, taking action.

There is a tension, however, in the relationship between social workers and service users in terms of care and control, which will be context specific and must be articulated clearly and precisely. The issues of compliance are more obvious with some user groups than others, yet partnership is as crucial in the assessment of risk as in the assessment of care. Social workers have to work through the complexity of the balancing of risk, control, autonomy and partnership. While limits to participation and partnership need to be clear and partnership promoted as far as possible within those limits, there is also a clear imperative to address inequality and structural disadvantage. Only in this way can partnership with service users embrace empowerment in an equal and meaningful way.

References

Adams, R. (2008) *Empowerment, Participation and Social Work* (4th edn), Basingstoke, Palgrave Macmillan.

Armstrong, S., Chistyakova, Y., Mackenzie, S. and Malloch, M. (2008) *Circles of Support and Accountability: Consideration of the Feasibility of Pilots in Scotland*, Glasgow, Scottish Centre for Crime and Justice Research.

Arnstein, S. (1969) 'A ladder of community participation', *American Institute of Planners Journal*, 35: 216–24.

Balloch, G. and Taylor, M. (2001) *Partnership Working: Policy and Practice*, Bristol, Policy Press.

Batchelor, S.A. and Burman, M.J. (2004) 'Working with girls and young women', in G. McIvor (ed.) *Women who Offend*, London, Jessica Kingsley.

Bayes, K. (2009) *Higher Aspirations, Brighter Futures: Overview of the National Residential Child Care Initiative*, Glasgow, Scottish Institute for Residential Child Care.

Beresford, P. and Branfield, F. (2006) 'Developing inclusive partnerships: user-defined outcomes, networking and knowledge – a case study', *Health and Social Care in the Community*, 14(5): 436–44.

Braye, S. (2000) 'Participation and involvement in social care: an overview', in H. Kemshall and R. Littlechild (eds) *User Involvement and Participation in Social Care: Research Informing Practice*, London, Jessica Kingsley.

Braye, S. and Preston-Shoot, M. (1995) *Empowering Practice in Social Care*, Buckingham, Open University Press.

Brown, W. and Kandirikirira, N. (2007) *Recovering Mental Health in Scotland: Report on Narrative Investigation of Mental Health Recovery*, Glasgow, Scottish Recovery Network.

Carr, S. (2010) *Personalisation: A Rough Guide* (rev. edn), London, Social Care Institute for Excellence.

Cox, J. (2007) 'Family group conferencing and "partnership"', in S. Hunter and P. Ritchie (eds) *Co-production and Personalisation in Social Care*, London, Jessica Kingsley.

Croft, S., Beresford, P. and Wulff-Cochrane, E. (2004) 'The future of social work', in D. Statham (ed.) *Managing Front Line Practice*, London, Jessica Kingsley.

Dewar, B., Jones, C. and O'May, F. (2004) *Involving Older People: Lessons for Community Planning*, Edinburgh, Scottish Executive.

Dowling, B., Powell, M. and Glendinning, C. (2004) 'Conceptualising successful partnerships', *Health and Social Care in the Community*, 12(4): 309–17.

Emond, R. (2008) 'Children's voices, children's rights', in A. Kendrick (ed.) *Residential Child Care: Prospects and Challenges*, London, Jessica Kingsley.

Ferguson, I. (2007) 'Increasing user choice or privatizing risk? The antinomies of personalization', *British Journal of Social Work*, 37: 387–403.

Forbes, J. and Sashidharan, S.P. (1997) 'User involvement in services: incorporation or challenge?', *British Journal of Social Work*, 27: 481–98.

Hill, M. (2000) 'Partnership reviewed: words of caution, words of encouragement', *Adoption & Fostering*, 24(3): 56–68.

Hothersall, S., Maas-Lowit, M. and Golightley, M. (2008) *Social Work and Mental Health in Scotland*, Exeter, Learning Matters.

Houston, S. (2010) 'Beyond homo economicus: recognition, self-realization and social work', *British Journal of Social Work*, 40: 841–57.

Hunter, S. and Ritchie, P. (2007) 'Introduction: with, not to: models of co-production in social welfare', in S. Hunter and P. Ritchie (eds) *Co-production and Personalisation in Social Care*, London, Jessica Kingsley.

Jeffery, C. (2010) *Older People, Public Policy and the Impact of Devolution in Scotland*, Edinburgh, Age Scotland.

Johnston, L., Lardner, C., Barton, A. and Martin, M. (2009) *Mapping Scotland's Disability Organisations*, available online at www.scotland.gov.uk/Resource/Doc/294586/0091088.pdf [accessed 27 June 2010].

Kemp, P. (2010) 'Introduction to mental health service user involvement', in J. Weinstein (ed.) *Mental Health, Service User Involvement and Recovery*, London, Jessica Kingsley.

Kemshall, H. (2010) 'Risk rationalities in contemporary social work policy and practice', *British Journal of Social Work*, 40: 1247–62.

Kendrick, A. (2000) *The Views of the Child: Article 12 and the Development of Children's Rights in Scotland*, available online at www.personal.strath.ac.uk/andrew.kendrick/index_htm_files/article12kendrick.pdf [accessed 27 June 2010].

Langan, M. (1998) 'Radical social work', in R. Adams, L. Dominelli, and M. Payne (eds) *Social Work: Themes, Issues and Critical Debates*, Basingstoke, Palgrave Macmillan.

Leadbetter, C. (2004) *Personalisation through Participation: A New Script for Public Services*, London, Demos.

Leadbetter, C. and Lownsbrough, H. (2005) *Personalisation and Participation: The Future of Social Care in Scotland*, London, Demos.

Leathard, A. (ed.) *Going Interprofessional: Working Together for Health and Welfare, London*, Routledge.

Marshall, T. (1999) *Restorative Justice: An Overview*, London, Home Office.

Milligan, I. and Stevens, I. (2006) *Residential Child Care: Collaborative Practice*, London, Sage.

Morris, J. (1997) 'Care or empowerment? A disability rights perspective', *Social Policy and Administration*, 31(1): 54–60.

National Forum on Ageing Futures Group (2009) *Unlocking Our Potential: Older People – A Key to Scotland's Future*, available online at www.qmu.ac.uk/copa/forums/NFA%20Futures%20Group.docs/National%20Forum%20on%20Ageing%20Futures%20Group%20Report%20Sep09.pdf [accessed 27 June 2010].

Needham, C. (2009) 'Policing with a smile: narratives of consumerism in New Labour's criminal justice policy', *Public Administration*, 87(1): 97–116.

Pearson, C. and Riddell, S. (2006) 'Introduction: the development of direct payments in Scotland', in C. Pearson (ed.) *Direct Payments and Personalisation of Care*, Edinburgh, Dunedin Academic Press.

Pycroft, A. (2006) 'Too little, too late?', *Criminal Justice Matters*, **64**(1): 36–7.

Quinn, N. and Knifton, L. (2005) 'Promoting recovery and addressing stigma: mental health awareness through community development in a low income area', *International Journal of Mental Health Promotion*, 7(4): 37–44.

Rummery, K. (2009) 'Healthy partnerships, healthy citizens? An international review of partnerships in health and social care and patient/user outcomes', *Social Science & Medicine*, 69: 1797–804.

SCCYP (Scotland's Commissioner for Children and Young People) (2008) *Sweet 16? The Age of Leaving Care in Scotland*, Edinburgh, SCCYP.

SCCYP (Scotland's Commissioner for Children and Young People) (2010) *Go Outdoors! Guidance and Good Practice on Encouraging Outdoor Activities in Residential Child Care*, Edinburgh, SCCYP.

Scottish Executive (2006) *Changing Lives: Report of the 21st Century Social Work Review*, Edinburgh, Scottish Executive.

Scottish Executive (2007) *All Our Futures: Planning for a Scotland with an Ageing Population*, vol. 2, *Full Strategy*, Edinburgh, Scottish Executive.

Scottish Government (2010a) *Self-directed Support: A National Strategy for Scotland*, Edinburgh, Scottish Government.

Scottish Government (2010b) *Reshaping Care for Older People: Information Booklet*, available online at www.scotland.gov.uk/Resource/Doc/1095/0097691.pdf [accessed 27 June 2010].

Scottish Restorative Justice Consultancy and Training Service (2008) *An Overview of Restorative Justice in Scotland*, available online at www.restorativejusticescotland.org.uk/RJ_in_Scotland_1.10_TextOnly.doc [accessed 27 June 2010].

Scourfield, P. (2007) 'Social care and the modern citizen: client, consumer, service user, manager and entrepreneur', *British Journal of Social Work*, 37: 107–22.

Stafford, A., Laybourn, A., Hill, M. and Walker, M. (2003) '"Having a say": children and young people talk about consultation', *Children & Society*, 17: 361–73.

Thomson, N. (2007) *Power and Empowerment*, Lyme Regis, Russell House.

Tritter, J.Q. and McCallum, A. (2006) 'The snakes and ladders of user involvement: moving beyond Arnstein', *Health Policy*, 76: 156–68.

Turner, M. and Balloch, S. (2001) 'Partnership between service users and statutory social services', in S. Balloch and M. Taylor (eds) *Partnership Working: Policy and Practice*, Bristol, Policy Press.

Turner, M. and Evans, C. (2004) 'Users influencing the management of practice', in D. Statham (ed.) *Managing Front Line Practice in Social Care*, London, Jessica Kingsley.

Twigg, J. (2000) 'The changing role of users and carers', in B. Hudson (ed.) *The Changing Role of Social Care*, London, Jessica Kingsley.

United Nations (1989) United Nations Convention on the Rights of the Child, available online at www2.ohchr.org/english/law/pdf/crc.pdf [accessed 27 June 2010].

Who Cares? Scotland (2010) *Give Me a Chance: Be Fair to a Child in Care*, available online at www.givemeachancescotland.org [accessed 27 June 2010].

Whyte, B. (2007) 'Restoring "stakeholder" involvement in justice', in S. Hunter and P. Ritchie (eds) *Co-production and Personalisation in Social Care*, London, Jessica Kingsley.

Wilson, G. and Daly, M. (2007) 'Shaping the future of mental health policy and legislation in Northern Ireland: the impact of service user and professional social work discourses', *British Journal of Social Work*, 37: 423–9.

Index

40/20 rule 173

A

ability 22
accountability 3, 4, 20–34
  legal 7, 22, 26
  lines of 24–31
  and professional autonomy 31–2
Act of Sederunt (Sheriff Court Ordinary
  Cause Rules) 1993 108
Act of Sederunt (Sheriff Court Rules
  Amendment) (Adoption and
  Children (Scotland) Act 2007) 2009
  109
Act of Union 1701 167
actuarial methods of risk assessment
  56–7
Adil, M. 37
adjudication 171
adoption 105, 109
Adoption and Children (Scotland) Act
  2007 104, 109
adoption orders 109
adult criminal justice *see* criminal
  justice
adult protection 4, 40–2, 136–51
  capacity, consent and deprivation of
    liberties 146–8
  contexts of vulnerability 137–9
  legal framework 139–46
  rights and representation 148–9
adult service users 4–5, 152–66
  accessing advocacy 157–8
  anti-discriminatory practice 154–5
  range of remedies 161–3
  self-directed support 155–7
Adult Support and Protection
  (Scotland) Act 2007 (ASPA) 2, 35,
  37, 40, 41, 41–2, 136, 139–50,
  152–3
Adults with Incapacity (Scotland) Act
  2000 (AwIA) 37, 39, 41–2, 125,
  136–7, 139–50, 152–3
advance statements 149

advocacy
  adult protection 148–9
  children's hearings 94–5
  listening to children 4, 101–17
  supporting people to access
    157–8
age of consent to medical treatment
  102
age of criminal responsibility 101, 106,
  173
age of marriage 102
Age of Legal Capacity (Scotland) Act
  1991 102, 105, 111
Age of Majority (Scotland) Act 1969
  102
Aldgate, J. 53–4
All Our Futures 212
Andrews, D. 193, 194
anti-discriminatory practice 80–1,
  154–5
Antisocial Behaviour etc. (Scotland) Act
  2004 (ASBA) 176, 178
apartheid 12
Arnstein, S. 203
Arthurworrey, Lisa 24–5
assessment 4, 52–69, 74–5
  for carers 120, 159–60
  children's hearings 90–1
  community care 119–20, 121–2,
    132
  and criminal justice 189–90,
    193–4
  GIRFEC system *see Getting it right
    for every child*
  of incapacity 147
  law and 54
  nature of 52–4
  policy context 58–65
  of risk 55–7
  steps in process 53
assessment orders 140, 143–4
  assessment in another place 140,
    144
  assessment in situ 140, 144

Association of Directors of Adult Social Services (ADASS) 123–4
Asylum and Immigration Appeals Act 1993 73
asylum seekers 73–4
Austrian, S.G. 53
autism spectrum disorders 153
autonomy
  adult protection and 136–51
  professional 31–2

B
Baby P 15, 20, 24
Baillie, T. 114
Balloch, S. 203
Banks, S. 16, 21, 23
banning orders 140, 141, 145, 149
Batchelor, S.A. 205
Bath and North East Somerset Council 155
Beckett, A. 47
Beckford, Jasmine 79
black and minority ethnic (BME)
  communities 70–2
  socialisation practices 75–81
  stereotypes of black families 75
  see also racial discrimination
Blair House 175
blame 21–2, 24–5
Bonta, J. 193, 194
Bowes, A.M. 75
Braye, S. 15, 17, 21, 202, 203–4, 204, 205, 206
British Association of Social Workers (BASW) 29, 80
  Code of Ethics for Social Work 8–9, 16, 152
Burman, M.J. 205

C
Calder, M.C. 55–6
capacity
  adults lacking 136–51
  and consent 146–8
care, ethics of 12–13
care plans 146
Care Standards Tribunal 24–5

CARENAP (Care Needs Assessment Package) 121
carers 7, 120
  assessment of 120, 159–60
  supporting unpaid carers 120, 158–61
  working with 4–5, 152–66
  young 160–1
Caring Together: The Carers Strategy for Scotland 2010–2015 120
Carr, S. 206
case reviews 26
Central Council for Education and Training of Social Workers (CCETSW) 8
Chand, A. 78, 79
change 2–3
Changing Lives: Report of the 21st Century Social Work Review 3, 6, 8, 48, 155–6, 206
  accountability 20–1, 25, 31, 32
Changing Lives User and Carer Forum 152, 156
child abuse
  children's hearings 93–4, 105–6
  cultural differences 78–80
child protection 15, 20, 54, 55, 66
  children's hearings 88–9, 91, 93–4
child witnesses 110–11
childhood, stages of 101–2
children
  eligibility and direct payments 125
  GIRFEC *see Getting it right for every child*
  listening to *see* children's voices
  partnership working 96, 209–10
  policies for 58
  socialisation practices 70, 75–81
Children Act 1975 106
Children Act 1989 175
Children (Scotland) Act 1995 54, 75, 80, 86, 168, 175–6
  listening to children 103–4, 105, 106, 108
Children and Young Persons (Scotland) Act 1937 85
Children's Charter 107, 115

children's hearings 2, 4, 85–100
  assessment and reports 90–1
  compulsory supervision 95–7
  conducting 91–5
  grounds for referrals 87, 88–9, 91,
    93, 97
  human rights and 97
  listening to children 105–6, 109–10
  participation 92–3
  privacy, confidentiality and exclusion
    93–4
  representation and advocacy 94–5,
    110
  social disadvantage 89
  social work in 87–9
  youth justice and 96–7, 167–70,
    174, 175, 176–8
Children's Hearings (Legal
  Representation) (Scotland) Rules
  2002 94, 95
Children's Hearings (Scotland) Bill 87,
  91, 92, 94, 95, 110, 167, 169, 173,
  177
Children's Hearings Service 87
children's reporter 88, 92, 112, 174, 176
children's rights officers 109, 110, 113
children's voices 4, 101–17
  how to listen 107–11
  occasions for listening 104–7
  reasons for listening 101–4
  roles involved in listening 111–14
  strategic approach 114
child's plan 62, 63, 64, 66, 67
Circles of Support and Accountability
  211
citizen advocacy 158
Citizen Leadership 156
Clark, C.L. 22–3, 31
client satisfaction monitoring 162
Climbié, Victoria 20, 24
close family/friends 138
Cocking, R.R. 77
codes of ethics/practice 8–9, 29–30,
  31, 45, 152
Code of Ethics for Social Work 8–9, 16,
  152
*Code of Practice for Social Service
  Workers* 8, 15–16, 29, 152

collaborative working *see* joint
  working
collectivistic cultures 76–8
Colwell, Maria 106
communication 143, 147
communication needs 155
community-based CTOs 146
community care 4, 118–35
  accountability 23–31
  assessment 119–20, 121–2, 132
  carers 120
  direct payments 42, 124–7, 128,
    129, 155, 161, 208
  free personal and nursing care 125,
    129–32
  outcomes focus 122–4, 132
  self-directed support 123, 125,
    127–9, 132, 155–7, 163
Community Care (Direct Payments) Act
  1996 124, 208
Community Care (Direct Payments)
  (Scotland) Act 1997 42
Community Care and Health (Scotland)
  Act 2002 120, 124, 129
Community Care Needs of Frail People
  120
community justice 190–1, 211
Community Justice Authorities 186
community payback orders 188
community reparation orders 190
Community Service by Offenders
  (Scotland) Act 1978 185
community service orders 185
competence 22
complaints procedures 27, 28, 161–3
compulsory supervision 95–7, 176–7
compulsory supervision orders 177
compulsory treatment orders (CTOs)
  146, 149
conciliation 162
confidentiality 14–15, 93–4
conflicts of interest 23, 158
consent
  age of consent to medical treatment
    102
  capacity and 146–8
consultation 32
consumerism 207

Convention of Scottish Local Authority
Services (COSLA) 63
co-production 123, 132, 206–7
Council of Europe rules 172–3
Crerar Review 37, 163
criminal courts
dealing with children and young
people 169–70, 174–5
services to 188–90
criminal justice 2, 5, 184–200
partnership working 192, 210–11
research evidence 192–7
social work in context 184–8
social work in practice 188–92
youth justice *see* youth justice
Criminal Justice and Licensing
(Scotland) Act 2010 106–7, 173,
187, 188
Criminal Justice Social Work
Development Centre for Scotland 179
criminal justice social work teams
185
criminal law 106–7, 110–11
Criminal Procedures (Scotland) Act
1995 169, 174–5
criminological theory 171–2
critical risk 130–1
Croft, S. 207
cross-cultural perspective 81
cultural relativism 79
culture 70, 139
cultural differences and socialisation
70, 75–81
Cunningham v *Shields* 108
curator ad litem 94, 105, 109, 112
Custody of Children Act 1939 102,
105
cutbacks 66

D
Daly, M. 209
Dar, N. 75
Davis, A. 40
*Dealing with Offending by Young
People* 178
defensible practice 44, 55
defensive practice 10, 44
deficit model 75

degree-level training 2
dementia 47, 153, 163
deprivation of liberties 148
desistance-focused practice 195–6
detention orders 144, 149, 150
devolution 1–2, 167, 186
Dewar, B. 212
difference 4, 70–84
dilemmas 1, 44–6, 47
direct payments 42, 124–7, 128, 129,
155, 161, 208
see also self-directed support
Disability Agenda Scotland 208
Disability Equality Duty 126–7, 154–5
disability organisations 208
Disability Rights Commission 127
disabled people 154
eligible for direct payments 124–5
partnership working with 207–8
discipline 78–80
disclosure of criminal conviction/record
173
Disclosure Scotland 173
discretion 15, 31
discrimination 11, 12
anti-discriminatory practice 80–1,
154–5
racial 4, 70–84
disposal (in criminal justice) 171
diversity 4, 70–2
see also discrimination
Dominelli, L. 73, 75
Douglas, K.S. 57
Dowling, B. 202
Down's syndrome 153
drug users 158–9
Dundee University 157
Dwivedi, K. 78
Dworkin, R. 11–12

E
ecological approach to assessment 52,
54
economic disadvantage 89
Edinburgh Users Forum 209
electronic tagging 47, 176–7, 180
eligibility criteria 124–5, 128, 129,
130–2

Ellis, K. 40
emergency detention orders 144
employer, accountability to 24–5
empowerment 54, 204–7
England
community care 123–4, 126, 128, 131–2
FACS criteria 131
Putting People First 118, 123–4, 131
youth justice 175–6
entry warrants 144
environment 138–9, 147
Equalities Act 2010 70, 72
Equality and Human Rights Commission 153
ethic of care 12–13
ethics
ethical dilemmas 44–6, 47
social work values and the law 3–4, 6–19
European Convention on Human Rights (ECHR) 2, 12, 26, 136, 193
children's hearings 86, 87, 90, 91, 92, 94, 97, 162
Evans, C. 205
evidence-based practice 65
exclusion
banning orders (exclusion of third party) 140, 141, 145
from children's hearings 93–4

F
Fair Access to Care Services (FACS) criteria 131
families 138
partnership working 96, 209–10
see also parents
family law 104–5, 108
Farrall, S. 195, 196
Fawcett, B. 40, 43
Ferguson, I. 201, 206–7
financial abuse 138
financial measures 141, 143
For Scotland's Children 58, 64
forewarning 14–15
form F9 108
Forrester, D. 96

Framework for Social Work Education in Scotland 29
free personal and nursing care 125, 129–32
Fresh Talent initiative 71
Fuller, L. 11

G
Gabe, J. 40
Gardiner, H. 81
Gelsthorpe, L. 189
Gendreau, P. 194
Geneva Declaration of the Rights of the Child 102
Germany, Nazi 11, 12
Getting it right for every child (GIRFEC) 52, 57, 58–67, 89, 90, 180
evaluation of 64
implementing 63–4
implications for social work 65–7
National Practice Model 59–63, 63–4, 65
strengths and weaknesses 65
values and principles 58–9
Give Me a Chance anti-stigma campaign 210
globalisation 55
good lives model (GLM) 196–7
Gopaul-McNicol, S.A. 80
Gorman, K. 189–90
Greenfield, P.M. 77
Griffiths, A. 93–4
guardianship orders 145, 149
Guidance on Assessment and Care Management 119
Guidance on Single Shared Assessment 121
Guide to Implementing Getting it right for every child 59

H
Habermas, J. 36, 46
HALE 45
Hallett, C. 90, 92
harm
adults at risk of 136–51
categories of 141

Having Your Say form 92
hearings papers 90–1
Henry, Tyra 79
Highland Council Pathfinder 63–4, 66
Highland User Group 209
Hill, M. 210
hospital CTOs 146
human capital 196
human rights 11, 97
Human Rights Act 1998 (HRA) 12,
    22, 26, 42, 86, 193
Hunter, S. 44, 203, 206

I
immigration 71, 73–4
Immigration Act 1988 73
Immigration and Asylum Act 1999 73
imposed care at home 140, 145
*Improving the Lives of Children in
    Scotland – Are We There Yet?* 172
incapacity 136–51
Ince, L. 74
independence 153
    community care and the promotion
        of 4, 118–35
independent advocates 109, 113, 157–8
independent living 118, 126, 127, 153,
    207–8
Independent Living Fund 208
Independent Living in Scotland (ILIS)
    126
independent review panel 28
independent sector 153, 163
Indicator of Relative Need (IoRN) 122
individualised action plans 191
individualistic cultures 76–8
informal carers *see* carers
informal discussion 161, 162
Ingram, A. 58
inquiries
    making inquiries in adult support
        and protection 140, 143
    public 24–5, 30, 37–8, 79, 106
institutional care *see* residential care
institutional racism 74–5
Integrated Assessment Framework 60
intensive support and monitoring (ISM)
    programmes 176–7, 180

interagency agreements 25
interdependence 77–8, 138
interim orders 148
International Federation of Social
    Workers (IFSW) 20, 30, 31
international standards 172–6
intervention orders 145, 149
investigations 28
*It's a Criminal Waste: Stop Youth
    Crime Now* 178

J
Jeffery, C. 212
Johnston, L. 208
Joint Improvement Team 121, 122–3
joint working 3
    accountability to other agencies 25–6
    GIRFEC system 62, 64, 66–7
    single shared assessment 121–2
    supporting carers 159
    youth justice 179–80
judgements, professional *see*
    professional judgements
judicial review 26, 162

K
Kandel, R.F. 93–4
Kemp, P. 208
Kendrick, M. 44
Kilbrandon Report and reforms 85,
    105, 106, 170, 171, 173, 185
Kiss, E. 13
Knifton, L. 209
Korbin, J.E. 78
Kosmitzki, C. 81
Kropp, P.R. 57

L
ladder of participation 203–4
Laming, H. 20, 25
Landau, R. 44–5
Langan, M. 205
law
    images of 10–12
    relationship between social work
        and 6–7, 16–17
lay tribunal 86, 91–2
lead professionals 59, 62, 64, 66–7

Leadbetter, C. 206–7
learning disabilities 156
legal accountability 7, 22, 26
legal principles 142–3
legal representation 112
  children's hearings 94–5, 110
  youth justice 171
liability 21–2, 24–5
listening to children *see* children's
  voices
local area coordinators 154
local authorities 24, 149, 169
  complaints procedures 28, 161–3
  duties and children's hearings 87
  implementing GIRFEC 63
  see also looked after children
Lockerbie, Dylan 37–8
looked after children 113, 169
  'after care' duties for 178
Lord Advocate's Guidelines 169

M
MacNeil, M. 65, 66
Macpherson Report 72, 74
Management of Offenders (Scotland)
  Act 2005 186
Marriage (Scotland) Act 1977 102
Marryat, L. 94–5
Maruna, S. 195, 197
maturational reform 195–6
McCallum, A. 204
McConnell, J. 71
McIntosh, M. 53–4
McLaren, H. 14–15
McMichael v *United Kingdom* 90
McNeill, F. 185, 186, 188, 189, 194–5,
  197
mediation 36
medical certificate of incapacity 147
medical model 54
*Meeting Need, Managing Risk and
  Achieving Outcomes* 180
mental health 154
  mental disorder, vulnerability and
    autonomy 136–51
  service users and partnership
    working 208–9
Mental Health Act 2007 41

Mental Health (Care and Treatment)
  (Scotland) Act 2003 (MHCTA or
  MHA) 37, 41–2, 137, 139–50,
  152–3, 157
Mental Health Tribunal for Scotland
  146, 148
Mental Welfare Commission 143, 149
Meyer, C.H. 52–3
Milligan, I. 209–10
mini mental state examination 147
'minimum intervention' principle 104
Minow, M. 13
Morris, J. 208
movement restriction conditions
  (MRCs) 176–7, 180
Muir, Brandon 37
Muldoon judgement 145
Multi-Agency Public Protection
  Arrangements 35
multidisciplinary strategic groups for
  youth justice 179
Muslims 71–2
My World Triangle 62, 65

N
named person
  children 58, 64, 66, 67
  mental disorder 149
narrative theory 195–6
National Care Standards 26–7
National Convenor of Children's
  Hearings Scotland 92
National Forum on Ageing Futures
  Group 212
*National Guidance on Self-Directed
  Support* 157
*National Minimum Standards for
  Assessment and Care Planning for
  Adults* 122
*National Objectives for Social Work
  Services within the Criminal Justice
  System* (2004) 189
*National Objectives and Standards for
  Social Work Services within the
  Criminal Justice System* (1991) 185,
  186
National Practice Model 59–63, 63–4,
  65

National Residential Child Care
    Initiative 210
*National Standards for Scotland's
    Youth Justice Services* 170
National Youth Justice Strategy Group
    179
Nationality Act 1981 73
Nationality, Immigration and Asylum
    Act 2002 74
natural law 11–12
Nazi Germany 11, 12
Needham, C. 211
needs
    needs-led provision 119
    risk and need 41
    risk/need assessment and criminal
        justice 193–4
    RNR model 196–7
neglect 93–4, 105–6
Ness, Caleb 37
'new accountability' 23
NHS Carer Information Strategies 120
NHS and Community Care Act 1990
    119, 203
'no order' principle 86
non-instructed advocacy 157
nursing care 129–32

O
offenders
    children and young people 88–9, 96–7
    partnership working with 210–11
    supervision of 185, 191, 192, 194–7
    see also children's hearings; criminal
        justice; youth justice
Offentlichkeit (public sphere) 36, 46–7
Office of the Public Guardian 143, 149
O'Hagan, K. 79
older people 2, 47, 125
    community care and accountability
        23–31
    free personal and nursing care 125,
        129–32
    working in partnership 212–13
ombudsman 27, 162
O'Neale, V. 74–5
oppression 205
Ormston, R. 94–5

Osmo, R. 44–5
outcomes 30
    focus of community care 122–4, 132

P
parents
    of children under supervision 95–6
    and children's access to hearings
        papers 91
    children's hearings and youth justice
        178
    partnership with 96, 210
participation 4
    children's hearings system 92–3
    ladder of 203–4
    listening to children 4, 101–17
    service planning and development
        203–4
Partners for Inclusion 156
partnership working 4, 14, 121, 156,
    161, 201–16
    adult criminal justice 192, 210–11
    children and families 96, 209–10
    development in Scotland 207–13
    empowerment 204–7
    meaning of 202–4
    youth justice 170–1
Parton, N. 44
Paterson, F. 186
Patrick, H. 148
payback 187–8
Pearson, C. 208
permanence orders 109
personal assistants (PAs) 125, 155, 163
personal budgets 42, 123, 124–9, 155
personal care 125, 129–32
personalisation 123–9, 131, 132, 201,
    206–7
Pollack, D. 21, 26
Positive Mental Attitudes 209
positive risk-taking 36, 39, 47–8
post-release supervision 191, 192
pre-sentence reports 189–90
Preston-Shoot, M. 21, 202, 204
*Preventing Offending by Young People:
    A Framework for Action* 180
primary human goods 196–7
prison overcrowding 186

prisoner throughcare and resettlement
191–2
privacy 93–4
probation orders 190
Probation (Scotland) Act 1931 185
probation services 185, 210–11
procedures 30
Procurators Fiscal Service 174
professional accountability 21, 22, 29–31
professional advocacy 157
professional autonomy 31–2
professional judgements 31–2
    dealing with dilemmas 44–6, 47
    risk, uncertainty and 35, 39–48
    structured professional judgement
        and risk assessment 57
*Promoting Positive Outcomes: Working
    Together to Prevent Antisocial
    Behaviour in Scotland* 180
proportionality concept 17
*Protecting Scotland's Communities:
    Fair, Fast and Flexible Justice* 187
protection 13
protection orders 144–5
Protection of Vulnerable Groups
    (Scotland) Act 2007 35
protocols 25
public accountability 21, 22–3, 26–7
public inquiries 24–5, 30, 37–8, 79, 106
Public Interest Disclosure Act 1999 16,
    24
public services ombudsman 27, 162
Public Services Reform (Scotland) Act
    2010 27, 37
public sphere 36, 46–7
punishment 78–80
Putting People First 118, 123–4, 131
Pycroft, A. 211
pyramid of statutory intervention 139–41

Q
Quinn, N. 209

R
R (Howard League for Penal Reform) v
    *Secretary of State for the Home
    Department and the Department of
    Health* 175

Race Relations Act 1976 70, 72, 80
Race Relations (Amendment) Act 2000
    72, 73–4, 80
racial discrimination 4, 70–84
range of remedies 161–3
Reamer, F.G. 45
reciprocity, principle of 143
Reducing Reoffending strategy 179
referrals to children's hearings 87,
    88–9, 91, 93, 97
*Reforming and Revitalising: Report of
    the Review of Community Penalties*
    187
Regulation of Care (Scotland) Act 2001
    2, 27
regulatory landscape 37–8
Rehabilitation of Offenders Act 1974
    (ROA) 168–9
relationships 13–14
    listening to children 115
removal to a place of safety orders
    140, 144–5, 150
reoffending 191
    reducing 192, 194–7
reparation 187–8, 190
reporter, children's 88, 92, 112, 174,
    176
reporting officer 109, 112
reports
    children's hearings 90–1, 110
    social enquiry reports 189–90
    written by children 110
representation
    adult protection 148–9
    children's hearings 94–5
    legal *see* legal representation
representative at a children's hearing
    94–5, 110, 113
resettlement, prisoner 191–2
Reshaping Care for Older People
    212–13
residential care
    imposed 140, 145
    public expenditure on 119
    with locked doors 148
    vulnerability and 138–9
resilience matrix 60, 61, 62
resilience theory 54

respect for persons 9, 10, 12
responsibility 21–2, 25
responsibility model 186
restorative justice 176, 190, 211
restricted environment 140, 146
Review Appeals Panels 162
Richards, A. 74
Richmond, M. 52
Riddell, S. 208
rights 7, 152–3
  adult protection 148–9
  human 11, 97
  partnership working with children
    209–10
  values and 9, 10, 11–16, 17
risk 3, 4, 35–51
  assessment of 55–7
  construction of 38–9
  positive risk-taking 36, 39, 47–8
  professional judgements, uncertainty
    and 35, 39–48
  regulatory landscape 37–8
  role of the public sphere 46–7
risk bands, in community care 130–1
risk literacy 46
risk/need assessment 193–4
risk-need-responsivity (RNR) model
  196–7
Ritchie, P. 203, 206
Robinson, G. 190
Rose, W. 53
Ross, R. 194
Royal Commission on Long Term Care
  129
Rummery, K. 202, 203

S
S v Miller 90
S v Principal Reporter and the Lord
  Advocate 110
SACRO 211
safeguarders 94, 106, 110, 113
safeguarding children see child protection
Scotland's Action Programme to
  Reduce Youth Crime 178
Scotland's Children: The Children
  (Scotland) Act 1995 Regulations and
  Guidance 170

Scotland's Choice 175, 187–8
Scotland's Commissioner for Children
  and Young People (SCCYP) 114–15,
  210
Scottish Association for Mental Health
  209
Scottish Children's Reporter
  Administration (SCRA) 90–1, 174
Scottish Consortium of Learning
  Disability 208
Scottish Council for the Regulation of
  Care (Care Commission) 27, 163
Scottish National Party (SNP)
  government 187
Scottish Parliament 1–2, 37, 167, 186
Scottish Prisons Commission 175,
  187–8
Scottish Public Services Ombudsman
  Act 2002 27
Scottish Recovery Network 209
Scottish Social Services Council (SSSC)
  2, 29, 163
  Codes of Practice for Social Service
    Workers 8, 15–16, 29, 152
secure accommodation 94, 177, 180
Secure Borders, Safe Havens:
  Integration with Diversity in
  Modern Britain 74
self-advocacy 157
self-determination 10, 152
self-directed support 123, 125, 127–9,
  132, 155–7, 163
Self-directed Support: A National
  Strategy for Scotland 127–8, 201
Self-Directed Support (Scotland) Bill
  128–9
senior managers 25
service delivery 3
  GIRFEC system 65
  service user involvement in planning
    and 203
service users 7
  accountability to 22, 27–9
  partnership working see partnership
    working
  user expertise 44
  working with adult service users see
    adult service users

services to the court 188–90
Sevenhuijsen, S. 13
Sex Discrimination Act 1975 70, 72
Shanley, M. 13
Shardlow, S. 9, 21
Shemmings, D. 54
Shemmings, Y. 54
sheriff 108, 113
Sheriff Courts 93, 148
short breaks 159
short-term detention orders 144, 149, 150
single correctional service 186
single shared assessment (SSA) 121–2
SK v Paterson 95
Smith, C. 9–10
social bonds 195–6
social capital 196
Social Care Institute for Excellence (SCIE) 132
Social Care and Social Work Improvement Scotland (SCSWIS) 27, 37, 162–3
social disadvantage 89, 171–2
social enquiry reports 189–90
social justice 11, 12, 152
social model
  of disability 207–8
  mental health and learning disability 54
social structure 171–2
social work
  centrality of values 8–10, 152
  liminal profession 40
  relationship with the law 6–7, 16–17
  training 2
Social Work Inspection Agency (SWIA) 27
Social Work (Scotland) Act 1968 (SWA) 2, 26, 28–9, 105, 185
  youth justice 167–8, 174
socialisation 171–2
  cultural differences in socialisation practices 70, 75–81
societal factors 139
solicitors, instructing 111
specific case formulation 195

stages of childhood 101–2
Stalker, K. 55
Stanford, S. 44
state
  accountability to the 22–3
  power 12
Stevens, I. 209–10
Stradling, B. 65, 66
Strengthening for the Future 87
strengths, assessing 193–4
strengths approach 54
  reducing reoffending 196–7
substantial risk 130–1
summary courts 175
supervision
  community sentences 190–1
  compulsory for children and young people 95–7, 176–7
  offenders 185, 191, 192, 194–7
  professional 32
Sutherland Report 129
Sutherland Review 129–30
Swain, P.A. 14

T
tagging, electronic 47, 176–7, 180
Talking Points framework 122–3
Taylor, C. 43
telecare 47
The Same as You? A Review of Services to People with Learning Disabilities 154–5, 157
throughcare, prisoner 191–2
Titterton, M. 37, 38, 39, 45, 46
Tombs, J. 186
transparency 22, 131
Tritter, J.Q. 204
Turner, M. 203, 205
Twigg, J. 205

U
UK Parliament 2
uncertainty 36, 39–40, 43–4
Union of the Physically Impaired Against Segregation 208
United Nations Committee on the Rights of the Child 103, 172

United Nations Convention on the
    Rights of the Child (UNCRC) 4, 54,
    86, 102–3, 168, 209
United Nations Convention on the
    Rights of Persons with Disabilities
    153
unpaid carers *see* carers
unstructured clinical assessment 56
users of services *see* service users

V
values 213
    cultural differences 76–8
    radical and traditional 202
    rights and 9, 10, 11–16, 17
    social work and the law 3–4, 6–19
Voices of eXperience (VOX) 209
vulnerability 13, 22, 40
    contexts of 137–9
    vulnerable adults *see* adult protection
Vulnerable Witnesses (Scotland) Act
    2004 110–11

W
Ward, T. 195, 196, 197
Warner, J. 40
Waterhouse, L. 97
welfare 13
    dilemmas 45–6
    principle and childen's hearings 86

Wellbeing Indicators 58, 59, 60, 61,
    62, 63, 65
whistle-blowing 15–16, 24
White, S. 43
Who Cares? Scotland 109, 110, 210
Whyte, B. 185, 186, 189, 211
Wicks, M. 47
Williams, P. 11
Williams, R. 201
Wilson, G. 209
women, empowering 205

Y
young carers 160–1
young people, partnership working
    with 209–10
youth courts 174
youth hearings 175
youth justice 5, 167–83
    and children's hearings 96–7,
        167–70, 174, 175, 176–8
    distinct philosophy of 170–2
    future developments 178–80
    and international standards 172–6
    in practice 176–8
youth justice coordinators 179
Youth Justice Programme
    Implementation Board 179
youth justice social workers 179
youth justice teams 179